The Glory of the End-Time

Dedicated to precious souls everywhere trying to make sense of what's going on in this crazy world.

By

Edwin & Jody Mitchell

All Scripture quotations are taken from
the Authorized King James Version of the Holy Bible.

The Glory of the End-Time

By Edwin and Jody Mitchell

Copyright © 2013

To order more books online contact:

Amazon.com or Amazon Europe

Books can also be obtained
by mail order through the authors.

Edwin and Jody Mitchell
704C East 13th Street, # 519
Whitefish, MT 59937 USA

Published by Josiah Publishing

Reproduction and/or translation of this book is encouraged, provided it is done without alteration and given freely.

Contents

Ch. 1: Born to Love 1

Ch. 2: God's Divine Plan of Redemption 19
          A Messiah Shall Arise

Ch. 3: Born Again 28

Ch. 4: The Cross of Christ and Regeneration 35

Ch. 5: The Mystery of Israel and the Church 41

Ch. 6: The Time of the End: Seven Power Packed Years 46

Ch. 7   Christ's End-Time Message 50

Ch. 8: Interpreting End-Time Events 56

Ch. 9: The Seventieth Week of Daniel 60

Ch. 10: The Great Tribulation 69

Ch. 11: The Resurrection of Life 94
          The Day of the Lord

Ch. 12: The Great Wrath of God 104

Ch. 13: The Time of Jacob's Trouble 110
          God Pleads with His Chosen People

Ch. 14: Jesus Christ Returns to Earth with All His Saints 122

Ch. 15: Christ's Thousand Year Reign 129

Ch. 16: The Resurrection of Damnation 143
          Evil is Vanquished Forever

Ch. 17: Eternal Life with the Father and the Son 154

Ch. 18: The Issues of Eternity 157

Ch. 19: A Call to Examination 173

Ch. 20: Seeking the Glory 188

Endnotes 200

Unlocking the Mystery...

"But we speak the wisdom of God in a mystery, even the hidden wisdom, which God ordained before the world unto our Glory."
1 Corinthians 2:7

End-time events—so Glorious in their purpose—are a confusing quandary to most. How can puny man, with His limited understanding, grasp the mystery of the coming Apocalypse prophesied to precede the creation of a brand new heaven and earth; a Paradise free from the corruption brought on by sin; and wholly restored to the perfection of beauty that God intended in the beginning?

To unlock the mystery, it is essential to go back to the genesis of life ...onward into the throws of transformation ...and then into an Eternity of unspeakable joy (infinitely more precious than anything this world has to offer) in the Presence of the Heavenly Father and His only Begotten Son, Jesus.

> "There's a Land of Begin Again on the other side of the hill,
> where we'll learn to love and live again,
> when the world is quiet and still.
>
> There's a Land of Begin Again and there's not a cloud in the sky,
> where we'll never have to grieve again,
> and we'll never say good-bye.
>
> When all your troubles just surround you,
> and around you skies are grey,
> If you can only keep your eyes on,
> the horizon not so far away.
>
> There's a Land of Begin Again . . ."[1]

In the coming pages we hope to travel with you on a journey of discovery.

Jesus said:

". . . Unto you it is given to know the mystery of the Kingdom of God . . ."
Mark 4:11

CHAPTER ONE

Born to Love

From the beginning it has been in the heart of our Heavenly Father to create a Divine Family with whom He can share rich eternal companionship. Oh, how He yearns to share the incalculable splendor of His Person and the endless riches of His Kingdom with a family of worshippers who choose to yield their lives completely to Him *(Ps. 84:11b; Lk. 12:32)*.

The Father's Firstborn Son

The *"Firstborn"* into this sacred communion was Jesus, the Father's *"only begotten Son" (Jn. 3:16)*. He is *"the express image of His [Father's] person" (Heb. 1:3)*: *"the beginning of the creation of God" (Rev. 3:14b)*.

"Who is the image of the invisible God, the firstborn of every creature." Colossians 1:15

Together with the Holy Spirit of Wisdom, Jesus was with the Father before *"ever the earth was" (Pro. 8:23)*.

"The Lord possessed Me in the beginning of His way, before His works of old. I was set up from everlasting, from the beginning, or ever the earth was. When there were no depths, I was brought forth; when there were no fountains abounding with water. Before the mountains were settled, before the hills was I brought forth: while as yet He had not made the earth, nor the fields, nor the highest part of the dust of the world. . . . Then I was by Him, as one brought up with Him: and I was daily His delight, rejoicing always before Him." Proverbs 8:22-26, 30

As like produces like, even so the Son proceeded from His Father in the *"brightness of . . . [God's] Glory" (Heb. 1:3)*, *"having neither beginning of days, nor end of life" (Heb. 7:3)*; *"equal"* to His Father in essence, form and attributes *(Phil.*

2:6); and subordinate to none other than the Almighty God that begat Him *(Jn. 14:28)*. The Father, Son and Holy Spirit are one.

"For there are three that bear record in heaven, the Father, the Word [Jesus Christ—Jn. 1:1-3], and the Holy Ghost: and these three are one." 1 John 5:7

In prayer, Jesus said:

". . . Thou, Father, art in Me, and I in Thee . . . . We are one."
John 17:21, 22b

The secret to this holy union between the Father and the Son is Christ's abandoned submission to the sovereign will of the One that begat Him *(Jn. 6:38; Heb. 10:7)*. No matter what the cost or consequence, Jesus does *"always those things that please Him [God]" (Jn. 8:29b)*. Even when pushed to the utmost extremity of suffering before His crucifixion, Jesus proved to wholeheartedly yield Himself in humble surrender *(Heb. 5:8)*, joyously trusting in the goodness and wisdom of God *(Ps. 40:7, 8; Heb. 12:2)*.

"Saying, Father, if Thou be willing, remove this cup from Me: nevertheless **not My will, but Thine, be done**." Luke 22:42

With boundless joy the Father delights in the faithfulness of His Son. Nothing of Himself, or of His Kingdom, has He withheld from Jesus. He gave Jesus the **preeminence** in all things, for Jesus is His Firstborn; the chosen Heir of His eternal Kingdom *(Heb. 1:2)*; and the **unrivaled Treasure** of the Father's Heart.

"The Father **loveth the Son**, and hath
given all things into His hand." John 3:35

It is through the Lord Jesus that all creation came into being.

"In the beginning was the Word [Jesus Christ], and the Word was with God, and the Word was God. The same was in the beginning with God. All things were made by Him; and without Him was not any thing made that was made." John 1:1-3

"All power . . . in heaven and in earth" is at Christ's command *(Mt. 28:18)*. He sits at "the right hand of the Majesty on High" *(Heb. 1:3)*; "far above all principality, and power, and might, and dominion, and every name that is named, not only in this world, but also in that which is to come" *(Eph. 1:21)*.

"For by Him [Jesus] were all things created, that are in heaven, and that are in earth, visible and invisible, whether they be thrones, or dominions, or principalities, or powers: all things were created by Him, and for Him: and He is before all things, and by Him all things consist. And He is the head of the body, the Church: Who is the beginning, the firstborn from the dead; that **in all things He might have the preeminence**." Colossians 1:16-18

Every blessing ... "every good gift and every perfect gift" that "cometh down from the Father of lights" *(Jam. 1:17)* ... all lasting fulfillment *(Jn. 6:35)* ... and even access to the Father come only **by and through His Son**.

"For it pleased the Father that in Him should all fulness dwell."
Colossians 1:19

Jesus said: ". . . I am the way, the Truth, and the life: no man cometh unto the Father, **but by Me**." John 14:6

As the Son is under the Father, "who is above all" *(Eph. 4:6)*, so likewise, the Father "hath put all things under" the "feet" of His Son *(Eph. 1:22; 1 Cor. 15:27)*. He even "committed all judgment unto the Son: that all men should **honour the Son, even as they honour the Father**" *(Jn. 5:22, 23a)*. Not to honor the **Divinity of the Son**, therefore, is not to pay homage to the Father that sent Him *(Jn. 5:23b)*.

"Wherefore God also hath highly exalted Him, and given Him a name which is **above every name**: that at the name of Jesus every knee should bow, of things in heaven, and things in earth, and things under the earth; and that every tongue should confess that Jesus Christ is Lord, to the **Glory of God the Father**."
Philippians 2:9-11

"And again, when He bringeth in the Firstbegotten into the world, He saith, And let all the angels of God worship Him." Hebrews 1:6

Creating Man for Love

Expanding upon His Divine Family, the Lord God formed man of the *"dust of the ground" (Gen. 2:7)*; and woman of the *"rib"* of man *(Gen. 2:22)*. Together, man and woman (Adam and Eve), were to **love**, worship and obey the Father and the Son, rejoicing in Their Presence, **loving one another** and enjoying creation eternally. They were to tend to the Garden of Eden, *"to be fruitful and multiply, and replenish the earth, subdue it: and have **dominion**" (Gen. 1:26, 28)*.

"And God said, Let us make man in Our image, after Our likeness: and let them have **dominion** over the fish of the sea, and over the fowl of the air, and over the cattle, and <u>over all the earth</u>, and over every creeping thing that creepeth upon the earth. So God created man in His own image, in the **image of God** created He him; male and female created He them." Genesis 1:26, 27

And just like their Creator, man and wife were made to **love and to be loved** in return.

"Beloved, let us <u>love one another</u>: for **love is of God**; and every one that **loveth** is **born of God**, and knoweth God. He that loveth not knoweth not God; for **God is love**." 1 John 4:7, 8

Placed within their earthen frame was a *"living soul"* with a will of its own designed to **live forever** in the Light of their **Father's love** *(Gen. 2:7)*; <u>provided</u>, they (like Jesus), gave the **love** that He first gave to them back to Him and to others by <u>remaining true to His commands</u>.

"Herein is love, not that we loved God, but that **He loved us**, and sent His Son to be the propitiation for our sins. Beloved, if God so loved us, we ought also to **love one another**." 1 John 4:10, 11

"Behold, what manner of **love** the Father hath bestowed upon us, that we should be called the sons of God . . ." 1 John 3:1a

Free to Soar in Glory with the God That Made Us

Adam and Eve were born free. They were not in bondage to any man, or to any sin or addiction, or to any evil spirit. They were given total liberty to live for the *"Glory"* and *"pleasure"* of the One who *"breathed"* into their nostrils the very *"breath of life"* (Gen. 2:7).

"Thou art worthy, O Lord, to receive Glory and honour and power: for Thou hast created all things, and for Thy pleasure they are and were created." Revelation 4:11

Man and wife were uniquely endowed by their Creator with beautiful gifts and talents to wholeheartedly *"serve the living and true God"* (1 Th. 1:9b). As time went on, however, they lost this precious liberty, yet it was God's intent from the beginning for them to possess it forever.

"And the Lord spake unto Moses, Go unto Pharaoh, and say unto him, Thus saith the Lord, Let My people go, that they may **serve Me**." Exodus 8:1

Test of Love

The surpassing Presence of the *"God of Glory"* was in the Garden to envelope Adam and his wife *(Ps. 29:3)*, but the retaining of this blessing (and all of His other wonderful blessings) was **conditioned** upon their obedience to His commands. Thus, this lovely garden paradise became a proving ground for testing man's fidelity to God's **Two Sided Covenant of Love**.

"Jesus answered and said unto him, If a man **love Me**, he will **keep My words**: and My Father will **love him**, and We will come unto him, and make Our abode with him." John 14:23

The test started with a single command with a penalty attached. If violated, sacred communion with the Father would be broken and death would ensue.

"And the Lord God commanded the man, saying, Of every tree of the garden thou mayest freely eat: but of the tree of the knowledge of good and evil, thou shalt not eat of it: for in the day that thou eatest thereof thou shalt surely die." Genesis 2:16, 17

Satan and the Fall of Man

The temptation to transgress (disobey God, sin) came in veiled form, for in those days evil also stalked the earth. There had been a great war in heaven and Lucifer, an anointed cherub, had been cast down to earth along with one third of the angels that followed him in rebellion against God *(Rev. 12:4a; Lk. 10:18; Eze. 28:14, 15, 17)*. Once corrupted and cast down, the bright countenance of this fallen angel became equally dark and utterly wicked. From thenceforth, he came to be known by many contemptible names like **Satan, the Devil, the Dragon and the great Deceiver** *(Rev. 12:9)*. All those drawn into his mutiny were changed from glorious angels into diabolical demon spirits subject to his command *(1 Pet. 5:8; Eph. 6:12; 2 Cor. 11:4; Mk. 5:1-16)*.

Possessed with a lust to exalt himself over the God that made him *(Isa. 14:12-14)*, and driven to seize dominion over the works of His Creator's hands; the Devil set out on a mission to capture power by seizing the dominion of the earth from man. Knowing that **obedience** was the **conditional link** in the chain that connected Adam to the power of God, Satan devised a scheme to draw man and wife into disobedience.

He entered into the body of a serpent and went to work on Eve with **lies** and **beguilement** to seduce her to eat of the forbidden fruit *(1 Cor. 11:3)*. First, he twisted the clear Word of God, falsely assuring her that she would not suffer the punishment of death for her disobedience, even though his own fall from heaven was a testimony of the surety of God's righteous judgments.

"And the Serpent said unto the woman, Ye shall not surely die."
Genesis 3:4

Then the Devil went on to cast a deceptive and disparaging shadow over God's beneficence by insinuating that the

Heavenly Father (who only is *"good"* and from whom *"every good gift comes"*) would withhold from His obedient children any *"good thing"* that would bring them fulfillment and blessing *(Mk. 10:18; Jam. 1:17)*.

"For God doth know that in the day ye eat thereof, then your eyes shall be opened, and ye shall be as gods, knowing good and evil."
Genesis 3:5

"For the Lord God is a sun and shield: the Lord will give grace and Glory: no good thing will He withhold from them that walk uprightly." Psalms 84:11

Tempting Eve with the same vanity that led to his own downfall, and appealing to her natural senses, Satan promised that the voluptuous fruit set before her eyes would make her *"wise"*—as exalted as a "god." Once beguiled through the Serpent's lies, Eve ate of the forbidden fruit; and she, in turn, led her husband into **disobedience**.

"And when the woman saw that the tree was good for food, and that it was pleasant to the eyes, and a tree to be desired to make one wise, she took of the fruit thereof, and did eat, and gave also unto her husband with her; and he did eat." Genesis 3:6

Separation from God

At that juncture, sacred communion with the Father was broken. Adam and Eve had disregarded the Love Covenant of Life, acting independently from God's commands. Such is the essence of sin and the severance it creates.

". . . Your iniquities have separated between you and your God, and your sins have hid His face from you . . ." Isaiah 59:2a

Surely all creation was hushed. Innocence was lost and infidelity conceived. The fear of punishment spread like a foreboding shadow over the enlivened consciences of Adam and Eve and the joyous climate of Eden totally changed. Man and wife tried to hide from the Holy One whose welcome Presence they had formerly embraced. Suddenly, they realized they were naked and feebly tried to cover their bodies with fig leaves and their disobedience with finger pointing and deception *(Job 31:33)*. Thus was born the loathsome habit of gainsaying (deceit, lying, cover-up).

"This is the nature and disposition of the old Adam . . . that he would always cover his nakedness with fig leaves; for when he was addressed by the Lord on account of his transgression, a reason immediately presented itself by which he thought to cover himself; namely, 'the woman whom Thou gavest me,' he said, 'gave it me, and I did eat.' Gen. 3:12. And, likewise, when Eve was addressed, she laid it to the serpent [saying, 'The serpent beguiled me, and I did eat.' Gen. 3:13]. But if they had wanted to plainly tell the fundamental cause of their transgression, it would have been: 'Our curiosity and pride brought us to it [Gen. 3:6] . . . hence we allowed ourselves to be persuaded, and did eat of it.' Had they thus answered the Lord, it would have been a true answer. The answer which they gave was true; but it was not yet the true kernel or fundamental cause of their fall and transgression."

Matthias Servaes,
Tortured & beheaded in the Catholic Inquisition, A.D. 1565[1]

Consequences of Covenant Breaking

But the grievous breach was known to God, as surely as infidelity is known in marriage. The Heavenly Father then made an open display of the horror of sin and the <u>wounding and hurt</u> it begets. Something had to die for this crime. A **scapegoat** was needed to bear the burden. So, for the first time ever recorded, **blood** flowed in Eden. God chose to use the skins of precious creatures to cover the shame of Adam and Eve's disobedience.

Satan accomplished his goal. Sin gave him the *"advantage"* and the penalties for disobedience went into force *(2 Cor. 2:11; Eph. 4:27)*. Joy turned to sorrow and <u>spiritual rule over the earth</u> was transferred from Adam to the Devil, who became the *"god of this world" (2 Cor. 4:4)*.

The Lord also vexed the woman with pain in childbearing as a perpetual remembrance of her emotional vulnerability to evil seductions; and the man was consigned to toilsome labor as a reminder of his fleshly inclination to favor the demands of his wife over the commandments of God.

To keep them from being ensnared again by Satan's same subtle cunning, God (in His great love and wisdom) placed man in authority over the woman.

"Unto the woman He said, I will greatly multiply thy sorrow and thy conception; in sorrow thou shalt bring forth children; and thy desire shall be to thy husband, and **he shall rule over thee**."
Genesis 3:16

Knowing the strengths and weaknesses of their make-up, God gave them this statute as a covering. His intent was to give them the greatest possible advantage for guarding their fidelity to Him; and as a result, abiding in the richness of His loving favor and the eternal blessings that follow obedience. It is from this wellspring of life that the **love** we share with each other is drawn.

"By this we know that we love the children of God, when we **love God**, and keep His commandments."   1 John 5:2

This beautiful Old Testament safeguard of male authority was later carried over into New Testament Christianity.

"But I suffer not a woman to teach, nor to **usurp authority over the man**, but to be in silence. For Adam was first formed, then Eve. And Adam was not deceived, but the woman being deceived was in the transgression. Notwithstanding she shall be saved in childbearing, if they continue in faith and charity and holiness with sobriety."   1 Timothy 2:12-15

Never again was the woman to use her cherished position as *"help meet"* to influence her husband to disobey the Gracious God that had given them His Word for their good *(Gen. 2:18)*.

". . . What doth the Lord thy God require of thee, but to fear the Lord thy God, to walk in all His ways, and **to love Him**, and to serve the Lord thy God with all thy heart and with all thy soul, to **keep the commandments of the Lord**, and His statutes, which I command thee this day for thy good?"   Deuteronomy 10:12, 13

And never again was the man or the woman to allow anything, any evil spirit, or any person—even kinsmen—to interfere with his or her principal obedience to the Lord.

"He that loveth father or mother more than Me is not worthy of Me: and he that loveth son or daughter more than Me is not worthy of Me." Matthew 10:37

Eternal Death

Then, the Righteous Judge cursed the earth and **took immortality from man.**

"And unto Adam He said, Because thou hast hearkened unto the voice of thy wife, and hast eaten of the tree, of which I commanded thee, saying, Thou shalt not eat of it: cursed is the ground for thy sake; in sorrow shalt thou eat of it all the days of thy life; thorns also and thistles shall it bring forth to thee; and thou shalt eat the herb of the field; in the sweat of thy face shalt thou eat bread, till thou return unto the ground; for out of it wast thou taken: for dust thou art, and unto dust shalt thou return." Genesis 3:17-19

From the creation of man, onward into the Old Testament era, and then into the New, the penalty for sin has been (and still is) death.

". . . The soul that sinneth, it shall die." Ezekiel 18:4b

"For the wages of sin is death . . ." Romans 6:23a

In like manner as Lucifer was cast down from heaven, so God's two precious children were similarly expelled from the Garden of Eden; thus preventing them from accessing the **Tree of Life.** Not only were their bodies now subject to physical death, but their souls became subject to a *"Second Death,"* meaning eternal banishment from the life of God *(2 Th. 1:9)*; and a never ending existence of torment in a *"lake which burneth with fire and brimstone" (Rev. 21:8).*

"And the Lord God said, Behold, the man is become as one of Us, to know good and evil: and now, lest he put forth his hand, and take also of the **Tree of Life**, and eat, and **live for ever**: therefore the Lord God sent him forth from the Garden of Eden, to till the ground from whence he was taken. So He drove out the man; and He placed at the east of the Garden of Eden Cherubims, and a flaming sword which turned every way, **to keep [guard] the way of the Tree of Life**." Genesis 3:22-24

From thenceforth, all posterity has been *"born"* into iniquity and suffers *"trouble as the sparks fly upwards" (Job 5:7)*. Afraid to suffer and afraid to die, humanity has been captive ever since.

". . . Who through fear of death were all their lifetime subject to bondage." Hebrews 2:15

"As it is written, There is none righteous, no, not one. . . . Destruction and misery are in their ways: and the way of peace have they not known. . . . For all have sinned, and come short of the Glory of God." Romans 3:10, 16, 17, 23

"Wherefore, as by one man [Adam] sin entered into the world, and death by sin; and so death passed upon all men, for that all have sinned." Romans 5:12

"One man's disobedience" brought all mankind into **bondage to sin and Satan** *(Rom. 5:19; Jn. 8:44; Rom. 7:23; Col. 1:13),* setting in motion the lifetime cycle of enmity, pain, sorrow, disease and ultimately death still at work to this very day.

"Know ye not, that to whom ye yield yourselves servants to obey, his servants ye are to whom ye obey; whether of sin unto death, or of **obedience** unto righteousness?" Romans 6:16

Lost Without Love

Ever since sin severed the lifeline between God and man the orbit of man's earthly life has turned on an axis of selfishness, rather than on a Godward axis polarized by **obedience** to divine commands. Broken fellowship with the Father made a place for Satan; lust became an illusive counterfeit for love; and unholy bonding with the demonic took place. Mesmerized by the transitory entrappings of a world governed by the Devil, the passions of man became earthbound, and the sacred chambers of his heart became defiled by idolatrous affections.

"Love not the world, neither the things that are in the world. If any man love the world, **the love of the Father is not in him**. For all that is in the world, the lust of the flesh, and the lust of the eyes, and the pride of life, is not of the Father, but is of the world."
1 John 2:15, 16

This led to the worship of "other gods" (demon spirits), each incapable of bringing lasting happiness. Caught on a roller coaster of sensual stimulation, and subject to the powers of darkness, man vainly spun his wheels on an endless quest for self expression and meaning, trying to find the **love** and **fulfillment** that only God can give.

"All we like sheep have gone astray; we have turned every one to his own way . . ."   Isaiah 53:6a

This struggle continues today; though misdirected worship often occurs in less visible forms than outward rituals like burning incense in front of statues and shrines. We of the 21st century also try to appease our poverty of spirit by embracing more subtle idols like wealth, pleasure, glamour and fame; or, by an excessive fascination with things like sports, entertainment and the latest technological gadgets. Each of these "gods" have a powerful appeal and offer temporary distraction. Yet, none are capable of filling the God shaped vacuum in our souls. We were created to *"know the Lord"* (Hos. 2:10), and apart from His abiding Presence, and the assurance of **His love**, we are as lost and desperate as a fish out of water; forever hungering, yet unable to obtain the enduring contentment we seek.

Those that kneel before the "god of wealth," for example, run headlong into its limitations; for money cannot buy love and the fluctuating global economy makes it an unreliable deity. Similarly, those that pursue the "god of pleasure" eventually find that lust has no end; indulgence breeds addiction; and sexual sins like fornication and sodomy invite disease and destruction. Those that worship the "god of glamour" learn that its rewards are short-lived because beauty fades with age. And those that pant after fame discover that stardom is fleeting, for the glory of one popular icon is eventually overshadowed by the rise of another.

Aware of a higher calling than what meets the naked eye, many people are asking questions and seeking answers. Who am I? Why am I alive? Is this all there is? Why is there so much suffering in the world? How could a loving God allow my loved one to die? What happens after death? Is the thought of heaven just a silly myth? Will we all get what we deserve in the end?

King Solomon, famous for being the wisest man that ever lived (other than Jesus Christ), similarly sought answers for the riddle of life and the emptiness that plagues the human soul. With great fervor, he set his heart to indulge every desire and whim, not withholding himself from any pleasure or great work. After marrying hundreds of wives, constructing palaces, planting vineyards, hiring servants, developing massive horse stables, soliciting personal entertainers, sitting down with notorious royalty, and becoming the wealthiest, wisest and most influential king *"above all that were in Jerusalem before"* him *(Ecc. 2:7)*—even building the magnificent Temple of Jehovah God—discovered that **apart from divine companionship**, life is vanity, sorrow and vexation of spirit *(See Ecclesiastes)*. After years of searching, his ultimate discovery was this:

"Let us hear the conclusion of the whole matter: Fear God, and **keep His commandments**: for this is the whole duty of man. For God shall bring every work into judgment, with every secret thing, whether it be good, or whether it be evil." Ecclesiastes 12:13, 14

Born into Sin

As the offspring of Adam, we, *"by nature,"* are born into this world as *"the children of wrath"* and *"disobedience" (Eph. 2:3; 5:6)*. We are subject to a sinful disposition, like unto Satan.

"Ye are of your father the Devil, and the lusts of your father ye will do. He was a murderer from the beginning, and abode not in the Truth, because there is no Truth in him. When he speaketh a lie, he speaketh of his own: for he is a liar, and the father of it."
John 8:44

In like manner as the Devil, our first inclination is to put ourselves before God, and to seek our own glory (ego), not God's *(Isa. 14:12-14; Gal. 5:26)*—all the while using lies and deceit to hide our selfishness. And when we don't get what we want; or, we feel wounded or unjustly treated; resentment and other forms of retaliation (even if they be on a lower level than outright murder) rise up. Rather than being solely surrendered to the guiding voice of the Lord *(Gen. 3:8)*, knowing only good, as was Adam in the beginning before Eve was deceived by the Serpent *(1 Tim. 2:14)*, we are open to both good <u>and</u> evil *(Gen. 2:9)*.

"Divers lusts" now war in our members, fighting for the control of our lives; driving us to the world for gratification; and bringing us under the influence of Satan, *"the prince of the power of the air, the spirit that now worketh in the children of disobedience"* *(Eph. 4:22; 2:2)*.

"For we ourselves also were sometimes foolish, **disobedient, deceived**, serving divers lusts and pleasures, living in malice and envy, hateful, and hating one another."
Titus 3:3

These *"<u>deceitful lusts</u>"* that **bind** us (including the greedy longings of our minds) are a *"law"* unto themselves, causing us to do things we ought not.

"I find then a law, that, when I would do good, evil is present with me. For I delight in the Law of God after the inward man: but I see **another law** in my members, warring against the law of my mind, and bringing me into captivity to the **Law of Sin** which is in my members."
Romans 7:21-23

"For the flesh lusteth against the Spirit, and the Spirit against the flesh: and these are **contrary the one to the other**: so that ye cannot do the things that ye would."
Galatians 5:17

The lusts that war in our flesh cause us to strive against the ***"Royal Law"* of Love and Obedience** originally written into man's heart and conscience by the Spirit of God *(Jam. 2:8; Rom. 2:14, 15)*.

"I delight to do Thy will, O my God: yea, Thy Law is within my heart." Psalms 40:8

If not resisted, these lusts destroy harmony and provoke rivalry. They turn natural desires into inordinate affections (concupiscence); causing us to demand things that displease God; and enticing us to disobey **His mandate of love** by striking out at others—especially those that are in right standing with God when we are not *(Col. 3:5; Rom. 13:10)*.

"For this is the message that ye heard from the beginning, that we should **love one another**. Not as Cain, who was of that wicked one, and slew his brother. And wherefore slew he him? Because his own works were evil, and his brother's righteous."
1 John 3:11, 12

Not only do the lusts of the flesh (with all of their selfish demands and convenient cover-ups) turn brothers into foes, they also cause divorce and provoke wars. Worst of all, they turn the precious souls that God created for **love** and companionship into His enemies, as well.

"From whence come wars and fightings among you? Come they not hence, even of your lusts that war in your members? Ye lust, and have not: ye kill, and desire to have, and cannot obtain: ye fight and war, yet ye have not, because ye ask not. Ye ask, and receive not, because ye ask amiss, that ye may consume it upon your lusts. Ye adulterers and adulteresses, know ye not that the friendship of the world is enmity with God? Whosoever therefore will be a friend of the world is the **enemy of God**." James 4:1-4

Godly Desire Versus Ungodly Lust

Surrender is the touchstone test for distinguishing between wholesome desire and ungodly lust. As long as a desire is godly in nature, and surrendered to the Lord, it is holy.

If not surrendered, however, even the most innocent desire instantly corrupts. It becomes a selfish demand—an idol. As such, it forms a barrier between man and God. It cuts him off from the **divine love** and fulfillment we inherently need, and opens him up to the seductive enchantments of Satan. The man may, indeed, get what he craves; but along with the fleeting stimulation, he shall suffer a bankruptcy of soul.

"And they tempted God in their heart by asking meat for their lust. And He gave them their request; but sent leanness into their soul."
Psalms 78:18; 106:15

Lust can be a deadly and deceitful evil. Once conceived in the heart, it can grow in power, and demand repeated (and increased) gratification *(1 Cor. 6:12).*

"But every man is tempted, when he is drawn away of his own lust, and enticed. Then when lust hath conceived, it bringeth forth sin: and sin, when it is finished, bringeth forth **death**." James 1:14-15

If not denied, ungodly lust becomes a tyrannical master over those that serve it.

"'At the beginning sin [lust] always comes disguised as liberty. Its lure is the seductive freedom which it promises from the trammels of conscience and the authority of law. But every man who ever yet accepted sin's offer of a free, unfettered life, discovered the cheat. Free to do the evil thing, to indulge the baser moods [the sensual appetites and egotistical demands]—so men begin, but they end not free to stop, bound as slaves to the thing they were free to do.'" [2]

Still dissatisfied after indulging their sin, captive souls are pressed by the Devil to rise up and *"seek it yet again" (Pro. 23:35b).*

"Having eyes full of adultery, and that cannot cease from sin. . ."
2 Peter 2:14a

There is no deceit, no guile, no maneuvering or manipulation in godly desire. When we embrace it, we are willing to patiently await its fulfillment; or, surrender it up to God altogether, if that be His perfect will. Contrariwise, if snared by lust, we demand its gratification and the sooner the better. Instead of having a sweet spirit of acceptance as to obtaining or releasing our desire, we are often quick to dismiss all consideration of relinquishment by furnishing a list of "noble" rationales to justify getting what we want. Some even use the pretense of serving God to mask their covetousness.

Racing Towards Destruction

No longer singly governed by the unseen **Law of Love** written into the conscience—and still in bondage to the unseen **Law of Sin and Death** at work in his members—man must now be governed by outward laws designed to restrain the fallen nature; and thereby "protect" society from its own destruction.

"Knowing this, that the law is not made for a righteous man, but for the lawless and disobedient, for the ungodly and for sinners . . ."
1 Timothy 1:9a

But the laws wherewith most are governed do not always have their origin in God; and they are enforced by flawed leaders still (in varying measure) corrupted by the Law of Sin within. So we have a world at war—escalating in evil—and racing towards its own destruction; just as it did in the days of Noah before the Great Flood.

"And God saw that the wickedness of man was great in the earth, and that every imagination of the thoughts of his heart was only evil continually. And it repented the Lord that He had made man on the earth, and it grieved Him at His heart. . . . And God said unto Noah, The end of all flesh is come before Me; for the earth is filled with violence through them; and, behold, I will destroy them with the earth. . . . And, behold, I, even I, do bring a flood of waters upon the earth, to destroy all flesh, wherein is the breath of life, from under heaven; and every thing that is in the earth shall die."
Genesis 6:5, 6, 13, 17

As sin *"waxed gross"* in past generations *(Mt. 13:15)*, even so, it burgeons today. As long as the Law of Sin and Death rules in the heart of man, we will always have men and women, old and young, waxing perverse in their imaginations and violent in their actions; using (to one degree or another) the precious liberty that God gave us for **ministering His love** to vent hatred and hurt instead.

"For, brethren, ye have been called unto liberty; only use not liberty for an occasion to the flesh, but by **love** serve one another. For all the Law is fulfilled in one word, even in this; Thou shalt **love thy neighbour as thyself**. But if ye bite and devour one another, take heed that ye be not consumed one of another." Galatians 5:13-15

The sexual vice and savagery that preceded the overthrow of former civilizations like Sodom and Gomorrah fills the earth once again. Headline news tells all. We now have abortion on demand; sodomy in the "church;" drug lords ruling the streets, satanic massacres in schools; the Vatican cover-up of massive pedophilia in their "priesthood;" and despots sitting on thrones of power in Washington D.C. and other lands. We also have children risen up against their parents *(Mt. 10:21)*. We have *"a man at variance against his father, and the daughter against her mother . . . (Mt. 10:35)*. We have *"nation . . . against nation, and kingdom against kingdom"* and these are but the *"beginning of sorrows" (Mt. 24:7a, 8)*. They are a frightful harbinger, warning us in advance, that the world in which we now live is hastening towards a comparable end.

"For if God spared not the angels that sinned, but cast them down to hell, and delivered them into chains of darkness, to be reserved unto judgment; and spared not the Old World, but saved Noah the eighth person, a preacher of righteousness, bringing in the Flood upon the world of the ungodly; and turning the cities of Sodom and Gomorrha into ashes condemned them with an overthrow, making them an ensample unto those that after should live ungodly."
2 Peter 2:4-6

CHAPTER TWO

God's Divine Plan of Redemption
A Messiah Shall Arise

Being a merciful and compassionate Father, the Lord did not abandon us in our depravity. He set in motion a Divine Plan of Salvation and Redemption, whereby our alienation from Him caused by Adam's <u>disobedience</u> could be healed; we could be **restored to His love**; and at the same time, His wrath could be appeased. He *"cursed"* the Serpent and **forecast a door of hope** that would divide the people of the earth into <u>two communities</u> *(1 Jn. 3:10)*: the children of obedience and eternal life—and the children of disobedience and eternal death—the saved and the damned.

But it would not be opened without a great struggle: the Devil and his followers perpetually warring against those that choose to resist his evil devices by submitting to God and keeping His commandments *(Jam. 4:7)*.

"And the Lord God said unto the Serpent, Because thou hast done this, thou art **cursed** above all cattle, and above every beast of the field; upon thy belly shalt thou go, and dust shalt thou eat all the days of thy life: and **I will put enmity between thee and the woman, and between thy seed and her seed**; it shall bruise thy head, and thou shalt bruise his heel." Genesis 3:14, 15

At an appointed time, the Heavenly Father planned to send His only Begotten Sinless Son Jesus down from heaven into the world, *"made of a woman" (Gen. 3:15; Gal. 4:4)*; *"in the likeness of sinful flesh" (Rom. 8:3)*, to shed His blood on a wooden Cross as a substitutional sacrifice to pay the penalty for our sins *(Isa. 53:4-6, 10; Gal. 3:13)*.

"But He was wounded for our transgressions, He was bruised for our iniquities: the chastisement of our peace was upon Him; and with His stripes we are healed." Isaiah 53:5

"By the sacrifice of Himself" (Heb. 9:26), Jesus would wash away our sins, thus making it possible for the gulf between us and our Maker to be closed forever (Isa. 59:2).

"For there is one God, and one mediator between God and men, the man **Christ Jesus**; Who gave Himself a ransom for all, to be testified in due time." 1 Timothy 2:5, 6

In His great wisdom, Almighty God would allow His own Beloved Son to suffer a humiliating, ignominious and excruciating death at the hands of sinners, so as to *"overcome . . . with love"* all that would welcome Him. He did this that we *"might see **love** and **love again** and of **love** to do likewise to other men."* [1]

"For when we were yet without strength, in due time Christ died for the ungodly. For scarcely for a righteous man will one die: yet peradventure for a good man some would even dare to die. But God commendeth **His love** toward us, in that, while we were yet sinners, Christ died for us." Romans 5:6-8

Born of a virgin, Jesus would be spoken of as *"the Son of man,"* but all who would receive and **believe on Him** would acknowledge Him for who He truly is: *"The Christ, the Son of the living God"* (Mt. 16:16, 14:33, 27:54; 1 Jn. 4:2, 3). He would be *"despised and rejected of men"* (Isa. 53:3); betrayed (Ps. 41:9; Mk. 14:10), and shamefully treated (even by the religious elite and those who should be closest to Him). Then, He would be condemned on false charges and crucified as a criminal (Ps. 27:12; Mt. 26:59-61; Isa. 53:12; Mk. 15:27, 28). But after three days, He would defy all the powers of darkness and rise again (Col. 2:14, 15). Death would not be able to hold Him in the ground.

". . . The Son of man shall be betrayed unto the chief priests and unto the scribes, and they shall condemn Him to death, and shall deliver Him to the Gentiles to mock, and to scourge, and to crucify Him: and the third day **He shall rise again**." Matthew 20:18, 19

"Crucified through weakness" (2 Cor. 13:4), He would rise in power and ascend back into heaven to sit down at the

"right hand of God" *(Mk. 16:19)*. Then, at a future time, He would return in Glory to put Satan underfoot *(Gen. 3:15)*, and rule as King over all the kingdoms of the earth *(Rev. 11:15, 20:4)*.

Only those willing to come into His Light and accept His Atonement during their appointed lifetimes, by confessing and forsaking their evil thoughts and deeds (and turning to Him for the power to overcome the corrupt nature they inherited from Adam), would be part of His coming Kingdom.

"Let the wicked forsake his way, and the unrighteous man his thoughts: and let him return unto the Lord, and He will have mercy upon him; and to our God, for He will abundantly pardon."

Isaiah 55:7

All others would perish forever.

"For God sent not His Son into the world to condemn the world; but that the world **through Him** might be saved. He that **believeth on Him** is not condemned: but he that believeth not is condemned already, because he hath not believed in the name of the only begotten Son of God. And this is the condemnation, that light is come into the world, and men loved darkness rather than light, because their deeds were evil." John 3:17-19

Those who did come into His Light, however, and obey His Gospel, would be set free from spiritual captivity to Satan *(Lk 4:18)*; healed; reconciled to the Heavenly Father *(2 Cor. 5:18)*; and given access to the **Tree of Eternal Life** from whence Adam was banned. These faithful believers, by virtue of their union with their coming Messiah, would be greater in spiritual power than the Devil *(Lk. 10:18-20; Mk. 16:17, 18; 1 Jn. 4:4)*; and ultimately, inheritors of the dominion that Adam lost over the earth through his disobedience *(Dan. 7:27; Rom. 4:13; Rev. 11:15)*.

Abraham & the Covenant of Circumcision

The plan was initiated with the selection of a man named Abraham, who (unlike Adam) was proven to *"keep the way of the Lord"* at all costs *(Gen. 18:19; 22:16-18)*. Through Abraham's son Isaac; Isaac's son Jacob (later named Israel); one of Jacob's twelve sons named Judah; and one of Judah's descendants named David *(Mt. 1:1-16; Isa. 11:1; Rom. 1:3, 4; Acts 13:22, 23)*; would be born the **Son of God** as the one and only Saviour whereby the Jewish people (the descendants of Jacob), and thereafter all mankind, could be brought back into everlasting communion with the Father (**eternal life**) once again.

The outward *"token of the Covenant"* was the **circumcision** of every male child in Abraham's household *(Gen. 17:10-13)*.

"And God said, Sarah thy wife shall bear thee a son indeed; and thou shalt call his name Isaac: and I will establish My Covenant with him for an **Everlasting Covenant**, and **with his Seed** after him." Genesis 17:19

Non-compliance with this **condition** of circumcision was accounted as a breach of Covenant, cutting the transgressor off from the household of promise.

"And the uncircumcised man child whose flesh of his foreskin is not circumcised, that soul shall be <u>cut off</u> from his people; he hath broken My Covenant." Genesis 17:14

"We Have Found the Messias" (John 1:41)

The Divine *"**Seed**"* foreshadowed in Gen. 3:15; promised to Abraham, Isaac and Jacob as an Everlasting Covenant; and foretold by the prophet Isaiah; was conceived in the womb of a Jewish virgin, *"when the fulness of the time was come" (Gal. 4:4),* just as God promised. He is *"Christ the Lord" (Lk. 2:11), "the Son of the living God" (Mt. 16:16).*

"Therefore the Lord Himself shall give you a sign; behold, a virgin shall conceive, and bear a Son, and shall call His name Immanuel [meaning, God with us]." Isaiah 7:14

"Now to Abraham and his seed were the promises made. He saith not, And to seeds, as of many; but as of one, And to thy **Seed**, which is **Christ**." Galatians 3:16

Jesus gave His life as a scapegoat to *"ransom"* those that **believe on Him** from the *"power of the grave" (Hos. 13:14; Mk. 10:45; Ps. 49:15; Jn. 11:25, 26)*. To the Jewish people did His Salvation first come *(Rom. 1:16)*.

"Now the birth of Jesus Christ was on this wise: when as His mother Mary was espoused to Joseph, before they came together, she was found with child of the Holy Ghost. Then Joseph her husband, being a just man, and not willing to make her a publick example, was minded to put her away privily. But while he thought on these things, behold, the angel of the Lord appeared unto him in a dream, saying, Joseph, thou son of David, fear not to take unto thee Mary thy wife: for that which is conceived in her is of the Holy Ghost. And she shall bring forth a Son, and thou shalt call His name JESUS: for **He shall save His people from their sins**."
Matthew 1:18-21

"This Jesus" (Acts 17:3), born in Bethlehem of Judaea to the Jewish nation* *(Mic. 5:2; Mt. 2:1)*, and preached as Saviour to *"all nations"* by the early apostles *(Mt. 24:14; 28:19)*, is also the prophesied *"Ruler"* that is going to sit on the Throne of the Jewish patriarch David in the Millennial Kingdom soon to come *(Mic. 5:2)*. He is the eternal *"King of Israel" (Jn. 12:13)*.

"And the angel said unto her, Fear not, Mary: for thou hast found favour with God. And, behold, thou shalt conceive in thy womb, and bring forth a Son, and shalt call His name JESUS. He shall be great, and shall be called the Son of the Highest: and the Lord God shall give unto Him the **throne of his father David**: and He shall reign over the House of Jacob for ever; and of His Kingdom there shall be no end."
Luke 1:30-33

"For unto us a child is born, unto us a Son is given: and the government shall be upon His shoulder: and His name shall be called Wonderful, Counsellor, The mighty God, The everlasting Father, The Prince of Peace. Of the increase of His government and peace there shall be no end, upon the **throne of David**, and upon

---

* In Biblical terminology, *"nation"* means bloodline. Hence, scripturally speaking, the descendants of Abraham, Isaac and Jacob are a nation in themselves *(Gen. 12:2)*, regardless of their country of residence. The term "Gentile" designates all people outside the Jewish bloodline.

His Kingdom, to order it, and to establish it with judgment and with justice from henceforth even for ever. The zeal of the Lord of hosts will perform this." Isaiah 9:6, 7

Jesus Christ perfectly fulfilled the Biblical portrait given to the Jews and more of His Masterplan of Salvation is yet to be revealed. He is the foreshadowed *"Star"* of the Old Testament that reveals Himself in the New.

"I shall see Him, but not now: I shall behold Him, but not nigh: there shall come a **Star** out of Jacob, and a Sceptre shall rise out of Israel . . ." Numbers 24:17a

"I Jesus have sent Mine angel to testify unto you these things in the churches. I am the root and the offspring of David, and the bright and Morning **Star**." Revelation 22:16

Spiritual Reality

Satan covets Almighty God's supreme Throne of Power for himself. For that reason, he has been at *"enmity"* with Christ (the prophesied *"Seed"* of the woman) since the Garden of Eden. Now, however, his angst is not only directed against the Lord Jesus; but also, against His true followers and the Jewish people at large. This bitter rivalry is the underlying spiritual motor that turns the wheels of all Christian persecution and anti-Semitism. In an ever increasing display of vengeance, the Serpent incites his own *"seed" (Gen. 3:15)*—the *"children of the Devil" (1 Jn. 3:10; Jn. 8:44)*—to reproach and attack Jews and Christians alike.

". . . Whoever today still doubts the reality, the existence of demonic powers, has failed by a wide margin to understand the metaphysical background of this war. Behind the concrete, the visible events, behind all objective, logical considerations, we find the irrational [spiritual] element: the struggle [of the children of God] . . . against the servants of the Antichrist." [2]

This ongoing conflict of powers explains why enduring peace is never realized in Israel. Unbroken peace cannot be secured in the Holy Land until the demon powers that have been at work on earth since the Garden of Eden are defeated. This conquest shall take place when Christ returns to earth to fight the Battle of Armageddon and establish His Millennial Reign.

". . . The War with Satan in which the redeemed . . . [are] engaged, [shall continue] right on to the time when the Lord Jesus . . . [is] revealed from heaven, in judgment upon these vast, and terrible powers, full of cunning malignity, and hatred to His people, and as truly at work behind the world of men, from the days of the Garden story to the end." Jesse Penn-Lewis with Evan Roberts [3]

God's Chosen People

Indeed, the Jews are a *"peculiar treasure unto . . . [God] above all people"* (Exo. 19:5), for it was unto them that the promises were first given; and it is through them that the Heavenly Father chose to bring His Son into the world (Rom. 9:4, 5). He even entrusted them with prophetic messages to alert them to His future plans and to tell them how to recognize their Messiah and distinguish Him from forthcoming counterfeits. He also gave them His laws to guide them in righteous living, like a *"schoolmaster,"* until their Promised Saviour finally came (Gal. 3:19, 24; Rom. 10:4).

Central to those laws was animal sacrifice, given as a means of atonement to cover their sins and as a perpetual reminder of the pain and injury that transgression begets. These prescribed sacrifices were to be in force only until Jesus came to take away their sinful nature forever by the sacrifice of Himself (Heb. 9:26); thus **giving God's chosen people a brand *"new spirit"*;** and transferring the written Word of right living from *"tables of stone"* to the inward folds of their hearts (2 Cor. 3:3).

"But this shall be the Covenant that I will make with the House of Israel; after those days, saith the Lord, I will put My Law in their inward parts, and write it in their hearts; and will be their God, and they shall be My people." Jeremiah 31:33

"A new heart also will I give you, and a new spirit will I put within you: and I will take away the stony heart out of your flesh, and I will give you an heart of flesh. And I will put My Spirit within you, and cause you to walk in My statutes, and ye shall keep My judgments, and do them." Ezekiel 36:26, 27

A Door of Hope to the Gentiles

But Jesus is not the Messiah of **believing** Jews exclusively. Rather, He is the Saviour of as many as will **accept** Him and **believe** on His name *(Rom. 10:9-12).*

"He [Jesus] came unto His own, and His own received Him not. But as many as **received** Him, to them gave He power to become the sons of God, even to them that **believe** on His name."
John 1:11, 12

That's why John the Baptist introduced Him like this:

". . . Behold the Lamb of God,
which taketh away the sin of the world." John 1:29b

It's also why—long beforehand—God said to Abraham:

". . . Behold, My Covenant is with thee, and thou shalt be a father of many nations." Genesis 17:4

Thus, **through Christ**, God gave all mankind (Jews and Gentiles) the same Glorious opportunity to be restored to everlasting communion with Him.

"For ye are all the children of God by **faith in Christ Jesus**. For as many of you as have been baptized into Christ have put on Christ. There is neither Jew nor Greek, there is neither bond nor free, there is neither male nor female: for ye are all one in Christ Jesus. And **if ye be Christ's, then are ye Abraham's seed**, and heirs according to the promise." Galatians 3:26-29; Also, Gal 3:7, 8

"For there is no difference between the Jew and the Greek: for the same Lord over all is rich unto all that call upon Him. For whosoever shall call upon the name of the Lord shall be saved."
Romans 10:12, 13

Before Christ came, everyone outside of the Jewish bloodline, except for a small number of Gentile proselytes, was stigmatized as being the *"Uncircumcision" (Eph. 2:11)*; meaning, *"aliens from the commonwealth of Israel, and strangers from the covenants of promise, having no hope, and <u>without God</u> in the world" (Eph. 2:12b).*

"But now **in Christ Jesus** ye [Gentiles] who sometimes were far off are made nigh by the blood of Christ. . . . For **through Him** we both [Jews and Gentiles] have access **by one Spirit** unto the Father. Now therefore ye [Gentiles] are no more strangers and foreigners, but fellowcitizens with the saints, and of the household of God." Ephesians 2:13, 18, 19

Hallelujah! Because of the *"precious blood of Christ, as of a lamb without blemish and without spot" (1 Pet. 1:19)*, we can all be saved from **spiritual death** and start all over again.

"For since by man came death, by man came also the resurrection of the dead. For as in Adam all die, even so **in Christ** shall all be made alive." 1 Corinthians 15:21, 22

"For <u>God so loved the world</u>, that He gave His only begotten Son, that **whosoever believeth in Him** should not perish, but have everlasting life." John 3:16

CHAPTER THREE

Glory Hallelujah!

Born Again

The door of access to the Father and His wondrous **love** swings wide open when we hear the Gospel, believe the Gospel, repent of our sins and receive the Spirit of Christ into our hearts *(Rom. 10:17; Mk. 1:15).*

"And because ye are sons, God hath sent forth the **Spirit of His Son into your hearts**, crying, Abba, Father." Galatians 4:6

At that Glorious moment, we become spiritually alive. We are *"**born again**, not of corruptible seed, but of incorruptible, by the Word of God, which liveth and abideth for ever" (1 Pet. 1:23).*

"Which were born, not of blood, nor of the will of the flesh, nor of the will of man, <u>but of God</u>." John 1:13

Hallelujah!

". . . Christ in you [and Christ in me], the **hope of Glory**." Colossians 1:27

Think of the jubilation when a child is born into this world. Magnify the elation to the uttermost and then you begin to get an idea of the celebration that takes place in heaven when the lost are thus brought into the Kingdom of God.

"Likewise, I say unto you, there is joy in the presence of the angels of God over one sinner that repenteth." Luke 15:10

Nothing in this world can be compared to the joy of Salvation. It is life from the dead!

"And you hath he quickened, who were **dead** in trespasses and sins." Ephesians 2:1

Oh, the joy of complete forgiveness from all of our past sins *(Rom. 3:24)*! As the clouds of guilt and shame roll away, our hungry hearts open up to the sunshine of **God's love** and we want to go out and tell the world all about it.

"O taste and see that the Lord is good: **blessed** is the man that trusteth in Him." Psalms 34:8

With everything in us, we want to praise His name!

"Bless the Lord, O my soul: and all that is within me, bless His holy name. Bless the Lord, O my soul, and forget not all His benefits: who **forgiveth all thine iniquities**; who **healeth all thy diseases**; who redeemeth thy life from destruction; who crowneth thee with lovingkindness and tender mercies; who satisfieth thy mouth with good things; so that thy youth is renewed like the eagle's." Psalm 103:1-5

We are loved and we are loving the Lord in return by **keeping** His commands. Plus, our inward mechanism to give and receive love (formerly dwarfed and perverted by lust, covetousness and selfishness) is on the mend, too.

"That Christ may dwell in your hearts by faith; that ye, being rooted and grounded in love, may be able to comprehend with all saints what is the breadth, and length, and depth, and height; and to know the **love of Christ**, which passeth knowledge, that ye might be filled with all the fulness of God." Ephesians 3:17-19

What a Friend we have in Jesus! He fills us with His love; heals our broken hearts; brings deliverance to our souls; restores health to our bodies and soundness to our minds. What a wonderful Saviour is He!

Jesus said: "The Spirit of the Lord is upon Me, because He hath anointed me to preach the Gospel to the poor; He hath sent Me to heal the brokenhearted, to preach deliverance to the captives, and recovering of sight to the blind, to set at liberty them that are bruised, to preach the acceptable year of the Lord." Luke 4:18, 19

"Beloved, I wish above all things that thou mayest prosper and be in health, <u>even as thy soul prospereth.</u>"   3 John 1:2

Like the merchant man that found *"One Pearl of Great Price,"* we have found our Messiah; and we are purposed to render everything that we are (and everything we have) in order to fully embrace Him *(Mt. 13:45, 46)*.

Now we're part of God's own Family made up of other faithful and <u>obedient</u> born again believers that are also enraptured by the Lord Jesus *(Mk. 3:32-35; Lk. 8:21)*. These are not Christians in *"tongue"* only; but most importantly, they are Christians in *"Spirit and in Truth"* *(1 Jn. 3:18; Jn. 4:23, 24)*. They are Christians in both word and deed. Some are alive today. Others are yet to come. And still others have already passed from this life, but in the life to come we shall all be united together *(1 Th. 4:13-18)*.

The Bible, the Holy Spirit and the will of God are now the compass we use when seeking direction for our lives. When we prayerfully follow them, regardless of our outward circumstances, peace and a deep sense of security and purpose abide. When we do not, the darkness we left behind returns like a haunting shadow, reminding us that we've been side-tracked and have returned to our old ways.

Glory Hallelujah! No more aimless wandering. We've made a landmark discovery: God has a specific and wonderful *"plan for our lives and the real adventure of being alive is to find it."*[1]

In trying to express the Glory of what happened to her when she wholly surrendered her life to Jesus and His Spirit came into her heart, one Christian sister wrote:

". . . Something miraculous had happened. The old fettering and tormenting husk had cracked and fallen off. . . . Life was utterly different and radiant from that hour. I do not mean that my whole nature was changed and self-absorption went. The new spiritual life of Christ develops slowly and only gradually changes the old temperament and character. Outwardly everything was exactly the same. . . . My dread of people was still there; and so was my complete ignorance of how to begin thinking about others and considering their interests. . . . But in some miraculous and mysterious way I had been lifted into a completely new mental and spiritual environment, out of the border land of outer darkness, into the light and **Glory of heaven**. It was as though a miserable, stunted plant had suddenly been transplanted from a tiny flowerpot, into a sunny, richly fertilized flowerbed. I was lifted out of the dreadful isolation of self-imprisonment and set down in the **love of God**."

Hannah Hurnard [2]

That pivotal experience started with earnest repentance and an acknowledgment of desperate need: *"Oh, I need Him. I need Him. No one else can help me."* [3] It was followed by a commitment to **hold nothing back from the Lord**; not a single fear, a single secret, a single relationship, or even a lifetime dream. Just...

"O God, if there is a God, if you will make Yourself real to me, **I will yield** . . ." [4]

Baptisms

After receiving the Spirit of Christ, we go on to be baptized in water by immersion and baptized in the Holy Ghost (the Holy Spirit). Water baptism is an ordinance of Christ signifying repentance and the total turn around of our lives *(Acts. 2:38)*. By it, we make an open declaration of our commitment to <u>die to the nature of sin</u> that we inherited from Adam; and from thenceforth to build brand new lives around Christ and obedience to His Word.* *(See Romans 6.)* The

---

* From the days of John the Baptist until now, scriptural water baptism has been administered only to those who hear, understand, believe and accept the Gospel for themselves. It is important to note that the baptism of babies is an unscriptural practice that has no Biblical command or precedent. Nowhere in the Bible is there a single record of infant baptism. This "sacrament"—performed in the Catholic Church and other pedobaptist denominations—is a direct contradiction to the Word of God. Infants and young children are in God's care, under the covering of at least one believing parent, until they come to an age of understanding when they can choose to accept, or reject, Christ for themselves *(1 Cor. 7:14)*. Baptism was a burning issue of the Reformation, resulting in a mass exodus of Catholics from their churches. Many of these born again believers were martyred at the hands of this institution to which they had formerly pledged their lives, thus revealing the antichrist spirit that works behind false doctrine *(1 Tim. 4:1)*.

Baptism of the Holy Spirit is a special endowment of *"power from on High"* that supernaturally equips us for ministry *(Lk. 24:49; 1 Cor. 12 & 14)*; enables us to be true *"witnesses"* of the Lord *(Acts 1:8)*; and does a beautiful work of sanctification in our lives amidst the *"fire"* of heated trials.

"I [John the Baptist] indeed **baptize you with water unto repentance**: but He [Jesus] that cometh after me is mightier than I, whose shoes I am not worthy to bear: He shall **baptize you with the Holy Ghost**, and with fire." Matthew 3:11

The Bible calls the Holy Spirit *"the Comforter"* because of His wondrous way of transforming suffering into joy. He gives us hope in our darkest hours and fills us with the **love of God**.

"And not only so, but we Glory in tribulations also: knowing that tribulation worketh patience; and patience, experience; and experience, hope: and hope maketh not ashamed; because the **love of God** is shed abroad in our hearts by the Holy Ghost which is given unto us." Romans 5:3-5

What an unspeakable Gift!! The Holy Spirit guides us *"into all Truth"* and brings to remembrance the words that Jesus taught *(Jn. 16:13)*.

Jesus said: "But the Comforter, which is the Holy Ghost, whom the Father will send in My name, He shall teach you all things, and bring all things to your remembrance, whatsoever I have said unto you." John 14:26

Redeemed from the Fall of Adam

As God's *"dear children" (Eph. 5:1)*, we then receive *"divine power"* and *"precious promises: that by these . . . [we] might be partakers of the **divine nature"*** once again *(2 Pet. 1:3, 4)*. Praise be unto God! All of us, Jews and Gentiles, have the same wonderful opportunity to be purged from the fallen nature of Adam and brought back into everlasting communion with the Father, wholly restored to the *"image of His Son" (Rom. 8:29)*.

"And as we have borne the image of the earthy, we shall also bear the image of the heavenly." 1 Corinthians 15:49

The Miracle of Rebirth

This miracle of **spiritual rebirth** and the **transformation** that follows is a great mystery. It can only be understood by faith and with the acknowledgement of spiritual reality *(Heb. 11:3)*.

"The wind bloweth where it listeth, and thou hearest the sound thereof, but canst not tell whence it cometh, and whither it goeth: so is every one that is **born of the Spirit**." John 3:8

Even Nicodemus, a distinguished *"master"* in Israel, had a hard time comprehending spiritual rebirth when Jesus introduced His teaching.

"Nicodemus saith unto Him, How can a man be born when he is old? Can he enter the second time into his mother's womb, and be born?" John 3:4

For that reason it was easy for Satan to remove sound doctrine on the born again experience from many churches; and in some cases, to replace it with a counterfeit "sacrament" that is falsely said to occur by means of infant baptism. Yet, the Bible teaches that spiritual rebirth is initiated only by means of the freewill choices of individuals that are old enough to repent, confess their sins, and give their lives to Christ. It is a fundamental **condition of Salvation**. Without being born again, Jesus said we can't even *"see the Kingdom of God,"* much less enter in to it.

Jesus said: ". . . Verily, verily, I say unto thee, Except a man be **born again**, he <u>cannot see</u> the Kingdom of God. . . . Except a man be **born of water and of the Spirit**, he <u>cannot enter</u> into the Kingdom of God. That which is born of the flesh is flesh; and that which is born of the Spirit is spirit. Marvel not that I said unto thee, **Ye must be born again**." John 3:3, 5-7

"Now if any man have not the **Spirit of Christ**, he is none of His."
Romans 8:9b

Only A Prayer Away...

Amazing as rebirth is—and it is amazing!—new life in Christ can begin for any of us with the simplest prayer faintly voiced in faith still so small and embryonic that it can be likened to the size of a tiny mustard seed *(Lk. 13:18, 19).*

"Heavenly Father: I repent. I am a sinner through and through. Please wash away everything in my life that separates me from You. Help me to start over, living an unselfish life of love and liberty, wholly surrendered to Your Son. Jesus, please come into my heart and create in me new life. I believe 'Thou art the Son of God; Thou art the King of Israel' (Jn. 1:49b)."

The Lamb's Book of Life

Once the Spirit of the Lord comes in, we become *"babes in Christ" (1 Cor. 3:1; 1 Pet. 2:2).* Our names are transferred from earthly rolls to heavenly rolls *(Jer. 17:13; Heb. 12:23).* They are *"written in the **Lamb's Book of Life**"* and remain there forever *(Rev. 21:27),* <u>provided</u> we go on to maturity by fighting *"the good fight of faith"* and laying *"hold on eternal life" (1 Tim. 6:12; Heb. 3:6, 14; Rev. 3:5).* *

". . . Rejoice, because your names are written in heaven!"
Luke 10:20b

Thus begins our journey out from a world governed by Satan, across the Jordan River (symbolizing the passing away of our old sinful lives in water baptism), into the Promised Land.

"Wherefore come out from among them, and be ye separate, saith the Lord, and touch not the unclean thing; and I will receive you, and will be a Father unto you, and ye shall be My sons and daughters, saith the Lord Almighty."   2 Corinthians 6:17, 18

In the words of a poignant hymn:

"The world behind me, the Cross before me, no turning back, no turning back . . ."   [Gal. 6:14; Lk. 9:62]. [5]

---

* See Chapter 20 for Biblical guidance on the initial steps of Salvation.

CHAPTER FOUR

The Cross of Christ and Regeneration

Born again *"of Spirit,"* we have a brand new genetic make-up (spiritually); and <u>as long as we abide in Christ</u> **by obedience to His Word** *(Jn. 14:23)*, we sin not, for His Seed is within us *(1 Jn. 3:6-9)*.

"Therefore <u>if</u> any man be **in Christ**, he is a **new creature**: old things are passed away; behold, all things are become new."
2 Corinthians 5:17

But the change from a self serving life supported by the world (albeit "religious" for some), to a life of self denial centered around the will of God, is no small transition *(Lk. 9:23)*. It involves a renunciation of vices like fornication, drunkenness and lying; as well as a **complete change** of nature and disposition, from a "wrong spirit" (so to speak), to what Scripture calls a *"right spirit" (Ps. 51:10)*, that truly reflects the image of Christ and the **love of God**.

"The trouble with us is not a list of wrongs that can be added up but the general state of wrongness. We may point to this or that in our lives and say that we will have done with it and doubtless we mean it. But we soon begin to find that our lives are not made up of separate pieces that can be separately mended. Life is one piece. If we make no radical change except to mend some particular fault we find ourselves giving way to it again because of some weakness at another point. It is **the whole of life that must be turned and changed**." [1]

This 180 degree <u>turn</u> is characterized by the **absolute surrender of ourselves unto God** to be entirely at His disposal *(2 Cor. 5:15; Gal. 2:20; 1 Pet. 4:2)*; just like our Lord Jesus, Abraham and King David, who (similar to the others) received this commendation from on High:

"I have found David the son of Jesse, a man after Mine own heart, which shall fulfil all My will." Acts 13:22b

The total giving of ourselves unto Jesus Christ as *"First Love"* requires a complete **death** to our old lives *(Rev. 2:4)*, and a revaluation of all things from His viewpoint, in Light of His Word. This includes those things which we are inclined to think good.

"Forasmuch as ye know that ye were not redeemed with corruptible things, as silver and gold, from your vain conversation received by tradition from your fathers." 1 Peter 1:18

Only as we submit ourselves choice-by-choice to this **daily work of the Cross** (by forsaking our old way of life in exchange for new lives in Christ), do we experience our promised deliverance *"from the power of darkness,"* (i.e. *"the power of Satan"*—*Acts 26:18),* and our translation *"into the Kingdom of . . . [God's] dear Son"* *(Col. 1:13).* By this wondrous working (though often painful), we **close the door on Satan** and **cease from sin** *(Rom. 6:7).*

"Forasmuch then as Christ hath suffered for us in the flesh, arm yourselves likewise with the same mind: for he that hath suffered in the flesh hath **ceased from sin**." 1 Peter 4:1, 2

". . . In the new birth, the infant believer has his sins forgiven. His spirit—formerly dead in trespasses and sins—is made alive by the Spirit of God and he receives power to become a son of God. He now begins to have the power to overcome the very things which enslaved him before. **What a marvelous change from victim of sin to victor, joint victor with Christ!** But nowhere does the Scripture or experience teach that the new birth automatically eliminates demon influence or bondage, or for that matter, all of the carryovers of the old man such as tempers, moods, lusts, envyings, selfishness, prejudice, to name a few. The born again believer must learn to **take up his Cross**, deny himself and die daily; he must walk in the Spirit lest he fulfil the lusts of his flesh. Hopefully, he will also press on to find his rightful place in the plan of God and effectual functioning in the Body of Christ. The process of growing up in Christ is usually painful, though the result is Glorious." Jesse Penn-Lewis with Evan Roberts [2]

This is what true conversion is all about: freedom from sin and Satan and reconciliation with God through Jesus Christ. It is a total threat to the Devil. That's why he has worked so hard to keep the effectual ongoing operation of the Cross (just like the born again experience) out of as many churches as possible.

"There is nothing external that can constrain or vex him [Satan] so long as he can possess the citadel of our hearts, and prevent the entry of Christ's nature, disposition, Spirit and power. If he can do this he has already gained the point of his craftiness; yes, if a man were baptized by Peter or Paul himself and received the bread of the Holy Supper from the Lord's own hand, and never saw the papal idolatry again, but retained one of the fruits of the Devil, whether hatred, or <u>party spirit</u> [denominationalism], envy, bitterness, avarice, revengefulness, pride, unchastity [lust], or any other wickedness, we must take knowledge with the Scripture that <u>his spirit is devilish</u>, and <u>his life hypocrisy</u>. For it is evident that **the whole man must be regenerated**, sincere, true, spiritually minded, godly, devout, holy, subject to Christ. As James said, Whosoever shall keep the whole Law, and yet offend in one point, he is guilty of all. Jas. 2:10."

Menno Simons, ex-Catholic priest, A.D. 1496-1561 [3] *

The Good Fight of Faith

The Apostle Paul likened this Glorious metamorphosis to an ongoing battle: flesh against spirit and spirit against flesh *(Gal. 5:17)*; <u>until</u> *"Christ be formed "* in us *(Gal. 4:19)*.

"<u>Till</u> we all come in the unity of the faith, and of the knowledge of the Son of God, unto a perfect man, unto the measure of the stature of the fulness of Christ."   Ephesians 4:13

Daily repentance and amendment of life, in combination with ongoing Bible study *(Ps. 119:11)*, obedience to the Word *(1 Pet. 1:22)*, and sustained uncompromised warfare to *"put*

---

* Chased by the Catholic institution and other religious opponents, Menno (a major influence in the Reformation) eluded capture. His underground writings revealed heresy and helped establish the persecuted Flock in Christ. Many of these saints were eventually martyred.

off" the old man and *"put on"* the new, are what we render unto God to propel us forward in our development from infancy to maturity.

"Wherefore laying aside all malice, and all guile, and hypocrisies, and envies, all evil speakings, as newborn babes, desire the sincere milk of the Word, that ye may grow thereby." 1 Peter 2:1, 2

"That ye **put off** concerning the former conversation the old man, which is corrupt according to the deceitful lusts; and **be renewed** in the spirit of your mind; and that ye **put on** the new man, which after God is created in righteousness and true holiness. Wherefore putting away lying, speak every man truth with his neighbour: for we are members one of another." Ephesians 4:22-25

This daily warfare requires complete honesty, no excuses (gainsaying)! First we are honest with ourselves *(Jam. 1:22);* then with the Lord *(Ps. 32:5)*; and thereafter with trustworthy brethren, when appropriate. There is no getting around this **condition**. We must humble ourselves and take this narrow Way of the Cross if we hope to receive the forgiveness of God, and thus be cleansed, healed, set free, and restored to right standing.

"But **if we walk in the light**, as He is in the light, we have fellowship one with another, and the blood of Jesus Christ his Son cleanseth us from all sin. If we say that we have no sin, we deceive ourselves, and the Truth is not in us. **If we confess our sins**, He is faithful and just to forgive us our sins, and to cleanse us from all unrighteousness." 1 John 1:7-9

"Confess your faults **one to another**, and pray one for another, that ye may be healed. The effectual fervent prayer of a righteous man availeth much." James 5:16

Though the open acknowledgement of sin can initially be scary, because it leaves us feeling foolish and vulnerable to distain, it is a liberating blessing—especially when done in the presence of brethren that are familiar with their own fleshly weaknesses. Rather than arousing their contempt, it has the opposite effect, engendering greater trust and respect. If done in simplicity and godly sincerity, it can even be used by God to compel others out from behind the oppressive walls of pride and defensiveness into the glorious Light of Christ.

". . . O fallen brother! Let my arms enfold thee, fallen sister! Let me trust and love you back to honour, Let me draw you to the Great Forgiveness, Not as one above who stoops down to save you, Not as one who stands aside . . . . Nay, as he who says, I, too, was poisoned . . . but now; arisen, I am struggling up the path beside you; Rise! and let us face these heights together."

The Discipline of Failure, A Poem [4] *

Heart Circumcision

The travail of soul through which the saints *"press"* into the Kingdom *(Phil. 3:14)*—and possess it *(Mt. 11:12)*—is the New Testament *"sign of circumcision"* we receive as a *"token"* of our sonship with the Father. No longer is the distinguishing mark of God's ownership the outward cutting of the flesh (as it was with Abraham); but rather, the inward **purging of our hearts** *"through the blood of the Everlasting Covenant"* of Christ *(Heb. 13:20b)*.

"And ye are complete in Him, which is the head of all principality and power: in Whom also ye are circumcised with the circumcision made without hands, in putting off the body of the sins of the flesh by the **circumcision of Christ**." Colossians 2:10-11

Without this divine supernatural work of renewal, the most noble of our works (as far as Salvation goes), and even our profession of the Christian faith, are vain *(Gal. 6:15)*.

---

* Nowhere in the New Testament are believers taught to confess their sins to a select "priesthood," as mandated in Catholicism. According to the Bible, born again Christians are all part of Christ's *"royal priesthood"* (1 Pet. 2:9). Hence, we are taught to confess our sins to God and to one another. There is particular humiliation that goes with open confession that has a wonderful way of helping us put an end to debilitating behavior problems. Left in the dark, they often continue unabated, buried under pretense, and kept in tact by pride.

"For he is not a Jew, which is one outwardly; neither is that circumcision, which is outward in the flesh: but he is a Jew, which is one inwardly; and **circumcision is that of the heart**, in the spirit, and not in the letter; whose praise is not of men, but of God."
Romans 2:28, 29

With this inward circumcision, however, we are **changed** from *"Glory to Glory"* amidst life's daily trials by *"the washing of regeneration, and renewing of the Holy Ghost"* (2 Cor. 3:18; Tit. 3:5b). Not until the Day of the Lord, when Jesus appears in the clouds to gather His own, will this magnificent transformation find its ultimate fulfillment (1 Cor. 15:52).

"Beloved, now are we the sons of God, and it doth not yet appear what we shall be: but we know that, when He shall appear, we shall be like Him; for we shall see Him as He is. And every man that hath **this hope** in him purifieth himself, even as He is pure."
1 John 3:2, 3

Until that great and Glorious Day of Resurrection, we *"press toward the mark for the prize of the high calling of God in Christ Jesus"* (Phil. 3:14); that *"when He shall appear, we may have confidence, and not be ashamed before Him at His coming"* (1 Jn. 2:28b).

"Having therefore these promises, dearly beloved, let us cleanse ourselves from all filthiness of the flesh and spirit, perfecting holiness in the fear of God."
2 Corinthians 7:1

CHAPTER FIVE

The Mystery of Israel and the Church

The Lord chose the Jews for wonderful reasons. It was not because they were *"more in number than any people,"* for they were *"the fewest of all people"* (Deu. 7:7), nor because they were *"better"* than others (Rom. 3:9). Rather, it was because He *"**loved**"* them and as a faithful God, *"He would keep the oath which He had sworn unto . . . [their] fathers"* (Deu. 7:8). Plus, He wanted a *"special people unto Himself"* (Deu. 7:6), like the patriarch Abraham, His own dear friend (Isa. 41:8; Jam. 2:23). This man had a *"faithful"* heart, commanded well his household and was steadfast in His Covenant with God (Neh. 9:8; Gen. 18:19). Through Abraham's Seed (that Seed being Christ), the Heavenly Father sought to garner to Himself a Divine Family from all nations of people; who, like their founding father Abraham, would hold nothing more dear to their hearts than their **first love for God** (Gen. 22:12, 16).

It was through such a nation as this that God chose to *"make known the riches of His Glory"* (Rom. 9:23). He chose to establish a *"**testimony in Jacob**"* so that succeeding generations of Jews and Gentiles might see a living demonstration of His grace and goodness upon the **children of obedience**; and as a result, likewise *"set their hope in God"* (Ps. 78:5-7). Through the Israelite community the Heavenly Father wanted all people the world over to behold the surpassing blessings He desires to lavish upon anyone and everyone whose undivided affections for Him are expressed by **obedience** to His commands (Ps. 84:11b).

For Salvation was never intended to be for *"the Jews only"* (Rom. 3:29); but rather, to *"the Jew first"* (Mt. 10:5, 6; 15:24). God wanted to use the example of their lives as a **powerful draw** to inspire others to likewise give their lives to the Messiah; and so become partakers with them of the *"blessedness"* that belongs to the *"household of God"* (Rom. 4:9-17; Eph. 2:11-22).

In a rebuke addressed to their unbelieving Jewish kinsmen, the Apostle Paul and Barnabas said:

". . . It was necessary that the Word of God should <u>first</u> have been spoken to you: but seeing ye put it from you, and judge yourselves unworthy of everlasting life, lo, we turn to the Gentiles. For so hath the Lord commanded us, saying, **I have set thee to be a light of the Gentiles**, that thou shouldest be for salvation unto the ends of the earth." Acts 13: 46, 47; Isaiah 60:3

The Land of Israel

In order to show the world a glimpse of this marvelous blessing God gave the Jewish people the land of Israel for an *"**everlasting possession**" (Gen. 17:8; 48:4; Exo. 32:13; Ps. 105:9-12)*; *"a land that floweth with milk and honey" (Deu. 11:9)*. This "Holy Land" (now the most coveted possession of the religious world) was originally taken from the heathen because of their defilements and satanic worship, and given to the Israelites for three specific reasons *(Deu. 9:5; Ezra 9:11)*: <u>one</u>, to set apart a country governed by the Law of God *(Deu. 27:2-10; Ps. 105:44, 45)*; <u>two</u>, to provide a safe homeland for His worshippers; and <u>three</u>, to prepare a place for the Messiah's coming Kingdom *(Isa. 24:23)*. It was to be *"the Glory of all lands" (Eze. 20:6)*, with its capital city, Jerusalem, established as the Throne of the Lord Jesus Christ *(Jer. 3:17; Isa. 2:2-5)*, its future monarch.

National Fall into Apostasy

But going all the way back to their wilderness wanderings, the Jews (for the most part) have been a headstrong and self-willed people; forsaking God's Law, assimilating into heathen cultures, glorying in the works of their own hands, and provoking the Lord to jealousy with their worship of other "gods" *(Deu. 9:7; 2 Ki. 21:15; Mal. 3:7)*. The majority have not *"**mixed**"* **faith** with the covenants and the promises they've been given, nor with the hearing of the Gospel message *(Heb. 4:2)*. For that reason their understanding has been darkened. **Unbelief** has blinded them to the reality of Jesus

Christ as the King of Israel and cut them off from the life of God *(2 Cor. 3:14, 15; 2 Cor. 4:4; Rom. 11:21-23).* Entrenched in the cares of the world; and putting education, career, politics, talent, nationalism and wealth before their intimacy with the Lord and obedience to Him; the great majority have been *"unmindful"* of *"the Rock that begat"* them *(Deu. 32:18).* Further still, they've been unyielding in their rejection of the Messiah and in their persecution of the remnant of their kinsmen that have embraced Him. Unbelief is so rife that few are willing to concede to the operation of God's providential hand in the outworking of their daily lives—and fewer still are willing to consider His past dealings in bringing calamities as judgment.

Consequently, over the course of time, they've lost their former Glory and respect among the nations. As a judgment, they are often viewed as *"an astonishment, an hissing, and a curse"* *(Jer. 25:18)*—even *"a reproach, among all the nations whither"* the Lord has *"driven them"* *(Jer. 29:18b).* Some of the contempt is a reaping of due shame brought on by <u>covenantal breaches</u> *(Rom. 2:24)*; yet, an alarming amount is outright anti-Semitism attributable to the relentless enmity of the Serpent's seed foretold in Gen. 3:15.

In spite of great opposition and adversity from their own liberal kinsmen, there are a number of unconverted Jews that still (the best they know how) adhere to Orthodox tradition. Some have done it at enormous personal cost. For example, a number of starving (yet devout) Jews held in Nazi concentration camps during the Holocaust fasted their meager ration of bread on the Day of Atonement (Yom Kippur) in order to be in compliance with Mosaic Law *(Lev. 23:27-32).*

Others, however, have become largely secular; losing sight of the Sabbath, abandoning the practice of circumcision, and discontinuing the annual observance of feasts like Passover. Throwing off all restraints, still others have sunk into the lowest of pagan practices; thus fulfilling the prophetic warning spoken by Moses at the end of his life, prior to the crossover of Joshua and the younger generation of Jews into the Promised Land.

"For I know that after my death ye will **utterly corrupt yourselves**, and turn aside from the way which I have commanded you; and **evil will befall you in the latter days**; because ye will do evil in the sight of the Lord, to provoke Him to anger through the work of your hands." Deuteronomy 31:29

Truly, these are the *"latter days."* Contrary to the Law of Moses *(Lev. 20:13; Deu. 23:17)*, Israel's high court sanctioned the annual observance of "Gay Pride" parades in Jerusalem in 2005. Former kings of Judah that came into power had the sodomites removed in compliance with God's Word *(1 Ki. 15:11, 12)*. But now, those that indulge in what the Bible calls *"vile affections"* have been granted legal privilege to flaunt their way down the streets of the Holy City in broad daylight *(Rom. 1:26-28)*. Rather than being urged to repent and turn to God for deliverance and healing from the oppressive and degrading chains of sexual perversity, they are being given a platform to abandon themselves to it.

The grief of the prophet Isaiah comes to mind. Mourning over what he saw in the spirit regarding the fallen state of Jerusalem, he cried:

"How is the faithful City become an harlot! It was full of judgment; righteousness lodged in it . . ." Isaiah 1:21a

"The shew of their countenance doth witness against them; and they declare their sin as Sodom, they hide it not. Woe unto their soul! For they have rewarded evil unto themselves." Isaiah 3:9

How woeful a tragedy! The Omnipotent God of the universe brought His magnificent Redemption and promises to the Jews first; yet lamentably, most have wandered far from Him *(Mt. 15:7-9)*. Instead of Jerusalem being identified as the *"City of the Lord, The Zion of the Holy One of Israel"* *(Isa. 60:14)*, it is presently *"spiritually . . . called Sodom and Egypt, where also our Lord was crucified"* *(Rev. 11:8b)*. As a result, the Land of Promise is again inundated with paganism and conflict.

Indeed, the Jewish people are a testimony. Now, however, (because of their waywardness), their lives not only attest to God's loving favor and manifold blessings, but also to His painful pleadings (i.e. chastisements and judgments). As a merciful Father, God is moving heaven and earth (so to speak) to compel a *"disobedient and gainsaying people"* to their knees in repentance *(Rom. 10:21)*; and thereafter, back into His arms and their destiny of eminence in His foreordained plan.

One Divine Family United *"in Christ"*

As we await that miracle of Redemption, we see our great God (that knows the end from the beginning) using the present alienation of His people to magnify His mercy. He is using it to bring to fulfillment the original Covenant He made with Abraham and a prophecy given to Moses long ago. For through the fall of the Jews, the door of Salvation has been opened unto the Gentiles, *"until the fulness of the Gentiles be come in"* *(Rom. 11:11, 25; Deu. 32:20)*. Then, *"if they abide not still in* **unbelief***"*; the Jewish people (now locked in darkness) shall *"turn to the Lord,"* repent and be brought back into the Divine Family; *"for God is able to graff them in again"* *(Rom. 11:23; 2 Cor. 3:16)*.

This unification of redeemed Jews and believing Gentiles through their common **faith in Jesus Christ** is **the *"Mystery"* of Israel and the Church** *(Eph. 3:3-6)*. Its fulfillment is the chief joy of the Father and the Son. It embodies the total Redemption of man from the fall of Adam to eternal oneness with the Godhead *(Jn. 17:21)*.

Once this occurs, evil and the destruction it has wrought; from the time when Lucifer conceived the first rebellion against God *(Eze. 28:15)*; to the casting of all evil doers (including the Devil and his angels) into everlasting torment in a *"lake of fire"* *(Rev. 20:1-3, 13-15)*; will be utterly vanquished. It is in anticipation of the fullness of this Glorious Redemption that *"the whole creation groaneth and travaileth in pain together until now"* *(Rom. 8:22)*.

"For the earnest expectation of the creature waiteth for the manifestation of the sons of God." Romans 8:19

CHAPTER SIX

The Time of the End
Seven Power-Packed Years

Bible prophecy tells of particular events and actions that must take place in order to set all creation free from the *"bondage of corruption"* brought on by sin and Satan; and to start afresh with all things new and beautiful *(Rom. 8:21).* The first has already transpired: the death, burial and Resurrection of the Lord Jesus Christ. Still awaiting fulfillment are: the thorough execution of just retribution against the shedding of all innocent blood and every unrepented evil ever committed *(Dan. 9:24; Rev. 6:10; 16:6)*; the establishment of the Jewish people in the Land of Israel under the rule of Christ with His saints *(Lk. 1:71-75)*; and the complete overthrow and punishment of all enemies of God, including Satan and his forces *(Rev. 19:20-21; 20:7-15; 1 Cor. 15:24, 25).*

The world as we now know it must come to an end, in like manner as the Old World came to an end in the days of Noah and the Great Flood. At that time, judgment came by water *(Gen. 6:17).* This time it will come by fire.

"For this they willingly are ignorant of, that by the Word of God the heavens were of old, and the earth standing out of the water and in the water: whereby the world that then was, being overflowed with water, <u>perished</u>: but the heavens and the earth, which are now, by the same Word are kept in store, **reserved unto fire** against the Day of Judgment and perdition of ungodly men."   2 Peter 3:5-7

Then, in like manner, comes the creation of new *"heavens and a new earth,"* unified *"in Christ"* *(Eph. 1:10)*, where mankind can once again rejoice in **God's loving favor** as at the beginning; walking openly before Him, and ruling as *"kings and priests"* under the authority of the Father and the Son *(Rev. 1:6).*

"But the Day of the Lord will come as a thief in the night; in the which the heavens shall pass away with a great noise, and the elements shall melt with fervent heat, the earth also and the works that are therein shall be <u>burned up</u>. . . . Nevertheless we, according to His promise, look for **new heavens and a new earth**, wherein dwelleth righteousness." 2 Peter 3:10, 13

"For, behold, I create **new heavens and a new earth**: and the former shall not be remembered, nor come into mind. But be ye glad and rejoice for ever in that which I create . . ."
Isaiah 65:17, 18a

Everlasting Righteousness

Seeing events leading up to this glorious time of the *"restitution of all things"* from afar off *(Acts 3:21)*, the Hebrew prophet Daniel said:

"**Seventy weeks** are determined upon thy people and upon thy Holy City, to finish the transgression, and to make an end of sins, and to make reconciliation for iniquity, and to **bring in everlasting righteousness**, and to seal up the vision and prophecy, and <u>to anoint the most Holy</u>." Daniel 9:24

Daniel then zeroed in on events pertaining to the last of these *"seventy weeks,"* describing a division in its center.

"And he shall confirm the covenant with many for <u>one week</u>: and in the **midst** of the week . . ." Daniel 9:27a

In Hebrew, the word "week" means "sevened." In the book of Genesis it was used to designate a seven year time period *(Gen. 29:27)*. Hence, according to Daniel's forecast, a power-packed **seven year period of time** [divided *"in the midst"*] is going to bring to a close the world as we now know it. This coming Apocalypse is what Bible-believing Christians refer to as the "**Seventieth Week of Daniel.**" It is an indispensable building block of doctrine. Every End-Time event finds its proper sequence within this prophetic structure. At its conclusion, the anointing of the *"most Holy,"* seen from afar by Abraham and Daniel *(Jn. 8:56)*, and brought into greater focus by the Apostle John, who spoke of it as

Christ's Thousand Year Reign *(Rev. 20:4)*, shall be Gloriously ushered in.

Two Big Questions: Timing & Sequence of Events

Eager to find out just when this closing **seven year** period would come (and what the future holds for faithful followers of the Messiah and the nation of Israel in particular), the disciples asked Jesus two questions; one before, and the other after, His Resurrection.

Before: ". . . What shall be the **sign of Thy coming** and of the **End of the world?**" Matthew 24:3b

After: ". . . Lord, wilt Thou at this time **restore again the Kingdom to Israel?**" Acts 1:6b

In response to these queries, the Lord Jesus unveiled His long hidden mystery, *"which in other ages was not made known unto the sons of men"* *(Eph. 3:5a)*. Already, bits and pieces had been given to the Old Testament prophets, but they only saw them through the eyes of faith and *"through a glass, darkly"* *(1 Cor. 13:12; Heb. 11:13)*. Some of the things are so sacred and spectacular that they've never even *"entered into the heart of man"* *(1 Cor. 2:9)*. Even *"the angels desire to look into"* them *(1 Pet. 1:12)*. Yet, our Lord Jesus Christ revealed them *"unto His holy apostles and prophets by the Spirit"* *(Eph. 3:5)*. Now, in fulfillment of a prophecy given to Daniel, the hidden distinctives are coming into even greater focus, indicating that *"the time of the end,"* and the new beginning that follows, are near.

"But thou, O Daniel, shut up the words, and **seal the book**, even to the **time of the end**: many shall run to and fro, and knowledge shall be increased." Daniel 12:4

Christ Opens the End-Time Book

Praise be unto God! Our exalted Lord Jesus Christ (and none other!) was given the sacred privilege of opening the End-Time Book sealed since the days of Daniel. Jesus received the Book from the Father's right hand and was given authority at an appointed time to break the *"seven seals thereof,"* thus setting in motion the seemingly surreal future events described therein. He revealed these events to the Apostle John in a vision and commanded him to write them down for all of us to see and understand *(Rev. 1:1, 11)*. They are recorded in what we now call the Book of Revelation *(Rev. 5:1-7)*.

By piecing together John's writings with Matthew 24, Mark 13, Luke 21 and many other passages of both the Old and New Testaments—and arranging them within the prophetic **structure of Daniel's Seventieth Week**—this End-Time mystery comes into view, with a picture of what is to be expected in this historic seven year period. It shall be like none other *(Dan. 12:1; Mt. 24:21)*.

"For in those days shall be affliction, such as was not from the beginning of the creation which God created unto this time, neither shall be. And except that the Lord had shortened those days, no flesh should be saved: but **for the elect's sake**, whom He hath chosen, He hath shortened the days." Mark 13:19, 20

CHAPTER SEVEN

Christ's End-Time Message

Christ's revelation of the *"time of the end"* is the apex of all Scripture. From Genesis to Revelation, passage after passage point to it. It is going to be a compact era of surpassing spiritual renewal and mighty exploits for the Church, as well as a time of unparalleled trouble and affliction around the globe. Who can but fathom the magnitude of travail that is prophesied to take hold of the world in order to birth brand new heavens and a new earth, void of sin and free from suffering and pain?

Right in the *"midst"* of it *(Dan. 9:27)*, Jesus is going to appear in the clouds with His mighty angels in a spectacular display of Glory. At that time, He is going to gather faithful believers of all generations (both the living and the dead) up with Him into heaven and there present us to the Father *(Mt. 10:32; 24:29-31; 2 Cor. 4:14; 1 Th. 4:16, 17; Rev. 7:9)*.

"These are going to be Glorious days for you, My chosen. . . . The Great Revelation is unfolding, and the ushering in of My Kingdom is at hand. . . . It shall indeed be a dark hour for the world, and humanity shall be enshrouded in a darkness such as in the days of the Flood. This shall be an even greater darkness, and there shall be anguish and travail. . . . But in this night . . . of man's rebellion and disobedience . . . the door shall be opened. It shall be opened by the Bridegroom, and they who are watching, and they who have maintained their lamps of witness shall go in. Others shall see and shall desire to enter, but shall be too late."

Prophecy of the Holy Spirit [1]

Once these faithfully awaiting saints go in with the Bridegroom, and the door shuts, there shall follow the greatest outpouring of fiery indignation ever known to man; thus purging the earth from evil in preparation for the coming change. It is around this *"**Blessed Hope**"* of deliverance from Wrath (and simultaneous resurrection into the Kingdom of heaven) that earnest Christians focus every day of their lives.

"Looking for that **Blessed Hope**, and the Glorious appearing of the great God and our Saviour Jesus Christ."   Titus 2:13

"Let your loins be girded about, and your lights burning; and ye yourselves like unto men that **wait for their Lord**, when He will return from the wedding; that when He cometh and knocketh, they may open unto Him immediately. Blessed are those servants, whom the Lord when He cometh shall find watching: verily I say unto you, that He shall gird Himself, and make them to sit down to meat, and will come forth and serve them."   Luke 12:35-37

Sea of Confusion

Due to the sensational nature of End-Time prophecy, it has skyrocketed to the "top of the charts" as one of the most intriguing (yet exploited) topics in all of Christendom. Shrouded in mystery, it confounds all of the sensibilities of the carnal mind, leaving us without an interpreter had we not been given the *"Spirit of Truth"* to show us *"things to come" (Jn. 16:13)*; and apostolic leaders to help us come to terms with the true *"sense" (Neh. 8:8; Eph. 3:3-5),* sequence, and purpose of events *"which must shortly come to pass" (Rev. 1:1).*

The timing of Christ's Appearance for the ingathering of His saints has become an issue of particular controversy. There seems to be no end to the diversity of teachings; some promising false hope of a premature escape from the pending pangs of persecution appointed to the saints prior to the Lord's Appearance for His Church; and others taking followers into the darkest hours of God's Great Wrath reserved for the ungodly in the aftermath.

Wearied by all the confusion, many professing Christians have been tricked by the Devil to withdraw from all possibility of controversy by minimizing the importance of apocalyptic text. Others have avoided it all together. Still others have gone as far as to state that a solid grasp on the End-Time is beyond reach and should therefore, for the sake of preserving "unity," be subject to *"private interpretation"* and catego-

rized as a "non-essential" (rather than an "essential") part of the true Christian faith *(2 Pet. 1:20)*.
These notions could not be further from the truth. End-Time teaching is anything but an "incidental" aspect of the Gospel. Contrariwise, the *"Blessed Hope"* is the Crown Jewel of it.

Speaking of this pivotal time, Jesus said:

> ". . . Let him that readeth **understand** . . ."
> Mark 13:14

The Apostle Paul later echoed:

> "But **I would not have you to be ignorant** . . ."
> 1 Thessalonians 4:13

We were given these charges for good reason. Sound grounding on the Word of God is our greatest means of preparation, as well as our greatest defense against deception; and not fragments torn from the fabric of Scripture only; but the whole Word *"rightly"* divided by the Spirit of Truth *(2 Tim. 2:15)*.

". . . The coming of the Lord is at hand. Establish your hearts in Him, and be ye faithful. . . . Never has it been more needful that ... [My children] hear Me. It is as vital at this hour as the contact between an army and their commander. Ye dare not risk being cut off. . . . I would prepare thee. I have truth to give thee that is vital to this hour. Ye need to receive it now so that ye shall not be perplexed." Prophecy of the Holy Spirit [2]

Who but the Devil would want to hold Christians **hostage to ignorance or heresy** at an Hour when keen discernment and readiness are prophesied to be of the utmost importance for the safe keeping of our souls? And who but the Devil would want to distance us from (rather than motivate us towards!) our Glorious inheritance in the Kingdom of God?

"And this know, that if the goodman of the house had known what hour the thief would come, he would have <u>watched</u>, and not have

suffered his house to be broken through. Be ye therefore **ready** also: for the Son of man cometh at an hour when ye think not."
Luke 12:39, 40

Watch and Pray

Three times in Mark Chapter 13 Jesus **commanded** us to *"watch"* for End-Time events as they unfold *(Mk. 13:33, 35, 37)*. We need to seriously heed this charge and become as adept in *"discern[ing] the signs of the times,"* as an experienced meteorologist is in forecasting climatic changes *(Mt. 16:3)*. The books of Daniel and Revelation need to be held close to our hearts; so much so, that we can distinguish which of the End-Time events they describe apply to the Church, and which do not. That way, we can prepare our hearts to weather the coming storms that shall affect us. If left in the dark; found lacking in faith *(Lk. 18:8)*; deceived by false teachings, *"false christs, and false prophets"* *(Mt. 24:24; Mk 13:22)*; or, distracted by the *"cares of this life"*; there is a strong possibility that we will be caught *"unawares"* and **left behind** *(Mt. 25:10-13)*. For those thus snared, the Lord shall come as *"a thief in the night"* *(1 Th. 5:2; 2 Pet. 3:10)*.

"And take heed to yourselves, lest at any time your hearts be overcharged with surfeiting, and drunkenness, and cares of this life, and so that Day come upon you unawares. For as a snare shall it come on all them that dwell on the face of the whole earth. **Watch** ye therefore, and **pray always**, that ye may be accounted worthy to escape all these things that shall come to pass [the Wrath], and to stand before the Son of man."   Luke 21:34-36

The Suffering that Precedes the Glory

We stand on the threshold of the most exciting and extraordinary time in all of history since the Resurrection of Jesus Christ. Astounding events are about to transpire. We need to understand <u>God's Glorious purposes</u> for them *(Dan. 12:10)*. We need to know exactly what Jesus meant when He commanded us to be *"ready."* We also need **a vision of the Glory that awaits us**. That (in combination with the daily work of the Cross and the power of the Holy Spirit)—if truly believed and acted upon—will strengthen us to courageously walk through whatever persecution and adversity shall precede our anticipated deliverance.

Yes, difficult times are on their way, but that's when the harvest of souls is most bountiful and the love between brothers and sisters grows in leaps and bounds. It's also when we experience what we all love to sing about: God's "Amazing Grace."

"For our light affliction, which is but for a moment, worketh for us a far more exceeding and eternal weight of **Glory**; while we look not at the things which are seen, but at the things which are not seen: for the things which are seen are temporal; but the things which are not seen are eternal." 2 Corinthians 4:17, 18

Accepting End-Time reality (and knowing how to respond "in Christ") is an awesome challenge for us all. But not if we keep our eyes fixed on Jesus and the *"Blessed Hope"* that is set before us. Come what may, the Lord promised that He would be with us "alway, *even unto the end of the world" (Mt. 28:20).* And if He be with us, we are up to the challenge.

"Fear thou not; for **I am with thee**: be not dismayed; for I am thy God: I will strengthen thee; yea, I will help thee; yea, I will uphold thee with the right hand of My righteousness."   Isaiah 41:10

Here is the testimony of a martyr that went before us, setting His seal to the Lord's promise to always be with us.

"I will tell to the world an incredible thing, namely, that I have found infinite sweetness in the bowels of the lion. . . . In a lonely corner I have had most Glorious company, and in the severest bond, great rest. All these things . . . the gracious hand of God has given me. Behold, He that at first was far from me, is now with me, and Him whom I knew but a little, I now see clearly; to whom I once looked from afar, Him I now behold as present; He for whom I longed, now offers me His hand; He comforts me; He fills me with joy; He drives from me bitterness, and renews within me strength and sweetness; He makes me well; He sustains me; He helps me up; He strengthens me. Oh, how good is the Lord, who does not suffer His servants to be tempted above that they are able! . . . Is there any like God the Most High, who sustains and refreshes

those that are tempted? He heals them that are bruised and wounded, and restores them altogether. Isa. 41; 43:20. None is like Him. Learn, most beloved brethren, how sweet the Lord is, how faithful and merciful; who visits His servants in trial (Isa. 43:2). ... He gives us a cheerful mind and peaceful heart."
Algerius, miserably burned to death in Rome, A.D. 1557 [3]*

"Fear not, little Flock" (Lk. 12:32a). The suffering that precedes the **Glory** is what new beginnings are all about!

"A woman when she is in travail hath sorrow, because her hour is come: but as soon as she is delivered of the child, she remembereth no more the anguish, for **joy** that a man is born into the world. And ye now therefore have sorrow: but **I will see you again**, and **your heart shall rejoice**, and your joy no man taketh from you." John 16:21, 22

---

* This courageous young student was subjected to great temptations and heinous torture. Yet, not even the entire senate of Venice, or the reigning pope, could persuade him to recant and deny the true Christian faith.

CHAPTER EIGHT

Interpreting End-Time Events

Enormous blessings, as well as frightful curses, go along with study of the Book of Revelation. On one hand, a special blessing is promised to those that hear it, read it and keep it *(Rev. 1:3)*. On the other, a perilous curse is pronounced against those that presumptuously tamper with the text in any way.

"For I testify unto every man that heareth the words of the prophecy of this book, If any man shall **add unto** these things, God shall add unto him the plagues that are written in this book: and if any man shall **take away from** the words of the book of this prophecy, God shall **take away** his part out of the Book of Life, and out of the Holy City, and from the things which are written."
Revelation 22:18, 19

Handling Revelation is like handling the genetic code for life, except in this case, eternal life. In genetics, a single alteration in the code can set off a series of changes which make the newborn unlike (instead of like) his parents. Even so, the changes, omissions and/or additions to the True End-Time Message can turn it into *"another gospel"* completely unlike the authentic Gospel given to us through the Revelation of Jesus Christ *(Gal. 1:6)*; thereby subverting the faith of many.

This is why carefulness is a must! What comes to mind is a perspective shared by a man who set up an Internet satellite beside his travel trailer on a wilderness excursion. He said he used a compass so as to point the dish at a particular angle based on latitude and longitude. If he got it "right on the mark," his computer picked up a signal and worked perfectly. But if the angle was slightly askew, he got nothing at all. He said precision was paramount because **fractional miscalculation** at the starting point eventuates in huge discrepancies in the latter end. Even so, a faulty platform for apocalyptic expectations that deviates in any degree from the Biblical panorama most often results in the outgrowth of numerous errors and misconceptions. *"A little leaven leaventh the whole lump"* (Gal. 5:9).

God forbid that we be found guilty of such miscalculations, *"intruding into those things"* not yet revealed unto us by His Holy Spirit (Co. 2:18).

"God is jealous over His mysteries, and He is not going to allow them to be mishandled, trifled with or rudely examined by those who do not have a right disposition of heart for them. There needs to be a **sense of reverence** and **appreciation** for divine mystery, and a **desire** that they be unveiled and revealed." [1]

Acknowledgment of **spiritual reality** is also crucial. Prophetic interpretation is far more than what we see before us in black and white, or hear with our natural hearing. It's also warfare: the *"Spirit of Truth"* versus the *"spirit of error"* (1 Jn. 4:6). Everything we garner as reliable must be rightly divided by the Holy Spirit and brought to the Touchstone of Scripture for cross confirmation; no violence done to the Spirit of the Word in its contextual application; and no *"damaging God's character"*[2] in an attempt to make ideas already cast in our imagination fit into the Biblical portrait.

As we delve in, we need to be mindful of the scope of conflict that we, as Christians, face in our struggle to *"come to the knowledge of the Truth"* (2 Tim. 3:7). Not only are we fighting demonic forces that would lead us astray and condition us for acceptance of the coming Antichrist, but also the *"lusts that war in . . . [our] members"* (Jam. 4:1).

In our humanity, we instinctively crave comfort and security (in a word, "normality") and recoil from the unknown, especially when it is surreal and may involve suffering for ourselves and those that we love. Unless we exercise extreme caution and maintain an attitude of faith and surrender to God's Will at all times, we can unwittingly fall prey to satanic influences, personal projections, and/or to the haphazard assimilation of untested doctrines that have already found recognition in the "Christian" community.

Spiritual slothfulness is another big problem for many. It's so much easier to rely on the doctrine of others that are seemingly expert in eschatology, than to personally delve into the Scriptures, especially when weighing the possibility of discovering truths that put us at odds with the religious status quo. Who among us relishes the idea of being branded as a "fanatic" or "outsider," particularly when it comes to the advent of Christ; a dimension of the faith brought into great disrepute by false End-Time teachers, Hollywood-styled sensationalists, the Jehovah's Witnesses, Branhamists and far-out doomsday prognosticators that set dates for Christ's Appearance that are never realized?

"But of that day and that hour knoweth no man, no, not the angels which are in heaven, neither the Son, but the Father." Mark 13:32

Regrettably, those that have trespassed in this way have fueled the contempt of a new crop of scorners (within and without many churches) that dismiss the relevance of the Book of Revelation, thus stepping into the shoes of the *"scoffers"* that the Apostle Peter warned would come.

"Knowing this first, that there shall come in the Last Days scoffers, walking after their own lusts, and saying, Where is the promise of His coming? For since the fathers fell asleep, all things continue as they were from the beginning of the creation." 2 Peter 3:3, 4

Cleanse Us, O Lord, & Open our Eyes

Knowing the seriousness of the matter, we encourage readers to join with us in the following prayers for Holy Spirit illumination and cleansing *(Eph. 1:17, 18)*. Be willing to start afresh, with all *"tables"* clean (so to speak); totally <u>independent</u> of past biases; and totally <u>dependent</u> on the *"Spirit of Truth,"* ready to build on God's Word from the ground up.

"For all tables are full of vomit and filthiness, so that there is no place clean. Whom shall He teach knowledge? And whom shall He make to understand doctrine? Them that are weaned from the milk, and drawn from the breasts. For precept must be upon precept, precept upon precept; line upon line, line upon line; here a little, and there a little." Isaiah 28:8-10

"Howbeit when He, the **Spirit of Truth**, is come, He will guide you into all Truth: for He shall not speak of Himself; but whatsoever He shall hear, that shall He speak: and **He will shew you things to come.**" John 16:13

In obedience to Christ's command to *"search the scriptures" (Jn. 5:39)*, join with us and the Bereans documented in the Book of Acts. These devout believers searched the Word daily for wisdom and understanding.

"These [Bereans] were more noble than those in Thessalonica, in that they **received the Word** with all readiness of mind, and **searched the scriptures daily**, whether those things were so."
Acts 17:11

Take out your reliable 1611 King James Bible and prayerfully follow along in this teaching. That way you can scripturally identify the major landmarks and warnings that have been setup to guide us in "soul-safety" through the *"Time of the End" (Dan. 12:4, 9)*.

Let all fears, doubts and former persuasions; as well as all apprehensions about the things to come, and how they may affect personal priorities, relationships and plans; be abandoned at the foot of the Cross, and subordinated to the Will of the Father. He can <u>surely</u> be trusted, for He holds the future in His hands and has every hair on our heads numbered *(Mt. 10:30)*.

"O Holy Spirit, Spirit of Truth, Thou Breath of God, Thou Wind of Heaven, come and blow upon Your servant until all the chaff of untruthfulness is carried away, and continue to blow until only the full grown kernel of Truth remains." [3]

". . . I believe with my whole heart in the [true Gospel of Jesus Christ], and will live and die therein. I hereby renounce all false doctrines, heresies, [evil religious spirits] and sects, which are not in accordance with God and His Word. And if I have erred in any respect through false doctrine, I pray the Almighty God, to forgive me through His great love and mercy [In Jesus' name, Amen]."
Jacques D'Auchy, betrayed & secretly murdered by Catholic decree for his bold defense of the Gospel, A.D. 1558 [4]

CHAPTER NINE

The Seventieth Week of Daniel

When approaching End-Time prophecy it is important to remember that Scripture interprets scripture. The Old Testament interprets the New Testament. Daniel interprets Revelation. Hence, as a starting point (as well as a continuum) believers need to have a grasp on the structure and purposes of Daniel's Seventieth Week. **Jesus commanded us to understand apocalyptic events in light of Daniel's prophecy** *(Mt. 24:15).* As long as we rely on Daniel's seven year template as our **foundational point of reference**, we can safely navigate through the rest of the Word piecing together the End-Time puzzle. Without it, we are like ships without a compass, lost in a sea of mystery, *"tossed to and fro, and carried about with every wind of doctrine" (Eph. 4:14).*

Cross confirmation of Daniel's prophetic framework stands center stage in chapters Thirteen and Fourteen of the Book of Revelation. Illuminated by the Holy Spirit, like an x-ray against a back drop of light, it shows itself in perfect alignment. Surrounding passages, like joints and ligaments, fill in the rest of the End-Time panorama; from the rise of the Antichrist, to the return of Christ to earth to fight the great Battle of Armageddon and establish His Thousand Year Reign *(Rev. 19:11-21; 20:4).*

At times these events unfold sequentially, and at others some of the puzzle pieces are scattered. Resolution and order can come to us, however, if we (as Bereans) search the Scriptures for overlapping passages that match in substance and format; while at the same time providing additional details (as unique as snowflakes) that make the things they describe, and their proper placement, more recognizable. Once discovered, we are then able to snap the pieces into place. As a result, piece by piece, a reliable landscape of events begins to take form.

Two Distinct Periods
The Mid-Week Resurrection: The Great Divide

Daniel's Seventieth Week is comprised of **two distinct periods** that are each approximately three and a half years long. Their duration is described twice each in Daniel and Revelation as *"time, times, and an half"* and/or *"forty and two months"* (Dan. 12:7; 7:25; Rev. 11:2; 13:5).* Each part is so vastly **different in purpose** (one from the other) that the Lord **divided** them *"in the midst"* with one of the most defining and unmistakable events of all time (Dan. 9:27): **the Appearance of His Son** for His Church (Mt. 24:30, 31; Mk. 13:26, 27). Distinguishing which of the passages in Daniel and Revelation refer to the first half of Daniel's Seventieth Week; and which passages to the latter half; requires an understanding of God's eternal purposes unique to each. Those eternal purposes are to be found in the Mystery of Israel and the Church.* *

A Harvest Scenario

In the Book of Revelation, this **Mid-Week Resurrection** is described as a Glorious ingathering of faithful believers into the Father's Heavenly Granaries, followed by a great outpouring of the *"Wrath of God"* upon the wicked that are left behind to suffer just retribution for their sins.

"And I looked, and behold a white cloud, and upon the cloud One sat like unto the Son of man, having on His head a golden crown, and in His hand a sharp sickle. And another angel came out of the temple, crying with a loud voice to Him that sat on the cloud, Thrust in Thy sickle, and reap: for the time is come for Thee to reap; for the harvest of the earth is ripe. And He that sat on the cloud thrust in His sickle on the earth; and **the earth was reaped**. [This is the Mid-Week Resurrection of saints.] And another angel came out of the temple which is in heaven, he also having a sharp sickle. And another angel came out from the altar, which had

---

*   In Biblical terminology the term "time" connotes a one year period. See Daniel 4:32 for an example of its usage.

* *   Refer to Chapter Five.

power over fire; and cried with a loud cry to him that had the sharp sickle, saying, Thrust in thy sharp sickle, and gather the clusters of the vine of the earth; for her grapes are fully ripe. And the angel thrust in his sickle into the earth, and gathered the vine of the earth, and cast it into **the great winepress of the Wrath of God**."
Revelation 14:14-19

Other passages containing the same structure run their course throughout the New Testament. Some use the same harvest scenario *(Mt. 3:12; 13:36-43)*, while others use different similitudes. Yet, they all point to the same sequence of events complete with its Mid-Week divide; and each contains information regarding the circumstances that precede and follow after it.

Christ's likening of the *"time of the end"* to the days of Noah and Lot is one of the most well known. Here again, we see the same severing of the wicked from among the just; the same ingathering of *"the righteous"* at the Mid-Week Resurrection; and the same outpouring of Wrath upon the earth that follows in its wake.

"For as the lightning, that lighteneth out of the one part under heaven, shineth unto the other part under heaven; so shall also the Son of man be in His day. . . . And as it was in the days of Noe [Noah], so shall it be also in the days of the Son of man. They did eat, they drank, they married wives, they were given in marriage, **until the day** that **Noe entered into the ark**, and the flood came, and destroyed them all. Likewise also as it was in the days of Lot; they did eat, they drank, they bought, they sold, they planted, they builded; but **the same day** that **Lot went out of Sodom** it rained fire and brimstone from heaven, and destroyed them all. Even thus shall it be in the day when the Son of man is revealed. . . . I tell you, in that night there shall be two men in one bed; the one shall be **taken**, and the other shall be **left**. Two women shall be grinding together; the one shall be **taken**, and the other **left**. Two men shall be in the field; the one shall be **taken**, and the other **left**." Luke 17:24, 26-30, 34-36

The First 3½ years of Daniel's Seventieth Week
The "Great Tribulation": "War with the Saints"

Although each 3½ year period of the "Week" has its own set of calamities, they are drastically different in severity and purpose. The most pronounced characteristics that set the first period of *"Great Tribulation,"* **before the Appearance of Christ for His Church,** apart from the second period, referred to as the *"Great Day of His Wrath" (Mt. 24:21; Rev. 7:14; Rev. 6:17),* are the **presence, persecution and purification of believers** under the tyranny of the Antichrist. It is for that reason that it is identified in both Daniel and Revelation as: *"War with the Saints."*

"I beheld, and the same horn made **war with the saints**, and prevailed against them. . . . And he [the Antichrist] shall speak great words against the Most High, and shall **wear out the saints** of the Most High, and think to change times and laws: and they shall be given into his hand **until** a time and times and the dividing of time [3½ years]." Daniel 7:21, 25

"And there was given unto him [the Antichrist] a mouth speaking great things and blasphemies; and power was given unto him to continue forty and two months [3½ years]. And he opened his mouth in blasphemy against God, to blaspheme His name, and His tabernacle, and them that dwell in heaven. And it was given unto him to make **war with the saints**, and to **overcome them**: and power was given him over all kindreds, and tongues, and nations."
Revelation 13:5-7

In these two passages we see that the Lord's primary instrument of testing for Christ's Church during this time is not seemingly random freaks of nature and other sorrows (though they be many and indeed *"perilous"—2 Tim. 3:1)*; but rather, in the **persecutions and sufferings** that Christians shall be called to endure because of their refusal to deny Christ, worship Satan and his Antichrist, and take upon themselves the **Mark of the Beast** for sustenance and survival *(Rev. 13:15-17).*

Undoubtedly, tribulation of every kind is a necessary form of chastening and testing that has its glorious outworking in our sanctification. But nothing so completely tests our fidelity to the Lord, and our "worthiness" of His eternal Kingdom, as our willingness to go with Him, not only to the Promised Land, but also, all the way to Calvary, if need be *(1 Pet. 2:19-21)*.

Believers that faithfully endure this test without denying Christ or departing from the Gospel (regardless of the cost or consequence) shall experience the Lord's deliverance at the Mid-Week Resurrection. But faithless and *"unprofitable"* professing Christians that *"obey not the Gospel of our Lord Jesus Christ"* and draw back in fear *(Mt. 25:30; 2 Th. 1:8; Heb. 10:35-39)*; or, who get swept up in the *"spirit of the world"* *(1 Cor. 2:12)*; shall become part of a great ***"falling away"*** *(2 Th. 2:3)*. As a result of their rebellion and spiritual laxity, they'll be **left behind** with unbelievers to suffer the **Great Wrath of God** that is unleashed on the earth during the second half of Daniel's Seventieth Week *(Mt. 24:36-51)*.

"And the destruction of the transgressors [the disobedient] and of the sinners [unbelievers] shall be together, and they that forsake the Lord [backsliders and apostates] shall be consumed."

Isaiah 1:28

The Glory of Tribulation

God's Glorious purposes during the *"Great Tribulation"* are three-fold.

<u>Number One</u>: **"To try them that dwell upon the earth,"** and thereby **separate the wheat from the tares** *(Rev. 3:10b; Mt. 13:36-43)*; the children of obedience and eternal life *(Heb. 5:9)*; from the children of disobedience and wrath *(Eph. 5:6; Col. 3:6; Rom. 2:8)*. During this *"hour of temptation, which shall come upon all the world"* *(Rev. 3:10)*, the thoughts, motives and deeds of every person alive shall be tried in a furnace of affliction; and the Gospel shall go forth in full power as God's only acceptable remedy for atonement and escape from the Wrath to come. All those that are brought to Christ, as well as those that already profess to be His, shall then be *"throughly purge[d]"* on His threshing floor. There it shall be

determined who shall be gathered unto Him and caught up into heaven at His appearance (Mt. 3:12); and who shall be left behind with the unbelievers; first to suffer the Great Wrath of God, and thereafter to be thrown into the Lake of Fire.

"When the Son of man shall come in His Glory, and all the holy angels with Him, then shall He sit upon the throne of His Glory: and before Him shall be gathered all nations: and **He shall separate them one from another**, as a shepherd divideth His sheep from the goats: and He shall set the sheep on His right hand, but the goats on the left. Then shall the King say unto them on His right hand, Come, ye blessed of My Father, inherit the Kingdom prepared for you from the foundation of the world. . . . Then shall He say also unto them on the left hand, Depart from Me, ye cursed, into everlasting fire, prepared for the Devil and his angels."
Matthew 25:31-34, 41

"As therefore the tares are gathered and burned in the fire; so shall it be in the end of this world. The Son of man shall send forth His angels, and they shall **gather out of His Kingdom all things that offend, and them which do iniquity**; and shall cast them into a furnace of fire: there shall be wailing and gnashing of teeth."
Matthew 13:40-42

Number Two: **To cleanse the Bride of Christ** of *"spot, or wrinkle, or any such thing"* in preparation to be received of the Bridegroom Jesus at His Appearance on the Day of the Lord (Eph. 5:27; Rev. 19:7, 8). Tribulation (inclusive of hardship, distress, persecution and adversity) creates a powerful threshing action in our lives that separates the eternal kernel of Christ's Presence within us from the chaff carried over from the world. This beautiful work of sanctification does its most extensive work amidst the pressure of heated trials, which cause our sins to surface like the dross in precious metals. Those that faithfully walk through it shall come forth as gold.

"Wherein ye greatly rejoice, though now for a season, if need be, ye are in heaviness through manifold temptations: that the **trial of your faith**, being much more precious than of gold that perisheth, though it be tried with fire, might be found unto praise and honour and Glory **at the appearing of Jesus Christ**." 1 Peter 1:6, 7

<u>Number Three</u>: **To sound a call to repentance and bring in a bountiful Harvest of Souls.**

Jesus said: "And this Gospel of the Kingdom shall be preached in all the world for a witness unto all nations; and <u>then</u> shall the End come." Matthew 24:14

Blessed are those that understand the Lord's grand design for His people during this perplexing time. Instead of shrinking in fear looking for a way to get out of it, they will be challenged to walk faithfully through it *(Deu. 4:30, 31)*.

"Yea, such fearless ones run through patience (mark, through), not out of, but <u>into</u>, the conflict that is set before us, and look not at the dreadful tyranny, but unto Jesus, the Captain, the Author and Finisher of our faith. Heb. 12:2." Hendrick Alewijns, Tortured & burned to death by Catholic Decree, A.D. 1569 [1]

"Many shall be purified, and made white, and tried; but the wicked shall do wickedly: and none of the wicked shall understand; but **the wise shall understand**." Daniel 12:10

The Second 3½ years of Daniel's Seventieth Week "The Great Day of His Wrath" (Rev. 6:17)

There are three distinctives that set this latter three and a half year period of Great *"Wrath"* apart from the first three and a half years of *"Great Tribulation."*

- <u>The first distinctive</u> is the **absence of the saints**.

Speaking to faithful believers, the Apostle Paul said: *"God hath not appointed us to Wrath (1 Th. 5:9).* Instead, Like Noah and Lot, we are promised deliverance from it; Christ Himself having taught us to seek to be counted *"worthy"* of its *"escape" (Lk. 21:36)*.

- <u>The second distinctive</u> is the **magnitude of God's dealings** in fulfillment of Daniel 9:24.

Once the saints are removed, the *"fiery indignation"* of the Lord shall sweep the earth *(Heb. 10:27)*. Those left behind continue to suffer the dictatorial rule of the Antichrist, as well as a series of unparalleled supernatural judgments unleashed in fury by God Himself. Violence and civil strife shall be rife *(Zec. 14:13)*.

• The third distinctive is God's dealings, not only with an impenitent mankind; but also with the **nation of Israel**, the **Jewish people** and the Holy City of **Jerusalem** in particular *(Lk. 21:20-24)*.

"And I heard the man clothed in linen, which was upon the waters of the river, when he held up his right hand and his left hand unto heaven, and sware by Him that liveth for ever that it shall be for a time, times, and an half [3½ years]; and when he shall have accomplished to scatter the power of the holy people, all these things shall be finished." Daniel 12:7

"But the court which is without the temple leave out, and measure it not; for it is given unto the Gentiles: and the Holy City [Jerusalem] shall they tread under foot forty and two months [3½ years]."
Revelation 11:2

These passages speak of a **final scattering of Jews** for *"double"* judgment **before a final ingathering of penitent Jewish survivors** [a remnant or "residue"] who come to the Messiah; and as a result, become full participants in Christ's Millennial reign from His Throne in Jerusalem *(Isa. 40:2; Zec. 12:10-14)*.

The Great Wrath shall be to Israel, what the Great Tribulation is going to be to the Church: a time of **sifting and separation**.

"Behold, the eyes of the Lord God are upon the sinful kingdom, and I will destroy it from off the face of the earth; saving that I will not utterly destroy the House of Jacob, saith the Lord. For, lo, I will command, and I will sift the House of Israel among all nations, like as corn is sifted in a sieve, yet shall not the least grain fall upon the earth. **All the sinners of My people shall die** by the sword, which say, The evil shall not overtake nor prevent us."
Amos 9:8-10

At its conclusion, however, converted Jews shall not be gathered up into heaven to be with the Lord like the Church at the Mid-Week Resurrection. Instead, they shall be gathered from around the world in a Second Exodus, and brought to the Land of Israel where each shall receive his appointed lot, according to God's long standing promise to His people *(Eze. 36:11)*.

"For thus saith the Lord God; Behold, I, even I, will both search My sheep, and seek them out. As a shepherd seeketh out his flock in the day that he is among his sheep that are scattered; so will I **seek out My sheep**, and will **deliver them** out of all places where they have been scattered in the cloudy and dark day. And I will bring them out from the people, and gather them from the countries, and will **bring them to their own land**, and feed them upon the mountains of Israel by the rivers, and in all the inhabited places of the country. . . . I will seek that which was lost, and bring again that which was driven away, and will bind up that which was broken, and will strengthen that which was sick: but I will destroy the fat and the strong; I will feed them with judgment. . . . Therefore will I save My flock, and they shall no more be a prey; and I will judge between cattle and cattle. And I will set up one Shepherd over them . . ." Ezekiel 34:11-13, 16, 22, 23a

Herein is the Mystery of Israel and the Church:

The *"Great Tribulation"* is primarily about a great harvest of souls, the purging by persecution of hypocrites from the Church, and the purification of the Bride of Christ in preparation for the Appearance of the Lord.

The *"Great Day of [God's] Wrath"* that follows in its wake is primarily about the destruction of the wicked, the purging by judgment of impenitent Jews from among His people, and the reconciliation of a remnant of surviving Jews to the God that chose them as His own *"peculiar treasure"* *(Exo. 19:5)*.

Both halves of the Week tie directly into the overthrow of Satan's rule and the unification of the Redeemed Church and Israel for joint rule under Christ, beginning with His Millennial reign, and continuing onward into His everlasting Kingdom.

CHAPTER TEN

The Great Tribulation
First Half of Daniel's Seventieth Week

Faithful Christian Overcomers are Here on Earth.

Now that the structure and purposes of Daniel's Seventieth Week have been set forth, let's take a look at the events that are to unfold during the *"Great Tribulation"* in their Biblical sequence. During this time the Lord Jesus Christ is going to break the first six seals of the End-Time Book *(Rev. 5:7-9; 6:1)*. At its close, He shall break the seventh seal and split the Week in half with His magnificent Appearance in the clouds.

The First Seal
The Rise of the Antichrist

Scripture says that in the Last Days, just prior to the Appearance of Jesus Christ for His sanctified Bride, two landmark events are to occur: one, a **great** *"falling away"* from the true Christian faith; and two, the **revelation of a single world leader** that represents to be the prophesied Messiah, but is actually a *"false christ"* *(Mt. 24:24; Mk. 13:22)*, or *"Antichrist"* *(1 Jn. 2:18)*. Though this despot is yet to be revealed, the **apostasy** started long ago at the outset of Christianity *(Acts 20:30; 2 Tim. 4:10)*. It picked up momentum thereafter with the rise of Catholicism; was carried through subsequent centuries through other wayward sects; continues its acceleration today; and shall surpass anything ever seen before as the approach of Jesus draws near.

"Now we beseech you, brethren, by the coming of our Lord Jesus Christ, and by our gathering together unto Him, that ye be not soon shaken in mind, or be troubled, neither by spirit, nor by word, nor by letter as from us, as that the **Day of Christ** is at hand. Let no man deceive you by any means: for that Day shall not come, except there come a **falling away first, and that man of sin be re-**

vealed, **the son of perdition**; who opposeth and exalteth himself above all that is called God, or that is worshipped; so that he as God sitteth in the temple of God, shewing himself that he is God."
2 Thessalonians 2:1-4

This *"son of perdition,"* also referred to as a *"Beast,"* or the *"First Beast"* *(Rev. 13:1, 12)*, will be a type of Nebuchadnezzar, in that he will be *"a king of kings,"* that rules *"wheresoever the children of men dwell"* *(Dan. 2:38)*. And just like Nebuchadnezzar, he will require all the world <u>under penalty of death</u> to worship an idolatrous *"image"* *(Dan. 3:5, 6; Rev. 13:15)*. Having been given power by Satan to rule over all people, he shall be used as the Devil's conduit to retaliate against God for Lucifer's humiliating *"fall from heaven"* by blaspheming the Almighty and making *"war"* with true believers *(Lk. 10:18; Rev. 12:13)*.

"And there was given unto him [the Antichrist] a mouth speaking great things and blasphemies; and power was given unto him to continue forty and two months [3½ years]. And he opened his mouth in blasphemy against God, to blaspheme His name, and His tabernacle, and them that dwell in heaven. And it was given unto him to make **war with the saints**, and <u>to overcome them</u>: and power was given him over all kindreds, and tongues, and nations."
Revelation 13:5-7

Just as Satan operated through the Serpent in the Garden of Eden, so the Devil will empower the Beast at the end of the world in hopes of using his last allotment of time to fulfill his diabolical obsession to be worshipped as God.

"Woe to the inhabiters of the earth and of the sea! For the Devil is come down unto you, having great wrath, because he knoweth that he hath but a short time." Revelation 12:12b

"And the Beast [Antichrist] which I saw was like unto a leopard, and his feet were as the feet of a bear, and his mouth as the mouth of a lion: and **the dragon [Satan] gave him his power**, and his seat, and great authority." Revelation 13:2

This *"Beast"* comes to power during times of increasing *"sorrows"* *(Mt. 24:8)*, making **false promises of peace** and prosperity. Suffering one calamitous natural disaster after another, economically depressed; laden with crime; terrorized by perpetual wars; immersed in civil strife; and buried in local, national, and international upheavals; all nations will accept this smooth talking seducer in hopes of being rescued from the growing chaos. He will be an **Ecumenical Champion** that promises a global socialist Utopia of *"peace and safety"* on <u>conditions</u> of total subservience to his economic, political and religious domain *(1 Th. 5:2, 3)*.

". . . He shall come in peaceably, and obtain the kingdom by flatteries." Daniel 11:21b

Feigning himself to be the true Christ described in Rev. 19:11-13, the Antichrist shall go forth *"conquering and to conquer"* *(2 Th. 2:4)*.

"And I saw when the Lamb opened one of the seals, and I heard, as it were the noise of thunder, one of the four beasts saying, Come and see. And I saw, and behold a white horse: and he that sat on him had a bow; and a crown was given unto him: and he went forth conquering, and to conquer." Revelation 6:1, 2

Taking the wealth and property of the "haves" and distributing it among the "have-nots" he shall win the hearts of the masses.

". . . He shall scatter among them the prey, and spoil, and riches . . ." Daniel 11:24

One World Community of Worshippers

Kings and paupers from all walks of life shall become subjects of *"Babylon the Great"* *(Rev. 17:5; 18:2)*, the international system that sustains the Beast's seat of power. At its heart lies a state run religious monopoly led by another *"Beast"* *(Rev. 13:11-15)*, a *"False Prophet"* *(Rev. 16:13; 19:20)*. This incredibly persuasive sorcerer shall be endowed with **supernatural powers** that enable him to rally a global community of worshippers that shall jointly serve the Antichrist.

"And I beheld another Beast coming up out of the earth; and he had two horns like a lamb, and he spake as a dragon. And he exerciseth all the power of the first Beast before him, and causeth the earth and them which dwell therein to worship the first Beast, whose deadly wound was healed." Revelation 13:11, 12

Already the world is being conditioned for subservience to this global religious network as liberal elements of all faiths merge in a **united push towards ecumenism**. Propelled by a *"spirit of whoredoms" (Hos. 4:12)*, this movement requires the setting aside of Biblical doctrines and ordinances in favor of what is now being deceptively promoted as "unity" for the sake of "peace and prosperity for all." Defenders of the nation of Israel, in their zeal for the safekeeping of a nation under constant enemy fire, are especially susceptible to this deception. **No God-fearing Christian should have anything at all to do with it** *(Rev. 18:4)*! Though its outward face may appear noble, Satan's underlying purpose for it is to draw Christ's sheep out from the true pastures into a Harlot Church (the *"whore"* of Revelation— *Rev. 17:1, 5, 15*), and to usher in the coming reign of the Antichrist. Eventually this religious monstrosity, as well as the socialist regime it supports, shall come crashing down. Like a modern day *"tower"* of *"Babel,"* complete with its own mythical stairway to heaven, *"Babylon the Great"* shall be brought to nothing *(Gen. 11:1-9)*.

"And he cried mightily with a strong voice, saying, **Babylon the Great** is fallen, is fallen, and is become the habitation of devils, and the hold of every foul spirit, and a cage of every unclean and hateful bird. For all nations have drunk of the wine of the wrath of her fornication, and the kings of the earth have committed fornication with her, and the merchants of the earth are waxed rich through the abundance of her delicacies." Revelation 18:2, 3

Temporary Peace for Israel

Inspired and empowered by the Devil, the Antichrist shall arise with a small band of supporters and gain worldwide recognition for his uncanny ability to broker a **Mid-East Peace Pact for the "protection" of Israel** *(Dan. 9:27; 11:21-*

24). Once the Antichrist seizes power <u>and</u> the peace pact is initiated, know for a certainty that the first seal has been broken. **The seven year countdown** of the End-Time clock (beginning with 42 months of Great Tribulation) **has begun!**

"And <u>after the league made with him</u> he shall work deceitfully: for he shall come up, and shall become strong with a small people."
Daniel 11:23

Seals Two, Three and Four
"Perilous Times"

"This know also, that in the Last Days **perilous times** shall come."
2 Timothy 3:1

The events that follow are graphically described in Revelation Chapter Six, as well as in Matthew 24, Mark 13 and Luke 21. During the Great Tribulation, war, famine and death shall take the lives of at least one quarter of the world's population *(Rev. 6:3-8).* That percentage exceeds one and a half billion people according to present day statistics. In addition to this, there shall be an escalation of climatic disasters that shall go from bad to worse. We are experiencing a foretaste of these *"sorrows."*

"And ye shall hear of wars and rumours of wars: see that ye be not troubled: for all these things must come to pass, but the end is not yet. For nation shall rise against nation, and kingdom against kingdom: and there shall be famines, and pestilences, and earthquakes, in divers places. All these are the beginning of sorrows."
Matthew 24:6-8; See also Mark 13:6-8

The prophet David Wilkerson caught a glimpse of what we are to expect in a vision he received back in 1973.

"I saw nature having labor pains. Supernatural signs and changes that can't be explained by men. Worldwide disasters that we're witnessing right now I see as labor pains in nature which are going to become more and more frequent and more intense the closer we get to the birth of the Kingdom of God. I saw major earthquakes coming to the United States. I saw worldwide famine especially in China, India and Russia. I saw the world's food supplies completely dwindled and millions starving. I saw coming a new kind of cosmic storm appearing as a raging fire in the sky leaving a kind of vapor trail. Tornadoes, hailstorms, floods and hurricanes are going to pound the earth with such intensity and violence that all of mankind is going to have to admit the world is under supernatural siege."[1]

Knowing what is on the horizon, Satan has already conjured up a lie to hide God's pleadings by blaming the escalating catastrophes on "Global Warming," often referred to as "Climate Change." This hoax (though thoroughly debunked) is staunchly defended with pseudo-science by those profiteering from this deception.

A Deluge of Evil Spirits

The greatest peril of all, however, (except for the persecution madness that pinnacles with the mandatory worship of the Beast) is going to be **deception**. Satan is going to unleash a barrage of *"seducing spirits"* as bearers of **false doctrine** (i.e. philosophies, ideologies, godless imaginings, etc.) in hopes of drawing even the most devout Christians into his net *(Mt. 24:24)*.

"Now the Spirit speaketh expressly, that in the latter times some shall depart from the faith, giving heed to **seducing spirits**, and **doctrines of devils**."   1 Timothy 4:1

False prophets, equally (if not more) cunning than those of former times are going to multiply, using every imaginable artifice to redefine the Gospel and thus capture the hearts of the *"simple" (Rom. 16:18)*, as well as the wary *(Acts 20:29-31)*.

"But evil men and **seducers** shall wax worse and worse, deceiving, and being deceived."   2 Timothy 3:13

"For **false Christs** and **false prophets** shall rise, and shall shew signs and wonders, to **seduce**, if it were possible, even the elect. But take ye heed: behold, I have foretold you all things."
Mark 13:22, 23

The deterioration has already begun. Cultivating "doctrine" in reverse of his Maker, the Devil is now working through false prophets and unrenewed church leaders to remove one bedrock of the Gospel after another from the foundation of the faith. At the same time, he is replacing them, *"precept upon precept; line upon line . . . here a little, and there a little"* with **lies disguised in Biblical vernacular**, but contrary in meaning and purpose *(Isa. 28:10)*. His aim is twofold: <u>one</u>, to create a universal belief system that changes the narrow way to eternal life presented in the New Testament into his *"broad"* way to perdition *(Mt. 7:13, 14)*; and <u>two</u>, to transform the face of our Lord Jesus Christ— first into a caricature—and ultimately into the *"image"* of the Antichrist *(2 Cor. 11:4)*.

The news media and the Ecumenical Movement are major tools in the Devil's hands for furthering this subversive propaganda. Once it has run its course, evil will be called good; lawlessness (meaning rebellion against the Law of the Lord) will be legislated as righteousness; true Christianity will be condemned as sedition; and *"the son of perdition"* (the Antichrist), *"as God"* will sit *"in the temple of God, shewing himself that he is God"* *(2 Th. 2:3b, 4)*.

"I know of nothing that so securely and firmly holds men in the sleep of sin till the Lord comes as a thief in the night, as to call good evil (Isa. 5:20), the Gospel a sect (of which all manner of evil and falsehoods are spoken), and to change the truth into lies. . . . [By this means true] Christians are called heretics and deceivers; every good work, virtue and righteousness is . . . misnamed, perverted, painted in such abominable colors, and the worst construction put upon them [true believers]. . . . The Devil, on the other hand does not appear half so ugly. . . . Disguised by a beautiful semblance of love, and changed and transformed into an angel of light [2 Cor. 11:13-15], as though he were sent of God, and were himself God. II Thess. 2:4. Then are . . . lies called nothing less than Gospel and truth; [while] Babylon is called the church of God."
The Proof of the Faith,
One of two books written in prison by Valerius Schoolmaster
Before his execution by papal decree, A.D. 1568 [2]

Be Not Deceived

Acutely aware of this pending danger, Jesus launched His End-Time teaching with this warning:

". . . **Take heed lest any man deceive you**: for many shall come in My name, saying, I am Christ; and shall deceive many."
Mark 13:5b, 6; Luke 21:8

Shining light on the meaning of that admonition, William Tyndale (martyred in the fifteen hundreds for his exposure of Catholicism and for his translation of the Holy Scriptures into English) expounded, saying:

"Christ saith that there shall come false prophets in His name and say that they themselves are Christ, that is, they shall so preach Christ that men must believe in them, in their holiness and things of their imagination <u>without God's Word</u>. . . . Behold how they are esteemed, and how high they be crept up above all, not into worldly seats only: but into **the seat of God, the hearts of men**, where they sit above God Himself. For both they and whatsoever they make of their own heads is more feared and dread, than God and His commandments. In them and their deservings put we more trust than in Christ and His merits. To their promises give we more faith, than to the promises which God hath sworn in Christ's blood." William Tyndale [3]

Only the Word of God ...the love of God ...the fear of God ...and a **jealous regard for Truth** can keep us from being deceived by the spirit of antichrist, and ultimately by the Antichrist Himself. Sound grounding in End-Time doctrine is essential.

"Ye therefore, beloved, seeing ye know these things before, beware lest ye also, being **led away with the error of the wicked**, <u>fall</u> from your own stedfastness. 2 Peter 3:17

". . . As the Church of Christ draws near to the <u>time of the End</u> . . . the full force of the Deceiver and his hosts of lying spirits will be directed upon the living members of the Body of Christ. . . . **Knowledge of Truth** is the primary safeguard against deception. The 'elect' must *know*, and they must learn to 'prove' the 'spirits' *until they do know* what is of God, and what is of Satan. The words of the Master, 'Take heed, I have told you,' plainly implies that personal knowledge of danger is part of the Lord's way of guarding His own, and believers who blindly rely upon 'the keeping power of God,' without seeking to understand how to escape deception, when forewarned to 'take heed' by the Lord, will surely find themselves entrapped by the subtle foe."

Jesse Penn-Lewis with Evan Roberts [4]

Love for the veracity of the Gospel will not be enough to rescue us, however. We also need a love for the bald-faced Truth **brought to bear upon the conscience** by the Holy Ghost; convicting us of our sins *(Jn. 16:8)*, unmasking our hypocrisy, and calling us to daily repentance and amendment of life. Without the **Cross of Christ** at work in our lives, we are wide open to the satanic sorceries of the Antichrist and False Prophet, sent in the sovereignty of God, as a judgment upon all those that are deficient in their zeal for Truth and the righteousness it begets *(2 Tim. 4:3, 4)*. Souls in such a state are extremely vulnerable to lies, especially when those lies are accompanied by false promises of relief from suffering in perilous times, and are followed by *"signs and lying wonders"* that seemingly affirm their origin as "divine."

"For the mystery of iniquity doth already work: only He who now letteth will let, until he be taken out of the way. And then shall that Wicked be revealed, whom the Lord shall consume with the spirit of His mouth, and shall destroy with the brightness of His coming: Even him, whose coming is after the working of Satan with all power and signs and lying wonders, and with all deceivableness of unrighteousness in them that perish; because they **received not the love of the Truth**, that they might be saved. And for this cause God shall send them **strong delusion**, that they should believe a lie: that they all might be damned who **believed not the Truth**, but had pleasure in unrighteousness. But we are bound to give thanks alway to God for you, brethren beloved of the Lord, because God hath from the beginning chosen you to Salvation through **sanctification of the Spirit** and **belief of the Truth**."

2 Thessalonians 2:7-13

Hallelujah! Bringing in the Sheaves

Though the earth shall be in travail due to manifold judgments and civil strife, the saints shall be rejoicing knowing that adversity is the most prolific time for winning souls. Great Tribulation, in combination with the preaching of the true Gospel of Jesus Christ, and a great outpouring of the Holy Spirit, shall produce an astounding harvest. Those that genuinely hunger and thirst after righteousness shall be filled *(Mt. 5:6)*.

After long years of sowing, a remnant of faithful believers will live to see the fruits of their labors. Some of their relatives, neighbors and friends, hardened in sin, shall fall to their knees in repentance. A number of those that formerly felt they had no need for God (or, thought they knew Him, but in truth lacked a "living faith") shall at last acknowledge their need and look up to the Lord Jesus Christ for Salvation. When *"all"* other avenues of *"hope"* are *"taken away"* *(Acts 27:20)*, a residue of wayward souls will finally stop pursuing the world and yield their lives to Christ.

From sea to sea, captives shaken by manifold disasters will be set free from Satan's chains and be gathered unto Christ, like ripe olive berries gathered from the boughs of the world's trees *(Isa. 17:6; 24:13)*.

What a privilege to be part of the last ingathering before Christ's Appearance! Even the direst sufferings seem small when compared to the jubilation of ushering one precious soul into the arms of the Lord Jesus Christ *(Lk. 15:3-10)*. Praise be unto God!

"They that sow in tears shall reap in joy. He that goeth forth and weepeth, bearing precious seed, shall doubtless come again with rejoicing, bringing his sheaves with him." Psalm 126:5, 6

The Fifth Seal
"War with the Saints" (Daniel 7:21; Revelation 13:7)

Not only shall there be calamities of unprecedented proportion, but also, persecution to the uttermost unleashed against Christ's Beloved Bride.

"And when He had opened the **fifth seal**, I saw under the altar the souls of them that were slain for the Word of God, and for the testimony which they held."   Revelation 6:9; See also Rev. 20:4

This acceleration of persecution will be of **satanic** instigation *(Rev. 13:4, 7)*, comparable in magnitude to the sufferings endured by the early Christians; and to the round up and mass martyrdom of Christ's faithful witnesses during the Roman Catholic Inquisition.

This last wave of violence, just like the Jewish pogroms of times past, shall proceed primarily from Nuremberg type edicts* made by the Antichrist and his False Prophet, and shall be carried out by those allied with his Beast System.

"And he [the Antichrist] shall speak great words against the Most High, and shall <u>wear out the saints</u> of the Most High, and think to **change times and laws**: and they shall be given into his hand until a time and times and the dividing of time [3½ years]."
Daniel 7:25

It shall be a contest of kingdoms unparalleled in the history of man.

"War is the key word of the Apocalypse; war on a scale undreamed of by mortal man; war between vast angelic powers of light and darkness; war by the dragon, and the deceived world powers upon <u>the saints</u>; war by the same world-powers against the Lamb; war by the dragon upon <u>the Church</u>; war in many phases and forms, **until the end** when the Lamb overcomes, and they also overcome who are with Him, called and chosen and faithful (Rev. xvii. 14)."   Jesse Penn-Lewis with Evan Roberts [5]

Mandatory Worship of the Beast and His Image

True Christianity shall be outlawed by decree and a **death penalty** shall be applied by the False Prophet to anyone that refuses to worship an *"image"* of the Antichrist.

---

* Race laws established in 1935 that stripped German Jews of their civil rights, casting them as "subjects," rather than as citizens, of Nazi Germany. These decrees eventually led to the deportation of Jews to Hitler's death camps, resulting in the Holocaust during World War II.

"And he had power to give life unto the image of the Beast, that the image of the Beast should both speak, and cause that as many as would not worship the image of the Beast should be **killed**."
Revelation 13:15

Informers shall include family, friends and foreigners; atheists and apostate Christians, too. Even neighbors and mentors will turn against faithful believers and hand them over to the authorities for prosecution.

"Trust ye not in a friend, put ye not confidence in a guide: keep the doors of thy mouth from her that lieth in thy bosom. For the son dishonoureth the father, the daughter riseth up against her mother, the daughter in law against her mother in law; a man's enemies are the men of his own house."
Micah 7:5, 6; See also Matthew 10:35, 36

"And ye shall be betrayed both by parents, and brethren, and kinsfolks, and friends; and some of you shall they cause to be put to death. And ye shall be hated of all men for My name's sake."
Luke 21:16, 17

The Mark of the Beast

Finally, socialism shall reach its peak. Everyone on earth that wants to transact business will be required to take on the **Mark of the Beast**. Sophisticated technology is already in place for embedding computer chips that could be used for this purpose. Everything from health care to housing—from food, to fuel, to finances—shall be under the control of the Antichrist.

"And he causeth all, both small and great, rich and poor, free and bond, to receive a **Mark** in their right hand, or in their foreheads: and that no man might buy or sell, save he that had the **Mark**, or the name of the Beast, or the number of his name."
Revelation 13:16, 17

Warning: Do Not Take the Mark!

The great challenge that shall face born again believers at this time shall be to heed the eternally consequential

warning given in Revelation **not** to consent <u>in any way</u> to the Antichrist's idolatrous imposition of demonic power by taking his **Mark**—even if that means death.

"And they overcame him [Satan] by the blood of the Lamb, and by the word of their testimony; and they loved not their lives unto the death." Revelation 12:11

"And the third angel followed them, saying with a loud voice, If any man <u>worship the Beast and his image</u>, and <u>receive his Mark in his forehead, or in his hand</u>, the same shall **drink of the wine of the wrath of God**, which is poured out without mixture into the cup of His indignation; and he shall be tormented with fire and brimstone in the presence of the holy angels, and in the presence of the Lamb: and the smoke of their torment ascendeth up for ever and ever: and they have no rest day nor night, who worship the Beast and his image, and whosoever receiveth the **Mark** of his name. Here is the <u>patience of the saints</u>: here are they that <u>keep the commandments of God</u>, and the <u>faith of Jesus</u>. And I heard a voice from heaven saying unto me, Write, Blessed are the dead which die in the Lord from henceforth: Yea, saith the Spirit, that they may rest from their labours; and their works do follow them."
Revelation 14:9-13

This passage of Scripture contains one of the most serious **warnings** and most exciting **promises** in the entire Bible. Those that bow down by any means to the Antichrist (or take on his **Mark**) shall be **damned**. Contrariwise, those that hold fast to their profession of Christ, without turning to the Beast System for sustenance and survival, shall *"endure unto the end"* and thus be *"**saved**"* (Mt. 24:13; Mk. 13:13).

God's Glorious Purpose for the Peril

It shall be a test *"to try them, and to purge, and to make them white, even to the time of the end"* (Dan. 11:35). What Satan means for *"evil,"* God shall use for *"good,"* to prosper His children, and **prepare them for the Glory** that is ahead (Gen. 50:2).

"Beloved, think it not strange concerning the fiery trial which is to try you, as though some strange thing happened unto you: but

rejoice, inasmuch as ye are partakers of Christ's sufferings; that, when **His Glory** shall be revealed, ye may be glad also with exceeding joy." 1 Peter 4:12, 13

Only those that are fully surrendered to the Cross of Christ shall be left standing after this *"fiery trial."* It shall be a **sifting** every bit as thorough as the sifting of the Apostle Peter in his last great confrontations with the Devil. No stone shall be left unturned as the Great Deceiver probes for a point of entry. He shall be searching for some kind of weakness, sensual vulnerability or blemish, whereby he can beguile believers to **disobey** the commandments of God by bowing down to Satan and denying Christ. He shall use the fear of suffering and death, as well as uncrucified lusts; unholy attachments to people, places, objects or ideologies; hidden idols; unfulfilled dreams; affinities for the world; unforgiveness, bitterness, revenge, or any other of the manifold breaches common to the unregenerate man.

"And the Lord said, Simon, Simon, behold, **Satan** hath desired to have you, that he may **sift** you as wheat: but I have prayed for thee, that thy faith fail not: and when thou art converted, strengthen thy brethren." Luke 22:31, 32

The Valley of Decision

"Multitudes, multitudes in the valley of decision: for the Day of the Lord is near in the valley of decision." Joel 3:14

Growing persecution (in combination with a dramatic decline in morals, social pressure to conform to the Beast System, and the rise of false prophets) shall bring the great *"falling away"* of professing Christians to a head *(2 Th. 2:3)*. No fall out in history shall be comparable to it. It shall be massive. Everyone shall stand in the *"valley of decision"* making life and death choices to either *"save"* their lives in this world; or, to *"lose"* them in order to gain the Kingdom to come *(Mk. 8:34-38; Jn. 12:25)*.

Just as Esau sold his birthright to Jacob in a moment of weakness *"for one morsel of meat"* *(Heb. 12:16; Gen. 25:29-34)*, even so, huge numbers of professing Christians, trying to assuage their sufferings, shall sell their birthrights in the Kingdom of Heaven for temporary relief. Even esteemed leaders that operate in a measure of hypocrisy shall be like trees plucked up by the roots when the storms come.

"Then shall they deliver you up to be afflicted, and shall kill you: and ye shall be hated of all nations for My name's sake. And then shall **many be offended**, and shall betray one another, and shall hate one another. And many false prophets shall rise, and shall deceive many. And because iniquity shall abound, **the love of many shall wax cold**." Matthew 24:9-12

Social church goers that are strangers to the Cross (having their faith in the mouth and not in deed; or, in the traditions of men, rather than in the doctrines of Christ and His apostles) shall be in grave danger of taking a devastating fall *(Mt. 7:24-27)*.

". . . No one fares worse in . . . [hardship and distress] than he who has not made good use of his time; such an one will then be visited with woe, distress, [fear] and misery; but to them that love God, all things work together for good; they are purified and tried by the refining fire." T.J.V. Braght [6]

Being weak in faith, and unprepared for hardship, lukewarm "Christians" shall violate the New Covenant; fall prey to sorcerous promises of respite; and bow down to the Antichrist and His Beast System *(Rev. 3:15-17)*.

"And such as do wickedly against the covenant shall he [the Antichrist] corrupt by flatteries . . ." Daniel 11:32a

Separation of the Wheat from the Tares
The Harlot Church

The price for following Christ shall climb sky high. As a result, two vastly different groups shall form. The largest (by far) shall be those that compromise their Christian integrity and merge into the state run Ecumenical Harlot Church. They shall be deceived to sacrifice their Salvation in exchange for a small measure of "normality" maintained by people of the world (i.e., buying, selling, planting, building, marrying, eating and drinking—*Lk. 17:26-30)*. *"Hell [shall] enlarge . . . herself, and open . . . her mouth without measure"* and a *"multitude . . . shall descend into it"* (Isa. 5:14).

"Corrupted" by the Antichrist's *"flatteries"* (seductions, lies), desperate for survival, and deceived by the False Prophet's ability to perform *"miracles"* (Rev. 13:11-14), **many** shall *"leave the paths of uprightness, to walk in the ways of darkness"* (Pro. 2:13).

"They went out from us, but they were not of us; for if they had been of us, they would no doubt have continued with us: but they went out, that they might be made manifest that they were not all of us". 1 John 2:19

The Church of the Two or More

The smallest group shall be those that choose to press through the narrow gate into the wide heaven. *"Rejoicing in hope; patient in tribulation . . ."* (Rom. 12:12), they shall wait courageously for the Appearance of the Lord (1 Th. 1:10; 2 Th. 3:5). Well grounded in the Gospel, they shall *"hold that fast"* which they have, allowing *"no man,"* not even the Antichrist, to take their promised *"crown"* (Rev. 3:11).

"Enter ye in at the strait gate: for wide is the gate, and broad is the way, that leadeth to destruction, and **many** there be which go in thereat: because strait is the gate, and narrow is the way, which leadeth unto life, and **few** there be that find it." Matthew 7:13, 14

Fierce persecutions shall drive this **End-Time Remnant** of Tribulation saints underground, where they shall worship the Lord *"in Spirit and in Truth"* in what is affectionately called: "The Church of the Two or More" (Jn. 4:23, 24; Mt. 18:20). Amidst the fires of affliction, they will be enjoying a beautiful union of spirits that comes by no other means than mutual surrender to the daily work of the Cross (ongoing repentance). The petty controversies, carnal demands, selfish ambitions and doctrinal errors that divide them shall progressively melt away *"till"* they come into the *"unity of the faith"* (Eph. 4:13), free from gainsaying (excuse making), compromise and religious whoredom (ecumenism). Day by day their *"rough"* and *"crooked ways"* shall *"be made smooth"* (Lk. 3:4, 5). Humbling themselves at the foot of the Cross, they shall confess their faults to the Lord and to *"one to another"* (Jam. 5:16; 1 Jn. 1:7-9), washing their robes in the *"blood of the Lamb."*

"And one of the elders answered, saying unto me, What are these which are arrayed in white robes? And whence came they? And I said unto him, Sir, thou knowest. And he said to me, These are they which came out of **great tribulation**, and have washed their robes, and made them white in the blood of the Lamb."
Revelation 7:13, 14

Though their lives shall be in constant danger, they shall experience "**amazing grace**" and a **bond of love** that can only be described as a taste of heaven itself. It shall parallel the depth of brotherhood forged by soldiers on the front lines of combat; and demonstrated in full splendor by the Christian martyrs during the Catholic Inquisition. Nothing, no nothing: not threats of deprivation, imprisonment, torture or death will be able to cause these faithful **few** to depart from Christ or to deny the love they share.

Setting an example for those of us that would follow after, one faithful martyr expressed this love in a letter that he wrote to his wife from prison, saying:

"Oh, that I might break my heart into pieces, and give it to you and our brethren! Oh, that I could help them with my blood; I should so gladly suffer for them!" Jerome Segers, A.D. 1551,
Tortured and burned at the stake by orders of Catholic tyrants [7]

Summing up the Glory of it all, T.J.V. Braght, a devout chronicler of the lives of the holy martyrs, said:

"They were endowed with such strength that even cruel and inhuman torture could not extort from them the names of their fellow brethren, so that, filled with divine and brotherly love, they sacrificed their bodies for their fellow believers. The brotherhood in general was thereby so enkindled with zeal and love, that each, despising the earthly and regarding the heavenly, prepared his heart for the sufferings to which his brethren were subjected, and by which he himself was daily threatened. They shunned no danger, in the way of sheltering their fellow believers, visiting them in prison, calling boldly to them in the place of execution, and comforting and strengthening them with words of Scripture." [8]

The Power of Testimony

As it was in times past, so shall it be in the days that lie ahead. Born again Christians that **truly know Jesus** (having demonstrated their first love for Him by keeping His commandments and ordinances—*Rev. 2:4; Jn. 14:15, 23*), shall wax *"strong,"* and by God's grace do astounding *"exploits."* Zealous for righteousness, and having a **vision of the Glory** that lies ahead, they'll even be a source of encouragement to others in need of a helping hand.

"But the people that do **know their God** shall be strong, and do exploits. And they that understand among the people shall instruct many . . ." Daniel 11:32b, 33a

Oh how the saints shall shine!

"And they that be wise shall shine as the brightness of the firmament; and they that turn many to righteousness as the stars for ever and ever." Daniel 12:3

The *"**Spirit of Glory and of God**"* shall so mightily rest upon them, that even their most ruthless opponents shall be put to shame *(1 Pet. 4:14)*.

"But before all these, they shall lay their hands on you, and persecute you, delivering you up to the synagogues, and into prisons, being brought before kings and rulers for My name's sake. And it shall **turn to you for a testimony**. Settle it therefore in your hearts, not to meditate before what ye shall answer: for I will give you a mouth and wisdom, which all your adversaries shall not be able to gainsay nor resist." Luke 21:12-15

Like Shadrach, Meshach, and Abednego (the three Hebrew captives who refused to bow down to the image of gold set up by King Nebuchadnezzar), faithful Christians shall also stand true. In the midst of the *"burning"* End-Time *"fur-*

nace" *(Dan. 3:17)*, when the fire is turned up *"seven times"* *(Dan. 3:19)*, others shall behold the *"Son of God"* in their midst and acknowledge that Jesus Christ is Lord *(Dan. 3:25)*. Even some of the most obstinate onlookers will break in repentance, for there is no greater demonstration of the <u>reality of Christ</u> than **absolute trust in God**, even in the face of death *(Phil. 1:28, 29; Job 13:15)*.

"Then Nebuchadnezzar spake, and said, Blessed be the God of Shadrach, Meshach, and Abednego, who hath sent His angel, and delivered His servants that **trusted in Him**, and have changed the king's word, and yielded their bodies, that they might not serve nor worship any god, except their own God."   Daniel 3:28

Patient endurance through suffering, in combination with forgiveness, <u>wins souls</u>!! As historians of the Catholic Inquisition have so profoundly stated:

> "Martyrdoms are effectual sermons."
> T.J.V. Braght [9]

Knowing this, the "valiants of faith" that went before us are said to have rushed to the scaffolds, hoping that through the *"voluntary surrender of their bod[ies] into the tyrants' hands,"* the lost and erring would *"come to the truth."* [10]

". . . I fain would, when I am to offer up my sacrifice, that they would place me on a wagon and carry me around town, and scourge me four times, that I might **let the light shine** . . . Rom. 1:16."   Clement Hendrickss,
Tortured and burned at the stake by Catholic decree, A.D. 1569 [11]

Glory to God for the unwavering faith and sacrificial love demonstrated by His overcomers!

"Greater love hath no man than this, that a man lay down his life for his friends."   John 15:13

Slain on the battlefield of Christ, all of the Lord's chosen martyrs shall surely receive the incorruptible *"crown"* *(1 Cor. 9:25)*.

The Abomination that Brings Desolation

Capturing the seat of Christ in the *"temple"* of men's hearts shall not be enough to satisfy Satan's obsession for supremacy *(2 Th. 2:4)*. His lust shall not be fulfilled until the throws of the fifth seal when he initiates his ultimate power grab: seizure of the *"Glorious Holy Mountain"* of God in Jerusalem *(Dan. 11:45)*.

"For thou [Lucifer] hast said in thine heart, I will ascend into heaven, I will exalt my throne above the stars of God: **I will sit also upon the Mount of the congregation**, in the sides of the north: I will ascend above the heights of the clouds; I will be like the Most High." Isaiah 14:13, 14

There, at the religious epicenter of the world, Satan is going to *"plant the tabernacles"* of his *"son of perdition"*—his counterfeit for God's only Begotten Son, Jesus Christ *(2 Th. 2:3; Dan. 11:45)*.

At that time, the Devil is going to endow the False Prophet with extraordinary powers of witchcraft for the express purpose of uniting the world in the construction of an image to the Antichrist.

"And he [the False Prophet] doeth great wonders, so that he maketh fire come down from heaven on the earth in the sight of men, and deceiveth them that dwell on the earth by the means of those miracles which he had power to do in the sight of the Beast [the Antichrist]; saying to them that dwell on the earth, that they should **make an image to the Beast** . . ." Revelation 13:13, 14a

This satanic image shall be setup on the Temple Mount and viewed throughout the world via television and/or the Internet (phone and computer); or, some other yet to be disclosed means.

"When ye therefore shall see the **abomination of desolation**, spoken of by Daniel the prophet, **stand in the holy place**, (whoso readeth, let him understand:) then let them which be in Judaea flee into the mountains." Matthew 24:15, 16

"But when ye shall see the **abomination of desolation**, spoken of by Daniel the prophet, standing where it ought not, (let him that readeth understand,) then let them that be in Judaea flee to the mountains." Mark 13:14

There can be no greater offense to God! Truly this is the final *"abomination that maketh desolate"* *(Dan. 11:31; 12:11)*; a desecration foreshadowed during the reign of Antiochus IV Epiphanes in the inter-testamental period when plunderers erected a statue of Zeus in the Holy of Holies. In defense of God's honor, Judas Maccabeus and his sons, together with their Jewish followers, waged and won guerilla warfare against their foes in approximately 165 BC. As a result, both the altar and Temple were cleansed and rededicated to the Lord. Jewish people annually celebrate this remarkable victory and the sanctification that followed in their festival of Chanukah.

Knowing the extraordinary zeal of the Maccabees, and a long line of other patriots of Israel; who **refused to** *"worship any god, except their own God"* *(Dan. 3:28b);* it is difficult to fathom any of their fellow Jews being deceived by the Antichrist's false promises of peace to compromise the Temple Mount. To concede to such an abominable desecration of the holiness of God; or, to go along with the rest of the world by bowing down to the Antichrist and taking on his damnable **Mark**, would be a sin of the utmost magnitude in the sight of these Israelite "greats!"

"And what shall I more say? For the time would fail me to tell of Gedeon, and of Barak, and of Samson, and of Jephthae; of David also, and Samuel, and of the prophets." Hebrews 11:32

This holy place (so staunchly defended by the Israelites in times past) has been reserved by our Heavenly Father for the worship of none other than His own Beloved Son during Christ's upcoming Thousand Year Kingdom Reign *(Isa. 2:2-4; 24:23; Zec. 8:3; 14:16, 17)*.

"At that time they shall call Jerusalem the Throne of the Lord; and all the nations shall be gathered unto it, to the name of the Lord, to Jerusalem." Jeremiah 3:17a

The Great Siege Against Israel

This blasphemous act of sacrilege provokes the Lord to jealousy. During the fifth seal it sets in motion a series of phenomenal judgments, beginning with a **Great Siege** on the nation of Israel instigated by Russia, Iran and other Islamic nations *(Eze. 38:1-9; Zec. 12:1-3; 14:1, 2)*. Like so many of the failed Mid-East peace-pacts of times past, the one established by the Antichrist for the protection of Israel shall also be broken. The anti-Semitism now in perpetual cultivation shall then be unleashed full throttle. It shall be a **second Holocaust**—even more devastating than the first.

"We looked for peace, but no good came; and for a time of health, and behold **trouble!**" Jeremiah 8:15

Jerusalem is going to be *"compassed with armies,"* in like manner as it was in the days of Nebuchadnezzar's famed siege *(2 Ki. 25:1, 2)*; and in like manner, the Jews are urged to *"flee"* out of the midst of it *(Jer. 6:1)*.

"And when ye shall see Jerusalem compassed with armies, then know that the **desolation** thereof is nigh. Then let them which are in Judaea flee to the mountains; and let them which are in the midst of it depart out; and let not them that are in the countries enter thereinto. For these be the **days of vengeance**, that all things which are written may be fulfilled. But woe unto them that are with child, and to them that give suck, in those days! For there shall be great distress in the land, and **wrath upon this people**. And they shall fall by the edge of the sword, and shall be led away captive into all nations: and Jerusalem shall be trodden down of the Gentiles, until the times of the Gentiles be fulfilled." Luke 21:20-24

God's chosen people, the Jews, were the first to have the Gospel of Christ preached unto them *(Rom. 1:16)*. Even so, they shall be the first nation of people punished in the Seventieth Week of Daniel for their impenitence and their rejection of the promised Messiah *(Rom. 2:1-11; 1 Th. 2:14-16)*.

"O Jerusalem, Jerusalem, thou that killest the prophets, and stonest them which are sent unto thee, how often would I have gathered thy children together, even as a hen gathereth her chickens under her wings, and ye would not! Behold, your house is left unto you **desolate**. For I say unto you, Ye shall not see Me henceforth, till ye shall say, Blessed is He that cometh in the name of the Lord." Matthew 23:37-39

The Sixth Seal
Stopping the Satanic Madness

Next comes a powerful climatic event portrayed as a **polar shift** that **shakes the whole world**, causing a *"great earthquake"* and bringing with it destruction; thus thwarting the frenzied persecution and martyrdom of Christians *(Mt. 24: 22; Rev. 6:9-11)*. Volcanic eruptions, tsunamis and other calamities shall follow in its wake *(Hag. 2:6, 7; Heb. 12:26)*.

"The earth shall reel to and fro like a drunkard, and shall be removed like a cottage; and the transgression thereof shall be heavy upon it; and it shall fall, and not rise again."
Isaiah 24:19, 20; See also Psalm 46:2, 3

This magnetic shift of the earth's spin axis not only affects the gravitational pull here, but also in the heavens, causing stars to fall out of orbit.

". . . Fearful sights and great signs shall there be from heaven."
Luke 21:11b

"And I beheld when He had opened the **sixth seal**, and, lo, there was a great earthquake; and the sun became black as sackcloth of hair, and the moon became as blood; and the stars of heaven fell unto the earth, even as a fig tree casteth her untimely figs, when she is shaken of a mighty wind. And the heaven departed as a scroll when it is rolled together; and every mountain and island were moved out of their places." Revelation 6:12-14
See also Matthew 24:29; Joel 2:30, 31; Acts 2:20

The dynamics of the sixth seal shall terrify the nations *(Hag. 2:21, 22a)*. **Darkness shall cover the face of the earth** and chaos shall ensue. People will be running for cover, saying to the mountains: *"Fall on us; and to the hills, Cover* *us" (Lk. 23:30b; Hos. 10:8).* Some will literally drop dead from heart attacks, petrified by fear *(Rev. 6:15, 16)*.

"And there shall be signs in the sun, and in the moon, and in the stars; and upon the earth distress of nations, with perplexity; the sea and the waves roaring; **men's hearts failing them for fear**, and for looking after those things which are coming on the earth: for the **powers of heaven shall be shaken**." Luke 21:25, 26

A Ray of Hope in the Midst of Peril & Darkness

At the same time another phenomenon of contrasting magnitude shall be transpiring: joy beyond expression shall be welling up within the saints like a dam ready to burst. Instead of having their hearts pounding with trepidation, they'll be leaping with anticipation. Discerning the *"signs of the times" (Mt. 16:3)*, God's children will be **looking up**, knowing that their *"Redemption draweth nigh" (Lk. 21:28)*. It's almost Mid-Week. Jesus is on the way to take them Home!

"Now learn a parable of the fig tree; When his branch is yet tender, and putteth forth leaves, ye know that summer is nigh: so likewise ye, when ye shall **see all these things**, know that it is near, even at the doors." Matthew 24:32, 33

Rather than giving way to panic and denying Christ in word, deed or doctrine in order to escape the perils of privation and persecution, these Cross-bearers shall hold out for their true Saviour, Jesus Christ, till the very end. To them, the acceleration of birth pangs shall not be reason to *"save"* their lives in this world; but rather, to *"lose"* them for **Christ's *"sake and the Gospel's,"*** in order to gain the Kingdom to come *(Mk. 8:35; Lk. 17:33)*. Knowing both the *"terror"* and the Glory of the Lord *(2 Cor. 5:11)*, they'll be in concert with all of nature sounding the Lord's last call to repentance before His Appearance in the clouds.

"Before the decree bring forth, before the day pass as the chaff, before the fierce anger of the Lord come upon you, before the Day of the Lord's anger come upon you. **Seek ye the Lord**, all ye meek of the earth, which have wrought His judgment; **seek right-**

eousness, seek meekness: it may be ye shall be hid in the Day of the Lord's anger." Zephaniah 2:2

Surely it shall be the heart's desire of every saint left standing to greet the Lord purged by the fires *(1 Pet. 1:7)*, washed in His blood *(Rev. 7:14)*, and surrounded by other precious souls won to His Kingdom through their faithfulness *(1 Th. 2:19)*.

"O that God would grant, that we all, without one missing, might behold one another, face to face, in the Kingdom of God!"
T.J.V. Braght [12]

CHAPTER ELEVEN

Glory Hallelujah!

The Resurrection of Life
The Day of the Lord

The Seventh Seal

Suddenly chaos turns to calm and there is silence in heaven. No wind whatsoever blows on the earth; not *"on the sea, nor on any tree" (Rev. 7:1)*. Jesus Christ is about to break the **seventh seal,** thus dividing Daniel's Seventieth Week in the *"midst" (Dan. 9:27)*.

"And when He had opened the seventh seal, there was silence in heaven about the space of half an hour."   Revelation 8:1

Once every effort to *"shake"* and awaken man to his fallen condition by means of Tribulation has been exhausted *(Heb. 12:25, 26)*; the saints have been thoroughly tried; and *"space"* for repentance has expired *(Ezra 9:8; Rev. 2:21)*; our faithful Lord Jesus is going to keep the promise He made to His overcomers. He is going to appear in the clouds and take His *"Glorious Church"* to the wondrous place He went to prepare for those that truly love Him *(Eph. 5:27)*.

"Let not your heart be troubled: ye believe in God, believe also in Me. In My Father's House are many mansions: if it were not so, I would have told you. I go to prepare a place for you. And if I go and prepare a place for you, **I will come again**, and receive you unto Myself; that where I am, there ye may be also."   John 14:1-3

In the same way Jesus ascended into heaven after His Resurrection, so *"shall He appear the second time" (Heb. 9:28)*.

"And when He [Jesus] had spoken these things, while they beheld, He was taken up; and **a cloud received Him** out of their sight. And while they looked stedfastly toward heaven as He went up, behold, two men stood by them in white apparel; which also said, Ye men of Galilee, why stand ye gazing up into heaven? This same Jesus, which is taken up from you into heaven, shall so come **in like manner** as ye have seen Him go into heaven."

Acts 1:9-11

144,000 Israelites Set Apart with a Special Seal

Before Jesus comes to gather the Church unto Himself, one final act must be fulfilled. An angel *"clothed with linen"* is going to go forth with a *"writer's inkhorn by his side"* to *"set a mark upon the foreheads" (Eze. 9:2, 3)* of *"an hundred and forty and four thousand of all the tribes of the children of Israel."* Thus *"sealed,"* this small remnant of select Jews shall be able to safely walk through the impending three and a half years of devastating Wrath. *"Vexed,"* as was Lot before the overthrow of Sodom, *"with the filthy conversation of the wicked" (2 Pet. 2:7, 8)*, they *"sigh and . . . cry for all the abominations that be done"* in the midst of Jerusalem *(Eze. 9:4)*.

"And after these things I saw four angels standing on the four corners of the earth, holding the four winds of the earth, that the wind should not blow on the earth, nor on the sea, nor on any tree. And I saw another angel ascending from the east, having the seal of the living God: and he cried with a loud voice to the four angels, to whom it was given to hurt the earth and the sea, saying, Hurt not the earth, neither the sea, nor the trees, till we have sealed the servants of our God in their foreheads. And I heard the number of them which were sealed: and there were sealed an hundred and forty and four thousand of all the tribes of the children of Israel."

Revelation 7:1-4

Possessing an integrity of spirit that is most precious to God, these chosen Israelites shall become the *"firstfruits"* of the *"**holy seed**"* which shall populate Israel when the Lord returns to earth after the Wrath to fight the battle of Armageddon and establish His Thousand Year Reign *(Isa. 6:11-13)*.

"These are they which were not defiled with women; for they are virgins. These are they which follow the Lamb whithersoever He goeth. These were redeemed from among men, being the **firstfruits** unto God and to the Lamb." Revelation 14:4

The Glorious Resurrection of Saints

The peel of a Trumpet shall then pierce through the silence and the *"Bridegroom's Voice"* shall be heard *(Jn. 3:29)*. Rejoice! It's *"Midnight"!* The Hour of deliverance has come!

"And at midnight there was a cry made, Behold, the Bridegroom cometh; go ye out to meet Him." Matthew 25:6

The faithful in Christ shall recognize the joyful sound immediately. They've been staying near to the Cross. They have been hearkening to the voice of the Great Shepherd. They've been keeping His commands and following the unction of His Spirit. They've been standing watch and have been in perpetual prayer. Having the *"lamps"* of their lives full of Holy Ghost oil and their wicks trimmed *(Mt. 25:4)*, they'll be ready to rush out and greet Him.

"Behold, He cometh with clouds; and every eye shall see Him, and they also which pierced Him: and all kindreds of the earth shall wail because of Him." Even so, Amen." Revelation 1:7

In a magnificent display of splendor, the firmament shall light up with Glory signaling His Appearance.

"For as the lightning, that lighteneth out of the one part under heaven, shineth unto the other part under heaven; so shall also the Son of man be in His day." Luke 17:24

Then Jesus shall descend from heaven with His mighty angels and the *"dead in Christ"* shall be the first to rise.

"For the Lord Himself shall descend from heaven with a shout, with the voice of the archangel, and with the **trump of God**: and the dead in Christ shall rise first: then we which are alive and remain shall be caught up together with them <u>in the clouds</u>, to **meet the Lord in the air**: and **so shall we ever be with the Lord**."
1 Thessalonians 4:16, 17

At that time, Jesus Christ is going to gather us into heaven and confess us before our Heavenly Father and His angels *(Mt. 10:32, 33)*. Then we shall hear welcome words like these:

"Thou art all fair, My love; **there is no spot in thee**."
Song of Solomon 4:7

". . . Well done, thou good and faithful servant: thou hast been faithful over a few things, I will make thee ruler over many things: **enter thou into the joy of thy Lord**." Matthew 25:21

Redeemed from the fall of Adam, we shall from thenceforth be <u>forever</u> united with each other and every true believer that ever lived in a bond of **unbroken fellowship** with the Father and Son. Glory to God! This unspeakable deliverance occurs *"immediately **after** the tribulation"* *(Mt. 24:29a)*, but **before** the fullness of God's Wrath is poured out upon the *"ungodly"* *(Lk. 17:26-29; Gen. 7:12, 13, 19:12-25; 2 Pet. 2:4-9)*.

". . . **After that tribulation**, the sun shall be darkened, and the moon shall not give her light, and the stars of heaven shall fall, and the powers that are in heaven shall be shaken. And <u>then</u> shall they see the Son of man coming **in the clouds** with great power and Glory. And <u>then</u> shall He <u>send His angels</u>, and shall gather together His elect from the four winds, from the uttermost part of the earth to the uttermost part of heaven." Mark 13:24-27
See also Matthew 24:29-31; Revelation 14:14-16

The Wondrous Ways of a Just God

Abraham well understood the principle of tribulation and triumph. He also understood that the deliverance of the righteous <u>precedes</u> the destruction of the wicked. It was on the basis of this understanding that he pled with the Lord for the lives of Lot and his family in the face of the impending doom of Sodom. Knowing the divine nature of the God he served, Abraham declared:

"That be far from Thee to do after this manner, to slay the righteous with the wicked: and that the righteous should be as the wicked, that be far from thee: Shall not the Judge of all the earth do right?" Genesis 18:25

In confirmation of this principle, one of the two angels sent to tell Lot to flee Sodom before the overthrow, said:

"Haste thee, escape thither; for **I cannot do any thing <u>till</u> thou be come thither**. Therefore the name of the city was called Zoar. The sun was risen upon the earth when Lot entered into Zoar. <u>Then</u> the Lord rained upon Sodom and upon Gomorrah brimstone and fire from the Lord out of heaven." Genesis 19:22-24

The same spiritual law of deliverance-before-destruction applies today. Just as Lot escaped the overthrow of Sodom and Gomorrah *"the same day"* he fled Sodom and entered into Zoar *(Lk. 17:27, 29)*; and Noah was delivered from the Great Flood *"the day"* he entered into the ark; even so, those that faithfully *"<u>endure unto the end</u>, the same shall be saved"* before the outpouring of God's Great Wrath *(Mt. 24:13)*.

". . . As the days of Noe [Noah] were, so shall also the coming of the Son of man be. For as in the days that were before the flood they were eating and drinking, marrying and giving in marriage, <u>until the day that Noe entered into the ark</u>, and knew not until the flood came, and took them all away; so shall also the coming of the Son of man be. Then shall two be in the field; the one shall be **taken**, and the other **left**. Two women shall be grinding at the mill; the one shall be **taken**, and the other **left**. <u>Watch</u> therefore: for ye know not what hour your Lord doth come." Matthew 24:37-42

United with the Lord ***"in the air"*** at ***"His appearing"*** *(1 Th. 4:17; 2 Tim. 4:1)*, these faithful believers shall ascend into the safety of His heavenly chambers *(Rev. 7:9-15)*; as did Noah and his family into the Ark; and Lot and his daughters into the city of Zoar; <u>until</u> the succeeding three and a half years of *"indignation"* (Wrath) that conclude Daniel's Seventieth Week *"be overpast."*

"Come, My people, enter thou into thy chambers, and shut thy doors about thee: hide thyself as it were for a little moment, **until the indignation be overpast**. For, behold, the Lord cometh out of His place to punish the inhabitants of the earth for their iniquity:

the earth also shall disclose her blood, and shall no more cover her slain." Isaiah 26:20, 21

Like the five wise virgins in Matthew 25 that patiently waited with all readiness for their Bridegroom, they will go *"in with Him to the marriage"* and the door will be *"shut"* (Mt. 25:10). Then, comes the Great Wrath of God Almighty.

"For they themselves shew of us what manner of entering in we had unto you, and how ye turned to God from idols to serve the living and true God; and to wait for His Son from heaven, Whom He raised from the dead, even Jesus, which **delivered us from the Wrath to come**." 1 Thessalonians 1:9, 10

The Resurrection of the Just: The First Judgment

The *"Day of the Lord Jesus"* is also referred to as the *"**Resurrection of Life**"* (Jn. 5:29), the *"**First Resurrection**"* (1 Cor. 5:5; Rev. 20:4-6), and the *"Resurrection of the Just'* (Lk. 14:14). The *"ungodly"* shall not rise in this initial *"Judgment"* (Ps. 1:5). It is a Day of immortalization and heavenly reception reserved solely for faithful believers that have confessed and forsaken their sins, finding mercy of the Lord (Pro. 28:13; 2 Cor. 5:4). **Another resurrection**, the Resurrection of the *"Unjust,"* referred to by Christ as the *"**Resurrection of Damnation**"* shall follow a thousand years later for those whose names cannot be found in the *"Book of Life"* (Acts 24:15; Jn. 5:29; Rev. 20:-6, 14, 15).

"Verily, verily, I say unto you, He that heareth My Word, and believeth on Him that sent Me, hath everlasting life, and **shall not come into condemnation**; **but is passed from death unto life**. Verily, verily, I say unto you, The hour is coming, and now is, when the dead shall hear the voice of the Son of God: and they that hear shall live. For as the Father hath life in Himself; so hath He given to the Son to have life in Himself; and hath given Him authority to execute judgment also, because He is the Son of man. Marvel not at this: for the hour is coming, in the which all that are in the graves shall hear His voice, and shall come forth; they that have done good, unto the **Resurrection of Life**; and they that have done evil, unto the **Resurrection of Damnation**." John 5:24-29

"And many of them that sleep in the dust of the earth shall awake, **some to everlasting life**, and **some to shame and everlasting contempt**." Daniel 12:2

The two distinct resurrections (representative of two distinct judgments), are as far apart in purpose as they are in years. The First Resurrection [the Resurrection of Life] is the **first day of Judgment** for the severing of the wicked from among the just and the recompensing of the righteous prior to the Great Wrath *(Lk. 14:14)*. The *"Resurrection of Damnation"* that occurs a thousand years later has a completely different purpose. It is the **final *"Day of Judgment"* reserved for the unjust**. At that time, all the impenitent souls that ever lived shall stand before a great White Throne to be judged *"according to their works"* by the Lord Jesus Christ and then sent forever into the Lake of Fire and Brimstone *(Rev. 20:11-15)*.

"The Lord knoweth how to **deliver the godly** out of temptations [the First Resurrection], and to **reserve the unjust** unto the [final] Day of Judgment to be punished." 2 Peter 2:9

Based upon Christ's parable of the shepherd that divides the sheep from the goats *(Mt. 25:31-46)*, in combination with the missing element of time in the three accounts we are given in Scripture of two resurrections *(Dan. 12:2; Lk. 14:14; Jn. 5:28, 29; Acts 24:15)*, many people have been under the errant impression that both occur simultaneously. Revelation 20:4-6, however, debunks that assumption and brings definition to the actual time frame of the two events.

Forever Changed

Motivated by the First Resurrection, true Christians everywhere purpose to walk in *"newness of life,"* as symbolized in believers baptism *(Rom. 6:3-5)*; *"not as though"* even the most devout among us have *"already attained, either were already perfect"*; but like the apostles, we *"follow after, if that . . . [we] may apprehend that for which also . . . [we are] apprehended of Christ Jesus" (Phil. 3:12)*.

We yearn for the Day when *"the trumpet shall sound"* and every trace of the lingering *"sin which doth so easily beset us"* is <u>completely</u> washed away *(1 Cor. 15:52; Heb. 12:1)*. A single moment in Christ's awesome Presence shall eternally liberate us from bondage to the *"Law of Sin and Death"* we inherited from Adam *(Rom. 8:2)*. Hallelujah! *"In the twinkling of an eye,"* we shall be forever changed!

"Behold, I shew you a mystery; We shall not all sleep, but we shall all be **changed**, in a moment, in the twinkling of an eye, at the <u>last trump</u>: for the trumpet shall sound, and the dead shall be raised incorruptible, and **we shall be changed**. For this corruptible must put on incorruption, and this mortal must put on immortality."
1 Corinthians 15:51-53

...No more struggles. ...No more stumbling. ...No more sickness, sorrow or death. Free at last! Free at last! Thank God Almighty, free at last!

"If the Son therefore shall make you free,
ye shall be free indeed." John 8:36

From then on, *". . . the righteous shine forth as the sun in the Kingdom of their Father"* *(Mt. 13:43a)*. Happy are they!

"Blessed and holy is he that hath part in the **First Resurrection**: <u>on such the second death hath no power</u>, but they shall be priests of God and of Christ . . ." Revelation 20:6a

Having *"passed from death unto life"* *(Jn. 5:24)*, we *"shall **never die**"* *(Jn. 11:25, 26)*. Not only shall we be like Jesus, but also, *"as the angels of God in heaven"* *(Mt. 22:30)*; for the Lord has promised to *"<u>change</u> our vile body, that it may be fashioned **like unto His Glorious body**"* *(Phil. 3:21)*.

"So also is the resurrection of the dead. It is sown in corruption; it is raised in incorruption: it is sown in dishonour; it is raised in Glory: it is sown in weakness; it is raised in power: it is sown a natural body; it is **raised a spiritual body**. There is a natural body, and there is a spiritual body." 1 Corinthians 15:42-44

Married to the Bridegroom Christ

The **"great mystery" of love and oneness** that God revealed through the union of man and wife in the flesh, shall then be realized in the Spirit between the Bridegroom Jesus and His cherished Bride (the Church).

"Let us be glad and rejoice, and give honour to Him: for the **marriage of the Lamb** is come, and His wife hath made herself ready. And to her was granted that she should be arrayed in fine linen, clean and white: for the fine linen is the righteousness of saints."
Revelation 19:7, 8

"For thy Maker is thine husband; the Lord of hosts is His name; and thy Redeemer the Holy One of Israel; the God of the whole earth shall He be called." Isaiah 54:5

Children of the Resurrection

Once in spiritual bodies, we no longer marry in the flesh.

"And Jesus answering said unto them, The children of this world marry, and are given in marriage: but they which shall be accounted worthy to obtain that world, and the Resurrection from the dead, **neither marry, nor are given in marriage**: neither can they die any more: for they are equal unto the angels; and are the children of God, being the **children of the Resurrection**."
Luke 20:34-36

Mormons, Muslims and others, whose beliefs put them at odds with this Biblical doctrine, are grievously misled. Addressing a controversy over this issue, Jesus said:

". . . Ye do err, **not knowing the scriptures**, nor the power of God. For in the Resurrection they **neither marry, nor are given in marriage**, but are as the angels of God." Matthew 22:29, 30
See also Mark 12:24, 25

Our Heavenly Father has eternal heavenly blessings (even greater than physical marriage) in store for those whose names are *"written in heaven"* (Heb. 12:23). Knowing this, King David rejoiced in God, saying:

"... In Thy presence is fulness of joy; at Thy right hand there are pleasures for evermore."　　　　　　　　　　　Psalm 16:11b

Christ Jesus: Our "Exceeding Great Reward"

All earthly pleasures pale in comparison to the never ending Glory awaiting us. Words can't describe how wonderful ...how beautiful ...how Glorious life will be as we abide in the Presence of the Almighty God and Jesus Christ eternally!!

...All other blessings aside: The Lord Himself is our *"**Exceeding Great Reward**" (Gen. 15:1)*!

Welcomed back into His "**Garden of Love**," we shall be forever with Him in Glory; along with all faithful believers that ever lived. There will be singing and joy amidst *"ten thousand times ten thousand, and thousands of thousands"* of heavenly beings *(Rev. 5:11)*.

"After this I beheld, and, lo, a great multitude, which no man could number, of all nations, and kindreds, and people, and tongues, stood before the throne, and before the Lamb, clothed with white robes, and palms in their hands; and cried with a loud voice, saying, Salvation to our God which sitteth upon the throne, and unto the Lamb. And all the angels stood round about the throne, and about the elders and the four beasts, and fell before the throne on their faces, and worshipped God, saying, Amen: Blessing, and Glory, and wisdom, and thanksgiving, and honour, and power, and might, be unto our God for ever and ever. Amen."
　　　　　　　　　　　　　　　　　　　　Revelation 7:9-12

We shall serve, worship and adore our Heavenly Father in the *"unity of the Spirit" (Eph. 4:3)*. Each of us shall be a unique and vital part of His everlasting dominion and never ending creation of eternal beauty through Jesus Christ *(Dan. 7:27; Rev. 21:3, 4)*. Praise ye the Lord!

" . . . As it is written, Eye hath not seen, nor ear heard, neither have entered into the heart of man, the things which God hath prepared for them that **love Him**."　　　　　1 Corinthians 2:9

CHAPTER TWELVE

The Great Wrath of God
The Second Half of Daniel's Seventieth Week

No Faithful Christians are left on Earth.

Words cannot describe how frightfully different and dark it will be for those left behind at the Mid-Week divide after the First Resurrection. For them, the Day of the Lord (the seventh seal) will not be one of rejoicing—but rather, one of anguish and terror, for it marks the beginning of God's Great Wrath. *(See Rev. chapters 8, 9, 11, 16 & 19:11-21.)*

"To them who by patient continuance in well doing seek for Glory and honour and immortality, **eternal life**: but unto them that are contentious, and do not obey the Truth, but obey unrighteousness, **indignation and wrath**." Romans 2:7, 8

Instead of having heads held high and arms outstretched to greet the Lord, like the saints that were caught up into heaven; they'll be cowering in fear, looking for places to hide.

"And the kings of the earth, and the great men, and the rich men, and the chief captains, and the mighty men, and every bondman, and every free man, hid themselves in the dens and in the rocks of the mountains; and said to the mountains and rocks, Fall on us, and hide us from the face of Him that sitteth on the throne, and from the Wrath of the Lamb: for the **great Day of His Wrath** is come; and who shall be able to stand?" Revelation 6:15-17

"And they shall go into the holes of the rocks, and into the caves of the earth, for fear of the Lord, and for the Glory of His majesty, when He ariseth to shake terribly the earth." Isaiah 2:19

"Blow ye the trumpet in Zion, and sound an alarm in My Holy Mountain: let all the inhabitants of the land tremble: for the **Day of the Lord** cometh, for it is nigh at hand; a day of darkness and of gloominess, a day of clouds and of thick darkness . . . . And the Lord shall utter His voice before His army: for His camp is very great: for He is strong that executeth His Word: for the **Day of the Lord** is great and very terrible; and who can abide it?"

Joel 2:1, 2a, 11

Left Behind

Once the Resurrected Saints have been delivered, the Great Wrath of God Almighty shall be unleashed throughout the world. No longer will the bright light of devout Christians transformed in disposition by the love of Jesus be present. Instead, there will be hungry and terror-stricken *"lovers of their own selves,"* fighting for survival in a time of moral collapse, unremitting calamity and devastating famine *(2 Tim. 3:1-5)*. Satan will incite man-against-man and violence shall be the order of the day. All the masks will be removed and the true *"nature"* of *"the children of wrath"* and *"disobedience"* will be fully manifest *(Eph. 2:3; 5:6)*.

The judgments at that time shall be fierce and unabated. There will be utter devastation as the earth is purged by fire and other means from the pollutions of sin *(2 Pet. 3:7; Isa. 24:19; Rev. 16:18-21)*. At last, God's magnificent purposes for the Seventieth Week of Daniel will be fulfilled *(Dan. 9:24)*. All innocent blood that was ever shed (including the blood of the Messiah and His beloved apostles, prophets and Christian martyrs) shall then be avenged *(Rev. 16:3-6)*. All unbelievers (the wicked) and unfaithful servants of Christ shall be punished together *(Isa. 1:28; Mat. 24:48-51)*; *"Babylon the Great"* (the evil religious and political systems of the world with all of their seducing entrapments and false worship) shall be vanquished *(Rev. 18:2, 9-24)*; and Satan's global dominion shall be ended.

God's Law of Righteous Judgment

Praise be unto God for His righteous judgments *(Rev. 16:5-7)*! He is a God of mercy and vengeance; delivering the penitent from the Wrath to come; and punishing the impenitent for the violence, blasphemy and shameful provocations they have wrought in the earth.

"O love the Lord, all ye His saints: for the Lord preserveth the faithful, and plentifully rewardeth the proud doer." Psalms 31:23

In this sure promise of future recompenses, all the righteous souls (yea, all the persecuted and downtrodden) that ever walked the earth have found great consolation.

"And whatsoever ye do, do it heartily, as to the Lord, and not unto men; knowing that of the Lord ye shall receive the reward of the inheritance: for ye serve the Lord Christ. But he that doeth wrong shall receive for the wrong which he hath done: and there is no respect of persons." Colossians 3:23-25

This is God's Law of Righteous Judgment. Every man shall eventually reap what he sows.

"Be not deceived; God is not mocked: for whatsoever a man soweth, that shall he also reap. For he that soweth to his flesh shall of the flesh reap corruption; but he that soweth to the Spirit shall of the Spirit reap life everlasting. And let us not be weary in well doing: for in due season we shall reap, if we faint not."
Galatians 6:7-9

"Some men's sins are open beforehand, going before to judgment; and some men they follow after" (1 Tim. 5:24). Either way, the Day of Reckoning shall come and justice will be served.

Unparalleled Fury

The Great Wrath is going to be "a time of trouble, such as never was since there was a nation even to that same time" (Dan. 12:1); no, "not since men were upon the earth" (Rev. 16:18). The world shall be "full of darkness" (Rev. 16:10), with "no brightness in it" (Amos 5:18-20).

In that Day, all of the idols worldwide are going to be "utterly" destroyed (Isa. 2:18). A "spirit of judgment" and a "spirit of burning" are going to sweep through Jerusalem in particular, purging away all innocent blood "from the midst thereof," and washing away the "filth of the daughters of Zion" (Isa. 4:4). "The names of the idols" shall then cease and the false *"prophets and the unclean spirit"* shall pass out of the Land of Israel *(Zec. 13:2)*.

Surrealistic details of the events that transpire begin with the opening of the seventh seal in Revelation Chapter Eight and conclude with the Battle of Armageddon at the end of Chapter Nineteen. They are also graphically described in Isa. 24, Isa. 34:1-10, Jer. 25:26-38 and other passages.

Quite unlike the Tribulation, this second half of Daniel's Seventieth Week shall primarily be comprised of **supernatural judgments** that come from the Lord Himself. There shall be curious scourges, freakish plagues and unremitting calamities *(Isa. 24:18)*, much akin to what took place in Egypt just prior to the Israelite Exodus *(Exo. 7:14-21)*. All kinds of other bizarre events shall take place, as well; like darkness at daytime *(Rev. 8:12; 16:10)*, yet scorching heat *(Rev. 16:12)*; *"hail and fire mingled with blood"* *(Rev. 8:7)*; good water turned fatally toxic *(Rev. 8:9-11)*; and grotesque sores upon the people who cave in to the Beast *(Rev. 16:2)*.

Eventually, iniquity shall pinnacle, just as it did in the days of Noah before the Great Flood *(Gen. 6:5-7; Joel 3:13; Rev. 14:18)*; to the extent that *"all the foundations of the earth,"* both morally and physically, are thrown *"out of course" (Ps. 82:5)*. Massive earthquakes, bloodied seas, burning vegetation, falling stars, polar shifts, giant hail stones, wars and radically diminished populations shall cause the face of the earth to change, along with its firmament, spirit and lighting *(Isa. 24:6)*. The terror will not relent until full *"reconciliation"* has been made for all the iniquities of mankind since the very beginning *(Dan. 9:24)*.

During the Tribulation, a quarter of the earth's population shall die by the sword, hunger and death *(Rev. 6:8)*. During the Wrath, multiplied numbers of the remaining three quarters left after the Tribulation shall also meet death by even greater catastrophes, <u>more frightful</u> than those that preceded them; and there will be no relief.

"Fear, and the pit, and the snare, are upon thee, O inhabitant of the earth. And it shall come to pass, that he who fleeth from the noise of the fear shall fall into the pit; and he that cometh up out of the midst of the pit shall be taken in the snare: for the windows from on high are open, and the foundations of the earth do shake. The earth is utterly broken down, the earth is clean dissolved, the earth is moved exceedingly." Isaiah 24:17-19

Though a great many people die *(Rev. 9:13-18)*, however, *"every living"* person left behind shall not be destroyed, as in the days when the Great Flood swallowed up all but Noah and his family. This was made known to Noah after the waters were dried up from the earth and he went forth from the Ark to build an altar to the Lord.

"And Noah builded an altar unto the Lord; and took of every clean beast, and of every clean fowl, and offered burnt offerings on the altar. And the Lord smelled a sweet savour; and the Lord said in His heart, I will not again curse the ground any more for man's sake; for the imagination of man's heart is evil from his youth; <u>neither will I again smite any more every thing living</u>, as I have done." Genesis 8:20, 21

Few, however, (if any) of the survivors shall want to go on, for the torment shall be great.

"And in those days shall men seek death, and shall not find it; and shall desire to die, and death shall flee from them." Revelation 9:6

Babylon the Great is Destroyed

Towards the end of the Wrath *"Babylon the Great"* shall be overthrown *(Rev. 17:16, 17; 18:2; Jer. 51: 58)*; Satan's religious, political and economic systems shall be *"utterly burned with fire" (Rev. 18:8)*; the *"Great Whore"* of Babylon, *"drunken"* with *"the blood of the martyrs of Jesus,"* shall be destroyed *(Rev. 17:1, 5, 6)*; and heaven shall rejoice.

". . . I heard a great voice of much people in heaven, saying, Alleluia; Salvation, and Glory, and honour, and power, unto the Lord our God: for true and righteous are His judgments: for He hath judged **the great whore**, which did corrupt the earth with her fornication, and hath avenged <u>the blood of His servants</u> at her hand. And again they said, Alleluia. And her smoke rose up for ever and ever." Revelation 19:1-3

No Record of Salvation

Despite the ever increasing peril, not once in the entire Book of Revelation <u>pertaining to this particular period of Great Wrath</u> do we find a single record of evangelism; or, of the Lord's divine pleadings, yielding a harvest of souls, as it will do during the Great Tribulation. All we find is blasphemy from whole populations of angry sinners gnawing their tongues for pain and shaking their fists at the God that made them. Four times in the passages describing the Great Wrath, Scripture says they *"repented"* **not** *(Rev. 9:20, 21; 16:9,11).*

"And I heard another out of the altar say, Even so, Lord God Almighty, true and righteous are Thy judgments. And the fourth angel poured out his vial upon the sun; and power was given unto him to scorch men with fire. And men were scorched with great heat, and **blasphemed the name of God**, which hath power over these plagues: and they **repented not** to give Him Glory."
Revelation 16:7-9

Removing the Vail of Darkness

Yet, we do know from Scripture, that a remnant of Jewish survivors is going to be broken in repentance. In Jeremiah, a beautiful portrait is painted of a residue of these Jews, comprised of both Judah and Israel, traveling together on a journey to Zion, hoping to find their Messiah there *(Jer. 50:4, 5).* But there is no mention of them receiving their promised Salvation until <u>after</u> the Battle of Armageddon, when the Seventieth Week of Daniel is brought to a close, and the Messiah returns to earth to establish His Thousand Year Reign *(Zec. 12:10-14; 13:1).* At that time, the Jews shall *"turn to the Lord"* and *"the vail"* of darkness that has blinded them to the Gospel of Christ shall be taken away *(2 Cor. 3:13-18).*

Before concluding this overview of the explosive events that bring the Great Wrath to its conclusion, let's pause and look more deeply into the wondrous way that God is going to bring His chosen people back into the bond of His Covenant through the fires of the coming Apocalypse—starting with the Book of Jeremiah...

CHAPTER THIRTEEN

The Time of Jacob's Trouble
God Pleads with His Chosen People

The Great Wrath was revealed to the prophet Jeremiah in a vision. Because so much of it pertains directly to the Jews; and only a remnant of them survives the devastation; he spoke of it as *"the time of Jacob's Trouble."*

"For thus saith the Lord; We have heard a voice of trembling, of fear, and not of peace. Ask ye now, and see whether a man doth travail with child? Wherefore do I see every man with his hands on his loins, as a woman in travail, and all faces are turned into paleness? Alas! for that Day is great, so that **none is like it**: it is even the time of **Jacob's Trouble**, but he shall be saved out of it."
Jeremiah 30:5-7

Consider the manifold pogroms the Jewish people have suffered in their history, including the horrendous Nazi Holocaust, and then meditate on the words: *"none is like it."* Jeremiah described the depth of despair long before the Book of Revelation ever filled in the demonic dimension of torment, saying that in those days *"death shall be chosen rather than life"* (Jer. 8:3a). Such a scenario is not hard to envision when pondered in light of the tragic number of Jewish suicides that took place in the World War II era. Can any of us begin to imagine the anguish of seeing our families ushered into gas chambers; or, our babies tossed into the air like sacks of potatoes and mercilessly shot down for sport by gloating German SS soldiers?

Once again, this kind of desperate conversation shall be the order of the day:

"In the morning thou shalt say, Would God it were even! and at even thou shalt say, Would God it were morning! for the fear of thine heart wherewith thou shalt fear, and for the sight of thine eyes which thou shalt see."   Deuteronomy 28:67

To get an idea of the severity of judgments that shall be meted out to the Jews in particular, one need only look into Deuteronomy 28. It begins with a list of the surpassing *"blessings"* that are promised to *"overtake"* God's chosen people, provided they keep the Covenant their forefathers made with God *(Deu. 28:1-14)*; including their final bonding with the Messiah *(Rom. 10:4)*. It is followed by a list of equivalent *"curses"* prophesied to *"overtake"* the posterity of those that break it *(Deu. 28:15-68)*. Therein, we not only get a glimpse of the fury that shall be unleashed during *"the time of Jacob's Trouble,"* but also, scriptural insight into the reasons for it; namely, **disobedience** and **Covenant breaking** *(Deu. 29:9-29)*. Extreme? Ponder this: out of a beastly lust to survive, desperate Jewish fathers and mothers that once fawned over their children are going to eat them to survive *(Deu. 28:53-57; Jer. 19:9)*.

Double Judgment

"Jacob's Trouble" begins with the Great Siege unleashed against the nation of Israel and the Holy City of Jerusalem *(Lk. 21:20-24)*. * This signal event occurs during the fifth seal, right after the image of the Antichrist is set up on the Temple Mount, and right before the Appearance of Christ for the catching away of His Bride. *"In that day" (Zec. 12:3)*, the Lord is going to make Jerusalem a *"cup of trembling unto all the people round about"* and there is going to be a great scattering of Jews to *"the four corners of the earth" (Zec. 12:2; Isa. 11:12)*.

". . . All the people of the earth [shall] be gathered together against it. . . . For I will gather all nations against Jerusalem to battle; and the City shall be taken, and the houses rifled, and the women ravished; and half of the City shall go forth into captivity . . . "
Zechariah 12:3b; 14:2a

Double judgment shall be brought to bear upon the Jewish people, beginning with a sudden blitzkrieg **Siege**;

---

* For more information on the Great Siege see pages 90-91.

and followed shortly thereafter by the catastrophic events that take place worldwide during the **Great Wrath**. Thus shall be fulfilled the words of the holy prophets *(Isa. 40:2)*.

"And first I will recompense their iniquity and their sin **double**; because they have defiled My land, they have filled Mine inheritance with the carcases of their detestable and abominable things."
Jeremiah 16:18

A Final Breaking

Wherever the Jews flee, the merciless sword of anti-Semitism shall follow, until every rebel in their number that is not moved by calamity or peril to repentance is destroyed *(Amos 9:9, 10)*.

"I will scatter them also among the heathen, whom neither they nor their fathers have known: and I will send a sword after them, till I have consumed them."
Jeremiah 9:16

The same satanic savagery detonated in Nazi Germany by the seed of the Serpent, and fueled across Europe, shall again express itself in fury. This time, however, it shall be on a global scale because every kindred and people will be subject to the tyranny of the reigning "Hitler"—the Antichrist himself. This **second Holocaust** shall exceed the first, in that there shall be no *"Righteous Among the Nations"* * to offer refuge or provide escape; no outside help. Three times in Jeremiah's lurid account of *"Jacob's Trouble"* the help of man is said to be absent.

"There is <u>none</u> to plead thy cause. . . . <u>All</u> thy lovers have forgotten thee. . . . This is Zion whom <u>no man</u> seeketh after."
Jeremiah 30:13a, 14a, 17b

There, in a howling *"wilderness"* of unparalleled judgment that offers no human assistance, God Almighty is going

---

* "Righteous Among the Nations": A title awarded by the nation of Israel at Yad Vashem, the Holocaust museum in Jerusalem, to some of the Gentiles that risked their lives to save Jews in the WWII era.

to plead "*face-to-face*" with His chosen people; destroying the impenitent; and thereafter, bringing into the New Covenant those that choose to return in sackcloth and ashes to the bosom of His Love.

"And I will bring you out from the people, and will gather you out of the countries wherein ye are scattered, with a mighty hand, and with a stretched out arm, and with fury poured out. And I will bring you into the wilderness of the people, and there will I plead with you face to face. Like as I pleaded with your fathers in the wilderness of the land of Egypt, so will I plead with you, saith the Lord God. And I will cause you to **pass under the rod**, and I will bring you into the bond of the Covenant: and I will **purge out from among you the rebels**, and them that transgress against Me . . ."
Ezekiel 20:34-38a

This final latter day purge shall be of such magnitude that only a *"remnant"* shall survive *(Zec. 13:9)*. Few in number, every man's life shall be considered his treasure—yea, *"more precious than fine gold" (Isa. 13:12)*.

"And it shall come to pass in that Day, that the **remnant** of Israel, and such as are escaped of the House of Jacob, shall no more again stay upon him that smote them; but shall stay upon the Lord, the Holy One of Israel, in Truth. The **remnant** shall return, even the **remnant** of Jacob, unto the mighty God. For though Thy people Israel be as the sand of the sea, yet a **remnant** of them shall return: the consumption decreed shall overflow with righteousness." Isaiah 10:20-22

Around this surviving *"remnant of Israel,"* and the 144,000 Jews *"sealed"* for protection prior to the Great Wrath *(Rom. 11:16-18; Eph. 2:19-22; Mt. 8:11)*, God is going to build His Divine Family; thus bringing to fulfillment their special destiny of exaltation as His own *"peculiar people"* at the outset of Christ's Millennial Reign *(Deu. 14:2; Deu. 26:19)*.

"And they shall be Mine, saith the Lord of hosts, in that Day when I make up My jewels; and **I will spare them**, as a man spareth his own son that serveth him." Malachi 3:17

Why Wrath Upon This People?

Scripture says: *"Unto whomsoever much is given, of him shall be much required" (Lk. 12:48).* This is certainly true of the Jewish people; for they have been given much! To them belong:

". . . The adoption [as God's 'peculiar treasure'—Exo. 19:5], and the Glory [of God's wondrous Presence], and the covenants [of betrothal and blessing], and the giving of the Law [a Divine Constitution teaching them exactly how to live healthy and fulfilled lives in His loving favor], and the service of God [the actual ministry and worship of the Most High], and the promises [announced through His holy prophets too numerous to list]; whose are the fathers [the great patriarchs of faith], and **of whom as concerning the flesh Christ came**, Who is over all, God blessed for ever. Amen."
Romans 9:4b, 5

Yes, the Messiah Himself was brought into the world as Saviour of *"many nations"* through the chosen lineage of the patriarchs Abraham, Isaac and Jacob *(Gen. 17:4, 5).* He is what makes them special! And though the world did not welcome and revere Him as such, what grieved God most was that His very own people didn't either.

"He was in the world, and the world was made by Him, and the world knew Him not. He came unto His own, and His own received him not."
John 1:10, 11

Not only did the Jews as a people reject their Messiah, demand His crucifixion and call for the release of a convicted killer instead *(Mk. 15:6-15; Acts 4:10);* but also, in their riotous frenzy, they even went as far as to call down the accountability for His *"innocent"* blood upon future generations of their own kindred.

"When Pilate saw that he could prevail nothing, but that rather a tumult was made, he took water, and washed his hands before the multitude, saying, I am innocent of the blood of this just person: see ye to it. Then answered all the people, and said, His blood be on us, and on our children."
Matthew 27:24, 25

Before Christ came, the Jews murdered the prophets sent to reprove their rebellion and call them to repentance. Afterwards, they attacked the apostles who sounded a similar call. They also intimidated, excommunicated, imprisoned and conspired to kill their born again kinsmen *(Jn. 12:10, 11, 42)*. Plus, they forbade the preaching of Christ's Gospel to Jews and Gentiles in the land of Israel *(Acts 4:17, 18)*—a prohibition <u>still</u> upheld in measure. To this very day, it is against the law in Israel for Messianic Jews to share the Gospel with Israelis under the age of eighteen!! For these reasons, *"wrath is come upon them to the uttermost."*

"For ye, brethren, became followers of the churches of God which in Judaea are in Christ Jesus: for ye also have suffered like things of your own countrymen, even as they have of the Jews: who both killed the Lord Jesus, and their own prophets, and have persecuted us; and they please not God, and are contrary to all men: forbidding us to speak to the Gentiles that they might be saved, to fill up their sins alway: for the **wrath is come upon them to the uttermost**." 1 Thessalonians 2:14-16

No wonder the Apostle Paul had such *"great heaviness and continual sorrow"* in his heart for his unbelieving Israelite kinsmen *(Rom. 9:2)*. He knew how very blessed *"above all people that are upon the face of the earth"* that God intended for them to be *(Deu. 7:6; 4:7, 8)*; and yet, how much suffering and anguish they would ultimately undergo at the hands of their enemies, because of their long standing record of rebellion and impenitence. Left unchecked, it eventually led to the sin that sums up all sin; namely, the rejection of their own Messiah.

Thank God, however, for the believing portion of Jews that have embraced their Messiah! A profound number came to Christ at the outset of Christianity and went on to become true *"witnesses"* of His divine nature and the Resurrection power in His name *(Acts 1:8, 22)*. ...Saints like John the Baptist and the apostles. The list goes on. There were members of the Sanhedrin, chief rulers, the head of a synagogue, *"a great company of the priests,"* and more *(Jn. 12:42; 19:38, 39; Acts 6:7; 18:8, 17)*. Others have followed. Hopefully, more are yet to come. But, for their sake, let it be *"before the fierce anger of the Lord"* comes *(Zep. 2:2)*.

Anti-Semitism

Sadly, under the "noble" pretext of avenging Christ of His "killers," there have been (and still are) so-called "Christian" groups* that have used the culpability of the Jews in regards to the Lord's crucifixion as an occasion to vent anti-Semitism. In so doing, they have cast an unfounded shadow over true Christians who would never take part in the persecution of God's chosen people; or, for that matter, in harming anyone else. Such reprehensible conduct is totally antithetical to the nature of Christ. In fact, true Christians suffer abuse (even martyrdom) from the same persecutors that have assailed Jews. Genuine Christians are known for their sacrificial love. They've historically gone the "extra mile" in reaching out to their fellowman; some even laying their lives down to succor and rescue Jews amidst the Holocaust and other pogroms.

This is not to excuse the Jewish people. Indeed, they are <u>accountable to God</u> for the crucifixion of Christ—and even more so than others. Standing at the judgment seat of Pilate, who boasted of having the *"power"* to either *"crucify"* or *"release"* Him, Jesus said:

". . . Thou couldest have no power at all against Me, except it were given thee from above: therefore he that delivered Me unto thee hath the **greater sin**."   John 19:11

Notwithstanding, the world must also remember that it was the Gentiles that mocked, scourged, spitefully entreated, spit upon, and ultimately carried out the Lord's execution

---

* These groups include: "Aryan" brotherhoods; Catholics influenced by prejudices seeded into the foundation of their heretical institution; Lutherans adversely affected by the anti-Semitic writings of Martin Luther, etc. The pernicious effects of this exploitation have been incalculable. The Nazi propaganda machine, for example, used Luther's railings to justify what Hitler called in Mein Kampf his *"work of the Lord"* to make Europe, and if possible the world, "Judenrein" (free of Jews).[1]

(Mt. 20:18, 19; Lk. 18:32, 33). Hence, not the Jews only, but "**all the world . . . [stands] guilty before God**" *(Rom. 3:19b).* Only genuine repentance and acceptance of Christ's atonement and Lordship can break this frightful continuum of sin.

In an attempt to call his Jewish kinsmen to repentance, one Messianic Jewish leader said:

"The resonance of the words 'Christ killer!' chills our corporate souls, for we have suffered much in the sounding of those terrible words. Every Jewish spokesman will expound on the absurdity of the charge of 'deicide,' yet, however much that rightful accusation has been unjustly and cruelly exploited . . . does it not remain true, nevertheless, that we killed Him? . . . Although the instrumentality was Roman, the determination was our fathers." [2]

Regardless of who did what, however, it is the **action of God** (not man!) to either avenge—or forgive—this greatest of all crimes. In the meantime, our part as true Christians is not to vent selective moral outrage against any particular group or ethnicity; but rather, to take responsibility for our own lives, by doing our best at every moment not to sin against the blood of Jesus. And when we do miss the mark, *"for there is no man that sinneth not"* (1 Ki. 8:46); we must speedily respond in repentance; lest we be judged *"guilty of the body and blood of the Lord"* ourselves.

Speaking of participation in the Lord's Supper, the Apostle Paul warned:

"Wherefore whosoever shall eat this bread, and drink this cup of the Lord, <u>unworthily</u>, shall be **guilty of the body and blood of the Lord**. But let a man examine himself, and so let him eat of that bread, and drink of that cup. For he that eateth and drinketh <u>unworthily</u>, eateth and drinketh **damnation** to himself, not discerning the Lord's body." 1 Corinthians 11:27-29

A Rush to the Altar

Knowing the culpability of the Jewish people in the crucifixion of Christ, and aware of the wrath and damnation that were to follow, the Apostle Peter held nothing back when preaching the Gospel to the Israelites *(Acts 3:13-15),* saying:

"Ye men of Israel, hear these words; Jesus of Nazareth, a man approved of God among you by miracles and wonders and signs, which God did by Him in the midst of you, as ye yourselves also know: Him, being delivered by the determinate counsel and foreknowledge of God, **ye have taken, and by wicked hands have crucified and slain**: Whom God hath raised up, having loosed the pains of death: because it was not possible that He should be holden of it." Acts 2:22-24

In response to this alarming charge, 3,000 souls came forward to the waters of repentance in order to *"save"* themselves from all identification with the *"untoward generation"* of Jews and Gentiles that took part in Christ's murder. So great was their conviction, that they *"were baptized . . . the same day,"* and from thenceforth *"continued stedfastly in the apostles' doctrine and fellowship"* (Acts 2:41, 42).

At that landmark gathering, *"fear came upon every soul"* (Acts 2:43). As a result, water baptism by immersion was embraced (in accord with Peter's preaching), as the door of release from accountability to the sins committed against Christ's *"innocent blood"* (Mt. 27:4). Belief on the Lord Jesus Christ, repentance from all sins (including those of our forefathers), and acceptance of His atoning act of Redemption is—and ever will be—the only means of Salvation and deliverance from the *"wrath to come"* (Mt. 3:7).

"He that believeth and is baptized shall be saved; but he that believeth not shall be damned." Mark 16:16

If Jews today do not rally "in spirit" around the souls that fled for refuge to the waters of repentance two thousand years ago, by similarly acknowledging their own sins, and renouncing the decision of their fathers to crucify Jesus; they are indicted together with them in that sin, and therefore, the consequence of it.

...Yes, anti-Semitism is a deplorable way of destroying the Jewish people. But failing to voice a bold call to repentance, when given the opportunity, is another; and the latter is eternal. Of course, that reproof needs to be sounded with a "right spirit" from genuinely concerned and penitent Christians well acquainted with *"how their own sin also implicated them in . . . [the Messiah's] death."* [3]

Mercy: The Hidden Pearl
Within the Oyster of Judgment

The history of the Jewish people is one of exceeding Glory, as well as of deep apostasy. The Old Testament is replete with accounts documenting repeated cycles of prosperity and blessing, followed by growing independence and an intermingling with pagan cultures. This usually led to the worship of other "gods" and the forsaking of the Lord and His Law. Next would come the warnings of the prophets and a call to repentance, which often times met with fierce resistance; leaving our merciful Heavenly Father no other option for compelling reconciliation than judgment.

Once brought low, His prodigals would then cry out in national repentance; make necessary restitution; and renew their vows of obedience. Sure enough, prosperity would return and the downward spiral would start again. Blessings were recovered, but **a very special tenderness was lost**, making it more difficult the next time around for the Israelites that strayed to humble themselves and return to God.

The profound resilience and gifting that God instilled in His chosen people further complicates matters. Quick "come backs," like the Didactic March in reverse,* have always moved the Jews two steps ahead, after falling one step back. This is indeed wonderful, except for the adamic vulnerability we all share to puff up in pride and accredit victory to our own doings, rather than to God's intervention. For these reasons, growing judgment has been required to kindle the same repentant response.

The bulk of "Christendom" suffers a similar malady; for in many ways it has also *"waxed gross"* when prospered; and behaves as a *"bullock unaccustomed to the yoke"* (Mt. 13:15; Jer. 31:18); hearing, but not heeding, God's Word (Jam. 1:22); or, even worse, changing it to adapt to uncrucified lusts (2 Tim. 4:3, 4). Only the blood of Jesus and the daily operation of His Cross can save us from this peril.

---

* Didactic March: Connotes "One step forward, two steps back," a philosophy Lenin voiced in a 1904 speech.

Once a pattern of recidivism is established, something of dynamic proportions must take place to awaken apostates to their fallen condition. In the case of the Jewish people in particular, that "awakening unto repentance" is going to necessitate an amplified re-visitation of the desperate feeling of abandonment that a great deal of European Jewry experienced in measure amidst the raging fires of the Nazi Holocaust.

". . . We [the Jewish people] will learn, out of our own experience, the **rejection** and **forsakenness** of our own Messiah in His sufferings. Just as we refused the intended revelation of God in the crucified Messiah, opportunity will be given us in our final judgment to glimpse Him anew in our own comparable sufferings—experienced this time by the entire nation in our latter days' extremity. . . . In the **absence of any hope regarding what man can do for us, or what we can do for ourselves**, God Himself will supernaturally and powerfully restore us in His mercy. The brokenness and the unprecedented repentance that will follow this, and the depth of our coming down before God at the revelation of His lovingkindness, will have had no precedent in our history (see Isa. 35:3-4; Ezek. 36:31; Zech. 12:10-14). We will tangibly experience **divine rescue out of hopeless despair**, a despair we would never have experienced except for the severity of that judgment! But it will be followed by a yet greater mercy that restores us out of the judgment. It is when we understand our past calamities as being the fulfillment of God's words of promised judgment that we have a basis of hope for the future restoration that He has also equally promised in His Word." [4]

There are no short cuts to this redemptive dimension of Wrath. The reckoning of Israel's past sins must be thorough *(Dan. 9:24)*; and the revelation of Jesus Christ as the true Messiah must be personal; born in desperate need and experienced in power. All hope that they can be saved by any other means than the Messiah Himself must be taken away before a broken remnant are going to turn to Him in a true spirit of repentance. Once this occurs, the Lord will lift from their hearts the *"vail"* of darkness that was spoken over them by their own prophets *(2 Cor. 3:13-17; Rom. 11:7-10; Ps. 69:22-24)*.

The Lord gave the Jews a unique heritage of His own choosing, but in so doing, He did not override their free will;

because the freedom of choice is the necessary element of mystery in our frame that makes it possible for us to give or withhold—receive or reject—His Love. Salvation for the Jewish people, just like Salvation for all people, can only be received by means of a **personal encounter** with the God that made us, followed by unfeigned repentance, and wholehearted acceptance of the Messiah. The chosen people have got to cross over the ford Jabbok on their own (so to speak), as did the patriarch Jacob, and wrestle alone with the Lord *"**face to face**,"* until they find Him in their uttermost extremity, at the *"breaking of the day,"* when Jesus returns to earth with all His saints to put their enemies underfoot *(Gen. 32:24-30).*

Seen through the lens of parental discipline, God's chastisements in our lives—as well as His future judgments in the lives of the Israelites—are ever redemptive and filled with promise.

> "Before I was afflicted I went astray:
> but now have I kept Thy Word." Psalms 119:67

He that did not spare His own Son the anguish of the Cross so as to atone for our sins, is the same God that is going to redeem a contrite and penitent remnant of His favored people through the fire of the coming Wrath; thus, saving them from *"a final and irremediable judgment—a fire that will not be extinguished and that is eternal."* [5]

"And I will bring the third part through the fire, and will refine them as silver is refined, and will try them as gold is tried: they shall call on My name, and I will hear them: I will say, It is My people: and they shall say, The Lord is my God." Zechariah 13:9

Herein is "Love Divine."

"Whoso is wise, and will observe these things, even they shall understand the lovingkindness of the Lord." Psalms 107:43

"O the depth of the riches both of the wisdom and knowledge of God! How unsearchable are His judgments, and His ways past finding out!" Romans 11:33

CHAPTER FOURTEEN

Glory Hallelujah!

Jesus Christ Returns to Earth
With All His Saints

Once the Great Wrath has accomplished a thorough work of cleansing, Jesus Christ **returns to earth** and touches His feet upon the *"Mount of Olives"* (Zec. 14:4, 5). Many people have confused the Day of the Lord with this later event, mistakenly thinking that both are the same. Clearly, they are not. When Christ **appears** in the clouds at the end of the Great Tribulation, He does not come to earth. Rather, He sends forth His angels to gather His elect together from the four winds *"to meet"* Him *"in the air"* (1 Th. 4:17; Mt. 24:29-31). From thence, they are taken to heaven and presented to the Father (Rev. 7:9). This is the First Resurrection, a Day set apart for the express purpose of gathering all devout believers that have *"**kept the faith**"* unto Christ.

"I have fought a good fight, I have finished my course, I have kept the faith: henceforth there is laid up for me a crown of righteousness, which the Lord, the righteous judge, shall give me at that Day: and not to me only, but **unto all them also that love His appearing**." 2 Timothy 4:7

The Great Battle of Armageddon

Later, approximately three and a half years after the saints are gathered *"in the air,"* **Jesus returns to earth as a Mighty Warrior** to fight the Battle of Armageddon (Jer. 25:30-33; Isa 66:15, 16). A vision of this triumphal event was put in words by a poet after she visited Union troops during the American Civil War, shortly before their conquest over slavery. Who among us can keep from standing at attention and shouting its victorious refrain? ..."*Glory! Glory! Hallelujah! His Truth is Marching On!*"

> "Mine eyes have seen the Glory of the coming of the Lord;
> He is trampling out the vintage
> Where the grapes of wrath are stored;
> He has loosed the fateful lightening of His terrible swift sword,
> His truth is marching on."
> Battle Hymn of the Republic, 1861[1]

At that time, "**_all the saints_**" are "**_with_**" Him.

"Then shall the Lord go forth, and fight against those nations, as when He fought in the day of battle. And His feet shall stand in that Day upon the Mount of Olives, which is before Jerusalem on the east . . . and the Lord my God shall come, and **all the saints with Thee**." Zechariah 14:3, 4a, 5b

Enoch, the seventh from Adam, saw this Day afar off and was glad:

"And Enoch also, the seventh from Adam, prophesied of these, saying, Behold, **the Lord cometh with ten thousands of His saints**, to execute judgment upon all, and to convince all that are ungodly among them of all their ungodly deeds which they have ungodly committed, and of all their hard speeches which ungodly sinners have spoken against Him." Jude 14, 15

"Arrayed in fine linen, clean and white" *(Rev. 19:8)*, these Resurrected Saints are the "*armies*" of heaven that shall come with Jesus to overthrow evil and usher in His Thousand Year Reign. Unlike the non-descript rider (the Antichrist) that the Apostle John saw seated upon a "*white horse*" at the outset of the Great Tribulation *(Rev. 6:2)*, this latter Rider is thoroughly identified as the true Christ by a series of descriptive titles.

"And I saw heaven opened, and behold a white horse; and He that sat upon him was called <u>Faithful and True</u>, and in righteousness **He doth judge and make war**. And He was clothed with a vesture dipped in blood: and His name is called <u>The Word of God</u>. And the **armies which were in heaven** followed Him upon white horses, clothed in fine linen, white and clean. And out of His mouth goeth a sharp sword, that with it He should smite the nations: and He shall rule them with a rod of iron: and He treadeth the winepress of the fierceness and Wrath of Almighty God. And He hath on His vesture and on His thigh a name written, KING OF KINGS, AND LORD OF LORDS." Revelation 19:11-16

Having beaten their *"plowshares into swords"* and their *"pruninghooks into spears"* *(Joel 3:10)*, Satan's army, comprised of the *"mighty men . . . with all men of war"* that survive the Wrath, are going to be led by the *"spirits of devils,"* operating in the *"kings of the earth,"* to a place called Armageddon. There they will raise insurrection against the Lord Jesus Christ and His army of saints *(Eze. 39:20; Rev. 16:14, 16)*.

Though the Devil fights back, however, and the *"heathen rage,"* and *"the kings of the earth . . . and the rulers take counsel together, against the Lord, and against His anointed"* *(Ps. 2:1, 2)*, as they did prior to Christ's crucifixion *(Acts 4:25, 26)*, He *"shall have them in derision"* *(Ps. 2:4)*. He shall *"speak unto them in His wrath, and vex them in His sore displeasure"* *(Ps. 2:5)*.

"Thou shalt break them with a rod of iron; Thou shalt dash them in pieces like a potter's vessel." Psalms 2:9

The Defender of Israel Fights for His Chosen People

At Armageddon, He that is called *"Faithful and True"* will personally *"plead"* with His enemies on behalf of *"Israel [His] heritage"* *(Joel 3:2)*.

In a Glorious display of mercy and grace, He shall keep His promise to the descendants of Abraham, Isaac and Jacob by rescuing the Jewish people from their enemies and turning the tables on all their foes who did them harm *(Lk. 1: 68-75)*.

"Thus saith thy Lord the Lord, and thy God that pleadeth the cause of His people, Behold, I have taken out of thine hand the cup of trembling, even the dregs of the cup of My fury; thou shalt no more drink it again: but I will put it into the hand of them that afflict thee; which have said to thy soul, Bow down, that we may go over: and thou hast laid thy body as the ground, and as the street, to them that went over." Isaiah 51:22, 23

All those that took part in furthering Israel's affliction; or, that gloated over the sufferings of God's chosen people in the day of their distress and calamity; shall be severely punished, reaping the wages of their own pride and exploitation.

". . . Thou [the descendants of Esau] shouldest not have looked on the day of thy brother [the Jews] in the day that he became a stranger; neither shouldest thou have rejoiced over the children of Judah in the day of their destruction; neither shouldest thou have spoken proudly in the day of distress. Thou shouldest not have entered into the gate of My people in the day of their calamity; yea, thou shouldest not have looked on their affliction in the day of their calamity, nor have laid hands on their substance in the day of their calamity; neither shouldest thou have stood in the crossway, to cut off those of his that did escape; neither shouldest thou have delivered up those of his that did remain in the day of distress. For the **Day of the Lord** is near upon all the heathen: <u>as thou hast done, it shall be done unto thee</u>: thy reward shall return upon thine own head. For as ye have drunk upon My Holy Mountain, so shall all the heathen drink continually, yea, they shall drink, and they shall swallow down, and they shall be as though they had not been. But upon Mount Zion shall be deliverance, and there shall be holiness; and the House of Jacob shall possess their possessions."
Obadiah 12-17

For though the Lord is wroth with His people for their rebellion *(Jer. 22:7-9)*, it is His intent, as a loving Father, to do them only good in the latter end *(Isa. 60:10; Jer. 30:16-22; Mic. 7:18-20)*.

"For a small moment have I forsaken thee; but with great mercies will I gather thee. In a little wrath I hid My face from thee for a moment; but with everlasting kindness will I have mercy on thee, saith the Lord thy Redeemer." Isaiah 54:7, 8

"Rejoice, O ye nations, with His people: for He will avenge the blood of His servants, and will render vengeance to His adversaries, and will be merciful unto His land, and to His people."
Deuteronomy 32:43

The Marriage Supper of the Lamb
Victory over Satan's Army

Consumed with the zeal of their Father's House, and unified with their Bridegroom in a common passion to obliterate evil and overthrow Satan's dominion, the Resurrected Saints are then given their long awaited opportunity to join the Lord in *"tread[ing] down the wicked"* as *"ashes"* under the soles of their feet *(Mal. 4:3)*.

"The righteous shall rejoice when he seeth the vengeance: he shall wash his feet in the blood of the wicked. So that a man shall say, Verily there is a reward for the righteous: verily He is a God that judgeth in the earth." Psalm 58:10, 11

"Let the saints be joyful in Glory: let them sing aloud upon their beds. Let the high praises of God be in their mouth, and a two-edged sword in their hand; to execute vengeance upon the heathen, and punishments upon the people; to bind their kings with chains, and their nobles with fetters of iron; to execute upon them the judgment written: **this honour have all His saints**. Praise ye the Lord." Psalm 149:5-9

This is *"**the Marriage Supper of the Lamb**,"* seen in the Spirit by the prophet Ezekiel, and later confirmed by the Apostle John *(Eze. 39:17-20)*.

"And I saw an angel standing in the sun; and he cried with a loud voice, saying to all the fowls that fly in the midst of heaven, Come and gather yourselves together unto the **supper of the great God**; that ye may eat the flesh of kings, and the flesh of captains, and the flesh of mighty men, and the flesh of horses, and of them that sit on them, and the flesh of all men, both free and bond, both small and great." Revelation 19:17, 18

At last, *"the blood of all the prophets which was shed from the foundation of the world,"* and the blood of the Christian martyrs, *"slain for the Word of God, and for the testimony which they held,"* shall be thoroughly avenged *(Lk. 11:50, 51; Rev. 6:9, 10)*.

"For, behold, the Lord cometh out of His place to punish the inhabitants of the earth for their iniquity: the earth also shall disclose her blood, and shall no more cover her slain."   Isaiah 26:21

The *"blasphemers"* of God *(2 Tim. 3:2)*; the *"enemies of the Cross of Christ"* *(Phil. 3:18)*; the *"despisers of those that are good"* *(2 Tim. 3:3)*; and *"the Devil that deceived them"* *(Rev. 20:3, 10)*, shall all be defeated and put underfoot *(1 Cor. 15:24-28)*. And though there will be some diehard survivors of the Battle of Armageddon *(Eze. 39:1-5)*, who still refuse to repent and give their lives unto Christ in Covenant Love, they shall be ruled *"with a rod of iron"* *(Rev. 12:5; 19:15)*.

From thenceforth, there will no longer be any need to *"convince"* anyone of the reality of God's Law of Righteous Judgment. Both Jews and Gentiles, great and small, will have perfect understanding of the *"wages of sin"* *(Rom. 6:23)*.

"For He put on righteousness as a breastplate, and an helmet of Salvation upon His head; and He put on the garments of vengeance for clothing, and was clad with zeal as a cloke. According to their deeds, accordingly He will repay, fury to His adversaries, recompence to His enemies; to the islands He will repay recompence. So shall they fear the name of the Lord from the west, and His Glory from the rising of the sun. When the enemy shall come in like a flood, the Spirit of the Lord shall lift up a standard against him." Isaiah 59:17-19

Satan is Bound for a Thousand Years

Thereafter, the Antichrist and the False Prophet, as the first to suffer eternal damnation (the Second Death), are thrown into a *"lake of fire burning with brimstone"* *(Rev. 19:20b)*. Then, Satan is *"bound"* *(Rev. 20:2)*, *"cast . . . into the bottomless pit, and shut . . . up . . . till the thousand years should be fulfilled"* *(Rev. 20:3)*. Despite his last futile efforts to exalt his *"throne above the stars of God"* *(Isa. 14:13)*, he shall be brought down to the lowest hell; yea, *"to the sides of the pit";* and the global ***"dominion"*** of Satan and his Antichrist shall be taken away *(Isa. 14:15; Dan. 7:26)*.

This will bring Daniel's Seventieth Week to a close.

Triumphal Change of Power

Then, the Lord will *"set . . . [His] Glory among the heathen" (Eze. 39:21, 22)*, and *"great voices in heaven"* shall be heard announcing the greatest change-over in governmental power ever known to man *(Rev. 11:15a; Dan. 7:22b)*, saying:

". . . The kingdoms of this world are become the kingdoms of our Lord, and of His Christ; and He shall reign for ever and ever."
Revelation 11:15b

Ruling and reigning with Him shall be every faithful saint that ever lived *(Rev. 1:6; 2:26, 27; 20:4)*. May we be included in their number! Amen and Amen!

"And the kingdom and dominion, and the greatness of the kingdom under the whole heaven, shall be given to the people of the **saints** of the Most High, whose Kingdom is an everlasting Kingdom, and **all dominions shall serve and obey Him**."   Daniel 7:27

CHAPTER FIFTEEN

Glory Hallelujah!

Christ's Thousand Year Reign

". . . As truly as I live, all the earth shall be filled with the Glory of the Lord." Numbers 14:21

What a Glorious era the Millennium shall be! Satan gone! His armies defeated and all enemies of righteousness subject to a rod of iron. From the start, it is going to be an era of triumph and celebration; both heaven and earth rejoicing. Daniel's prophesy is fulfilled. It's time *"to bring in everlasting righteousness, and to seal up the vision and prophecy, and to **anoint the most Holy**"* (Dan. 9:24b).

"Let the heavens rejoice, and let the earth be glad; let the sea roar, and the fulness thereof. Let the field be joyful, and all that is therein: then shall all the trees of the wood rejoice before the Lord: for He cometh, for He cometh to judge the earth: He shall judge the world with righteousness, and the people with His Truth."
Psalm 96:11-13

Eagerly awaiting their Messiah's victorious descent from the *"Mount of Olives"* with *"all His saints"* into Mount Zion will be the *"hundred and forty and four thousand"* chosen Israelites *"sealed"* prior to the Wrath (Zec. 14:4, 5; Rev. 7:3, 4; Jude 14; Rev. 14:1). They'll be singing a *"new song"* (Rev. 14:3), and just like Jesus said, they'll be saying: *"Blessed is He that cometh in the name of the Lord"* (Mt. 23:39b). This time, however, the Saviour of Israel shall come to His people in Glory, rather than *"lowly, and riding upon an ass"* (Zec. 9:9; Mt. 21:5).

"Blessed be the Lord God, the God of Israel, who only doeth wondrous things. And blessed be His Glorious name for ever: and let the whole earth be filled with His Glory; Amen, and Amen."
Psalm 72:18, 19

"Being the firstfruits unto God and to the Lamb" (Rev. 14:4), the 144,000 representatives of *"all the tribes of the children of Israel"* shall form the nucleus of the new Jewish nation (Rev. 7:4), with its magnificent capital in Jerusalem, and its anointed Monarch, none other than Christ the King (Mic. 4:6, 7).

The Second Exodus

Added around this *"holy seed"* (Isa. 6:9-13), shall be the rest of the Jewish people that survive the Wrath (Isa. 35:10; Eze. 34:11-16). After being recompensed <u>double</u> judgment for their sins, and many of them scattered and violently taken as captives into foreign countries, this beleaguered remnant shall be gathered from around the world (Isa. 11:11, 12; Jer. 23:3, 6-8). *"Fishers"* and *"hunters"* commissioned by Christ shall bring them back to the Holy Land promised to Abraham and his seed as *"an everlasting possession"* (Gen. 17:8).

"Hear the word of the Lord, O ye nations, and declare it in the isles afar off, and say, He that scattered Israel will gather him, and keep him, as a shepherd doth his flock. For the Lord hath redeemed Jacob, and ransomed him from the hand of him that was stronger than he. Therefore they shall come and sing in the height of Zion, and shall flow together to the goodness of the Lord, for wheat, and for wine, and for oil, and for the young of the flock and of the herd: and their soul shall be as a watered garden; and **they shall not sorrow any more at all**." Jeremiah 31:10-12

Epic in magnitude, this monumental deliverance can only be likened to the Israelite Exodus from Egypt that made its mark in history long ago. The Great Shepherd shall spare nothing in order to seek out His Flock. Every dispersed Jewish survivor shall be gathered home to the new Israel (Amos 9:8-10; Isa. 43:5-7). Glory Hallelujah!

"Therefore, behold, the days come, saith the Lord, that it shall no more be said, The Lord liveth, that brought up the children of Israel out of the land of Egypt; but, The Lord liveth, that brought up the children of Israel from the land of the north, and from all the lands whither He had driven them: and I will bring them again into their

land that I gave unto their fathers. Behold, I will send for many **fishers**, saith the Lord, and they shall fish them; and after will I send for many **hunters**, and they shall hunt them from every mountain, and from every hill, and out of the holes of the rocks."
Jeremiah 16:14-16

Some people have mistakenly concluded that the Second Exodus described in Jeremiah 16:14-16; 23:7, 8; Isa. 11:11, 12 and other passages was fulfilled in the era of the Nazi Holocaust and its aftermath. At that time, massive numbers of European Jews poured into the Holy Land and in 1948 Israel was established as a nation. Careful examination of other parallel passages, however, reveals that it was not. Many of the other happenings <u>attached</u> to this final return from captivity are still pending, namely: the reign of Christ on earth; universal acceptance of Jesus as *"the Lord our Righteousness"* by the Jewish people; and peace in the land of Israel.

"Behold, the days come, saith the Lord, that I will raise unto David a righteous Branch, and **a King shall reign** and prosper, and shall execute judgment and justice in the earth. In His days **Judah shall be saved**, and **Israel shall dwell safely**: and this is His name whereby He shall be called, <u>the Lord our righteousness</u>. Therefore, behold, the days come, saith the Lord, that they shall no more say, The Lord liveth, which brought up the children of Israel out of the land of Egypt; but, The Lord liveth, which brought up and which led the seed of the House of Israel out of the north country, and from all countries whither I had driven them; and they shall dwell in their own land."   Jeremiah 23:5-8

Salvation Comes to All Jews

Looking upon the Son of God *"whom they . . . pierced,"* overwhelmed by a *"spirit of grace and of supplications,"* and broken in repentance and remorse, these distraught survivors shall go into mourning *"as one that is in bitterness for his firstborn" (Zec. 12:10).*

"Then shall ye remember your own evil ways, and your doings that were not good, and shall lothe yourselves in your own sight for your iniquities and for your abominations."   Ezekiel 36:31

As tears of repentance fall from their eyes, the dam built through generations of their forefathers rebellion shall burst wide open, and out shall flow the crimson tide of Christ's redeeming blood.

"In that day there shall be a fountain opened to the House of David and to the inhabitants of Jerusalem for sin and for uncleanness."
Zechariah 13:1

As a result, the Jewish people, <u>one and all</u>, will embrace Jesus as Messiah; as the *"Son of the Blessed" (Mk. 14:61)*; the *"King of Israel" (Zep. 3:15)*; and so, **"all Israel shall be saved"** *(Rom. 11:26).*

"In those days, and in that time, saith the Lord, the children of Israel shall come, they and the children of Judah together, going and weeping: they shall go, and seek the Lord their God. They shall ask the way to Zion with their faces thitherward, saying, Come, and let us join ourselves to the Lord in a **perpetual Covenant** that shall not be forgotten." Jeremiah 50:4, 5

Hallelujah! What a time of rejoicing this shall be!

"Now if the fall of them be the riches of the world, and the diminishing of them the riches of the Gentiles; how much more their fulness? . . . For if the casting away of them be the reconciling of the world, what shall the receiving of them be, but **life from the dead**?
Romans 11:12, 15

From thenceforth they *"shall not do iniquity"* any more *(Zep. 3:13)*, nor be a reproach to the God that formed them *(Eze. 36:23)*; for He shall *"turn away ungodliness from Jacob,"* and *"take away their sins" (Rom. 11:26, 27).*

"In those days, and in that time, saith the Lord, the iniquity of Israel shall be sought for, and there shall be none; and the sins of Judah, and they shall not be found: for **I will pardon them whom I reserve**." Jeremiah 50:20

After suffering ***"double"* judgment** as punishment for their sins, they shall then *"possess the **double"* in blessing**.

"Showers of blessing" and *"everlasting joy shall be unto them"* *(Isa. 61:7; Eze. 34:26).*

"For thus saith the Lord; like as I have brought all this great evil upon this people, so will I bring upon them all the good that I have promised them."   Jeremiah 32:42

"Comfort ye, comfort ye My people, saith your God. Speak ye comfortably to Jerusalem, and cry unto her, that her warfare is accomplished, that her iniquity is pardoned: for she hath received of the Lord's hand **double** for all her sins."   Isaiah 40:1, 2

The Everlasting Covenant of Peace

One of the most remarkable blessings of all shall be the complete transformation of the Jewish people. According to His promise, the Lord will *"take away the stony heart"* out of their flesh, give them a *"new spirit"* *(Eze. 36:26)*, and *"put . . . [His] fear in their hearts, that they shall not depart"* from Him *(Jer. 32:40)*. Thus shall be established the *"Everlasting Covenant"* of Peace *(Eze. 37:26, 27),* given first to Abraham *(Gen. 17:7)*; passed on to Isaac and his seed *(Gen. 17:19)*; and received in the Last Days by both believing Jews and Gentiles through the blood sacrifice of Jesus Christ.

"For finding fault with them, He saith, Behold, the days come, saith the Lord, when I will make a New Covenant with the House of Israel and with the House of Judah: not according to the Covenant that I made with their fathers in the day when I took them by the hand to lead them out of the land of Egypt; because they continued not in My Covenant, and I regarded them not, saith the Lord. For this is the Covenant that I will make with the House of Israel **after those days**, saith the Lord; **I will put My laws into their mind, and write them in their hearts**: and I will be to them a God, and they shall be to Me a people: and they shall not teach every man his neighbour, and every man his brother, saying, Know the Lord: for **all shall know Me**, from the least to the greatest. For I will be merciful to their unrighteousness, and their sins and their iniquities will I remember no more."   Hebrews 8:8-12

Then, the saints and redeemed Israel shall bear the same inward *"token"* of **heart circumcision** that sets the children of God (the children of obedience) apart from all others. That token mark is **undivided love** for the Heavenly Father and Jesus Christ, His only Begotten Son.

"And it shall come to pass, when all these things are come upon thee, the blessing and the curse, which I have set before thee, and thou shalt call them to mind among all the nations, whither the Lord thy God hath driven thee, and shalt return unto the Lord thy God, and shalt <u>obey His voice</u> according to all that I command thee this day, thou and thy children, with **all thine heart**, and with **all thy soul**; that then the Lord thy God will turn thy captivity, and have compassion upon thee, and will return and gather thee from all the nations, whither the Lord thy God hath scattered thee. If any of thine be driven out unto the outmost parts of heaven, from thence will the Lord thy God gather thee, and from thence will He fetch thee: and the Lord thy God will bring thee into the land which thy fathers possessed, and thou shalt possess it; and He will do thee good, and multiply thee above thy fathers. And the Lord thy God will <u>circumcise thine heart</u>, and the heart of thy seed, to **love the Lord thy God** with **all thine heart**, and with **all thy soul**, that thou mayest live." Deuteronomy 30:1-6

After reconciliation for the iniquities of the Jewish people has run its course via judgment *(Dan. 9:24)*; and they are reconciled to the Father by the blood of Jesus; He shall *"restore again the Kingdom to Israel"*—thus answering the big question put to the Lord by His disciples shortly after His Resurrection *(Acts 1:6)*. Then, the Jews shall finally experience their promised *"peace" (Ps. 122)*; the *"peace of God, which passeth all understanding" (Phil. 4:7)*. This is a divine gift that no political or spiritual leader <u>other than the Lord</u> can give *(Eph. 2:14)*; for it is the fruit of right standing with God.

"Mercy and Truth are met together; **righteousness and peace** have kissed each other." Psalms 85:10

Free from the burden of sin, and purged from the *"rebels"* formerly *"among"* them *(Eze. 20:37, 38)*, they shall have peace of mind and peace throughout their Land.

"And I will make with them a **Covenant of Peace**, and will cause the evil beasts to cease out of the land: and they shall dwell safely in the wilderness, and sleep in the woods. And I will make them and the places round about My hill a blessing; and I will cause the shower to come down in his season; there shall be showers of blessing. And the tree of the field shall yield her fruit, and the earth shall yield her increase, and they shall be **safe in their land**, and shall know that I am the Lord, when I have broken the bands of their yoke, and delivered them out of the hand of those that served themselves of them. And they shall no more be a prey to the heathen, neither shall the beast of the land devour them; but they shall **dwell safely**, and **none shall make them afraid**."

Ezekiel 34:25-28

In Redeemed Israel, even the animals shall live in harmony, for the Lord has said: *"They shall not hurt nor destroy in all My holy mountain"* (Isa. 11:9a; 60:18).

"The wolf also shall dwell with the lamb, and the leopard shall lie down with the kid; and the calf and the young lion and the fatling together; and a little child shall lead them. And the cow and the bear shall feed; their young ones shall lie down together: and the lion shall eat straw like the ox. And the sucking child shall play on the hole of the asp, and the weaned child shall put his hand on the cockatrice' den." Isaiah 11:6-8

Peace on Earth

With the Lord Jesus Christ, the *"Prince of Peace"* (Isa. 9:6), and His new government of *"peacemakers"* ruling and reigning from Jerusalem (Mt. 5:9), the entire world shall also share in a thousand years of uninterrupted peace. Among them shall be the Resurrected Saints, including the esteemed holy martyrs, and participating Jews.

". . . And I saw the souls of them that were beheaded for the witness of Jesus, and for the Word of God, and which had not worshipped the Beast, neither his image, neither had received his **Mark** upon their foreheads, or in their hands; and they lived and **reigned with Christ a thousand years**." Revelation 20:4b

Armed conflict shall cease and the doxology of the heavenly host, heard by the shepherds on the eve of our Saviour's birth, shall be realized.

"Glory to God in the highest, and on earth peace, good will toward men." Luke 2:14

"In His days shall the righteous flourish; and **abundance of peace** so long as the moon endureth. He shall have dominion also from sea to sea, and from the river unto the ends of the earth. They that dwell in the wilderness shall bow before Him; and His enemies shall lick the dust. The kings of Tarshish and of the isles shall bring presents: the kings of Sheba and Seba shall offer gifts. Yea, all kings shall fall down before Him: all nations shall serve Him. For He shall deliver the needy when he crieth; the poor also, and him that hath no helper." Psalms 72:7-12

No longer shall men *"beat . . . [their] plowshares into swords"* and their *"pruninghooks into spears,"* as they did in preparation for Armageddon *(Joel 3:10)*. Instead, all manner of weaponry shall either be burned with fire *(Eze. 39:9)*, or turned back into life-supporting implements of agriculture.

"And it shall come to pass in the Last Days, that the Mountain of the Lord's House shall be established in the top of the mountains, and shall be exalted above the hills; and all nations shall flow unto it. And many people shall go and say, Come ye, and let us go up to the Mountain of the Lord, to the House of the God of Jacob; and He will teach us of His ways, and we will walk in His paths: for out of Zion shall go forth the Law, and the Word of the Lord from Jerusalem. And He shall judge among the nations, and shall rebuke many people: and they shall beat their swords into plowshares, and their spears into pruninghooks: nation shall not lift up sword against nation, **neither shall they learn war any more.**"
Isaiah 2:2-4; See also Micah 4:1-3

Praise God! Jesus is going to turn the world right side up in accord with the Father's grand design in the beginning.

"The vile person shall be no more called liberal, nor the churl said to be bountiful." Isaiah 32:5

Then, evil shall no longer be called good, nor good evil *(Isa. 5:20)*, but Truth shall be spoken *"plainly"* and *"the ears of them that hear shall hearken" (Isa. 32:3, 4)*. Christ's beloved saints, formerly so despised by the world because their manner of life was a reproof to it, shall then be honored by former opposers *(Rev. 3:8, 9)*; and *"the sons"* of those that *"afflicted"* the Jews shall *"come bending"* unto them *(Isa. 60:14)*.

The Restoration of Israel & Clean-up of the World

Under the Lord's oversight a massive program of supernatural proportions shall be launched to clean-up from the devastating effects of Daniel's Seventieth Week. Resources from all over the world shall pour into Jerusalem *(Isa. 60:5-10)*. With these revenues, the Israelites and their Gentile helpers:

". . . Shall build the old wastes, they shall raise up the former desolations, and they shall repair the waste cities, the desolations of many generations." Isaiah 61:4

The Land of Israel shall once again be *"tilled and sown"* *(Eze. 36:9; Isa. 65:21-23)*, and *"the cities shall be inhabited, and the wastes shall be builded"* *(Eze. 36:10)*; and the Lord shall *"multiply . . . man and beast"* upon its mountains; *"and they shall increase and bring fruit"* *(Eze. 36:11)*. Thus shall be fulfilled the promise He made to His people long ago, saying:

". . . Behold, I am for you, and I will turn unto you . . . . and I will settle you after your old estates, and will do <u>better</u> unto you than at your beginnings: and ye shall know that I am the Lord."
Ezekiel 36:9a, 11b

Garden of Love and Delight

Jerusalem itself, the greatly coveted (but plundered) city, shall then become *"the joy of the whole earth"*—for *"the Lord of hosts shall reign in Mount Zion, and in Jerusalem, and before His ancients Gloriously"* *(Isa. 24:23b)*.

"Great is the Lord, and greatly to be praised in the City of our God, in the Mountain of His holiness. Beautiful for situation, the joy of the whole earth, is Mount Zion, on the sides of the north, the City of the great King." Psalm 48:1, 2

Christ Himself is going to *"beautify the place of . . . [His] sanctuary; and . . . make the place of . . . [His] feet Glorious"*

(Isa. 60:13b). From there, He will bring everlasting consolation to His people *(Isa. 66:13).*

"For the Lord shall comfort Zion: He will comfort all her waste places; and He will make her wilderness like Eden, and her desert like the Garden of the Lord; joy and gladness shall be found therein, thanksgiving, and the voice of melody." Isaiah 51:3

Under His righteous reign, *"the voice of weeping shall be no more heard in . . . [Jerusalem], nor the voice of crying"* *(Isa. 65:18, 19).* Instead, there shall be the sound of a blessed people praising God and enjoying the precious treasures of everyday life.

"Thus saith the Lord of hosts; There shall yet old men and old women dwell in the streets of Jerusalem, and every man with his staff in his hand for very age. And the streets of the City shall be full of boys and girls playing in the streets thereof."
Zechariah 8:4, 5

Never again shall heathen despots, oppressors, moral liberals or hireling shepherds rule over God's chosen people, for the Lord has said:

". . . I will restore thy judges as at the first, and thy counsellors as at the beginning . . . " Isaiah 1:26a

Among these judges shall be the apostles that faithfully followed the Lord Jesus ***"in the regeneration,"*** and so, are counted worthy to *"sit upon twelve thrones, judging the twelve tribes of Israel"* *(Mt. 19:28; Lk. 22:29, 30).*

The Testimony of Jacob Re-Established (Ps. 78:5)

What a magnificent time it will be when the Lord Jesus Christ returns to earth to bring *"health and cure"* to His people, and *"reveal unto them the abundance of peace and Truth"* *(Jer. 33:6).*

At that time, passersby from other nations shall no longer look upon the desolation of Israel (and Jerusalem in particular), asking: *"Wherefore hath the Lord done thus unto this great City?" (Jer. 22:8b)*; and hear the refrain: *"Because they have forsaken the Covenant of the Lord their God, and worshipped other gods, and served them" (Jer. 22:9b)*. Instead, they shall look upon a restored State...

"And they shall say, This land that was desolate is become like the **Garden of Eden**; and the waste and desolate and ruined cities are become fenced, and are inhabited." Ezekiel 36:35

It shall be a **testimony of Redemption** to humanity; and, a source of jubilation to the Lord!

"Then the heathen that are left round about you shall know that I the Lord build the ruined places, and plant that that was desolate: I the Lord have spoken it, and I will do it." Ezekiel 36:36

"And it shall be to Me a name of joy, a praise and an honour before all the nations of the earth, which shall hear all the good that I do unto them: and they shall fear and tremble for all the goodness and for all the prosperity that I procure unto it." Jeremiah 33:9

No more anti-Semitism. No more contempt for the Jews.

". . . All that see them shall acknowledge them, that they are the seed which the Lord hath blessed." Isaiah 61:9b

At last the Promised Land shall radiate the idyllic ambiance of Eden, as God intended; and all the world shall know that mercy and grace (extended through the blood of the Everlasting Covenant of Christ), brings favor and blessing on earth; and thereafter, eternal life.

At that time, Israel shall be *"a land flowing with milk and honey" (Exo. 13:5)*, a region of plenty, *"without scarceness,"* where there is no *"lack"* for God's people of *"any thing in it" (Deu. 8:9)*. Plus, most importantly, it shall be revered as a heavenly Shangri-La where the entire population of Jews acknowledges: *"The Lord our Righteousness" (Jer. 23:6)*.

Once again, a special people, bearing the image of the great God that formed them, shall walk openly before the Lord in the cool of the day with a clear conscience, as did Adam and Eve at the first, before their disobedience *(Gen.*

1:26-2:25). Blessed with peace and prosperity, and exercising righteous dominion under Christ with the glorified Saints; the Israelites shall then be a **beacon of hope** to the nations round about; for the *"Glory"* of the Lord shall be *"seen upon"* them *(Isa. 60:2)*. He shall be exalted and the Jews shall fulfill their destiny as His ***"witnesses"*** to the world *(Isa. 43:10-12)*. As a result, *"the Gentiles shall come to . . . [their] light, and kings to the brightness of . . . [their] rising"* *(Isa. 60:3)*. Many people of diverse nations are going to literally chase them down in the streets so as to go with them to Jerusalem to worship the One that makes His *"face to shine"* upon His obedient servants *(Ps. 31:16)*. For then, as now, the gates of Salvation shall be *"open continually"* to all those that choose to enter in by the Door, Jesus Christ *(Isa. 60:11; Jn. 10:9)*.

"Yea, many people and strong nations shall come to seek the Lord of hosts in Jerusalem, and to pray before the Lord. Thus saith the Lord of hosts; In those days it shall come to pass, that ten men shall take hold out of all languages of the nations, even shall take hold of the skirt of him that is a Jew, saying, We will go with you: for we have heard that God is with you."   Zechariah 8:22, 23

Thus shall be fulfilled the Feast of Tabernacles, which, in the natural realm, is an annual celebration of the year's final crop. But in the spiritual realm, it is representative of the coming multinational celebration of the Lord's Last Harvest of souls.

"And it shall come to pass, that every one that is left of all the nations which came against Jerusalem shall even go up from year to year to worship the King, the Lord of hosts, and to keep the Feast of Tabernacles."   Zechariah 14:16

Those nations, however, *"of all the families of the earth"* that are not converted during Christ's Millennial reign, shall suffer want of rain at the first *(Zec. 14:17)*, and eternal damnation as their ultimate end *(Rev. 20:7-9, 15)*.

God's Divine Family
The Mystery of Israel and the Church Fulfilled

Capping off the splendor will be the unification of the Redeemed Church, together with Judah and Israel *(Eze. 37:21-22)*, as one Divine Family. They shall <u>jointly</u> rule under the Messiah, Jesus Christ, beginning in Jerusalem in the Millennium *(Isa. 2:2, 3)*, and continuing onward throughout eternity. *". . . Unto <u>Him</u> shall the gathering of the people be"* *(Gen. 49:10b)*.

". . . And there shall be one fold, and one Shepherd."
John 10:16b

This is the *"mystery"* that runs through the writings of the prophets and apostles. Novel as it was in the days that the Apostle Paul brought it to light, we shall see it fulfilled to the uttermost in the Glorious days of Christ's Thousand Year Reign.

"How that by revelation he made known unto me [Paul] the **mystery**; (as I wrote afore in few words, whereby, when ye read, ye may understand my knowledge in the **mystery of Christ**) which in other ages was not made known unto the sons of men, as it is now revealed unto His holy apostles and prophets by the Spirit; that the Gentiles should be <u>fellowheirs,</u> and of the same body, and partakers of His promise **in Christ** by the Gospel."   Ephesians 3:3-5

Yes, born again Gentile believers will have their full share with the Jews in the magnificent inheritance promised to Abraham *(Gal. 3:14)*. Both will be joined as <u>one Glorious family</u>, rejoicing forever in the Presence of Christ, and of God the Father *(Eph. 1:9-11; 2:11-22; 3:3-21)*.

"For the Lord will have mercy on Jacob, and will yet choose Israel, and set them in their own land: and the strangers shall be joined with them, and they shall cleave to the House of Jacob."
Isaiah 14:1

Then, at last, the Lord's Banquet House shall be *"furnished with guests"* in accord with His heart's desire *(Mt. 22:1-*

14); and Christ's prayer that we *"may be made perfect in one" (Jn. 17:23),* as He and the Father are one *(Jn. 17:21),* shall be answered.

.". ... [For] many shall come from the east and west, and shall sit down with Abraham, and Isaac, and Jacob, in the Kingdom of heaven. . . . And, behold, there are last which shall be first, and there are first which shall be last."　　　　Matthew 8:11; Luke 13:30

CHAPTER SIXTEEN

The Resurrection of Damnation
Evil is Vanquished Forever

Once *"the thousand years are expired,"* Satan will be *"loosed out of his prison"* for *"a little season"* to *"deceive the nations"* that remain defiant in their opposition to the Lord. From their ranks, he shall rally a great army, *"the number of whom is as the sand of the sea,"* to wage the final war between good and evil: the last insurgency against the Father and the Son *(Rev. 20:1-3, 7, 8)*.

Satan's devices, however, shall be foiled; for while encamped around *"the beloved City"* of Jerusalem, his armies shall be *"devoured"* by fire that comes down from Almighty God. Thereafter, the Devil shall be *"cast into the Lake of Fire and Brimstone, where the Beast and the False Prophet are, and shall be tormented day and night for ever and ever"* *(Rev. 20:9, 10)*.

"And I heard a loud voice saying in heaven, Now is come Salvation, and strength, and the Kingdom of our God, and the power of His Christ: for **the accuser of our brethren is cast down**, which accused them before our God day and night." Revelation 12:10

Hallelujah! Hallelujah! Hallelujah! The prophecy given in Genesis 3:15 shall be fulfilled to the uttermost. Jesus Christ, King of kings and Lord of lords, the promised *"Seed"* of the woman; shall thoroughly *"bruise"* the head of the Serpent under His Holy feet, that the Devil rise not again *(Rom. 16:20)*.

Warning to "Saints" and Sinners

Thereafter, follows the *"Resurrection of Damnation"* *(Jn. 5:29);* entirely unlike the *"First Resurrection"* of faithful believers *(Rev. 20:5, 6)*, in that it is reserved for **"they that have done evil,"** yet failed to repent *(Jn. 5:29; Acts 24:15; Dan. 12:2b)*.

"But the rest of the dead lived not again until the thousand years were finished . . ." Revelation 20:5a

" The Hypocrite's Hope Shall Perish" (Job 8:13b)

In their number shall be **unbelievers** *(Rev. 21:8)*, as well as **religious *"hypocrites,"*** that *"obey not the Gospel of our Lord Jesus Christ"* *(Mt. 24:48-51; 2 Th. 1:8, 9)*. Like the thieves and robbers spoken of by the Lord, this latter assemblage of professing Christians shall be those that have not submitted themselves to the *"circumcision of Christ"* *(Col. 2:11)*. They will have attempted to enter into His Kingdom through *"some other way"* than through the *"strait gate"* of surrender, suffering and self-denial symbolized in believers baptism *(Jn. 10:1; Col. 2:11; Mt. 7:13, 14)*.

"Strive to enter in at the strait gate: for **many**, I say unto you, will seek to enter in, and shall not be able. When once the Master of the house is risen up, and hath shut to the door, and ye begin to stand without, and to knock at the door, saying, Lord, Lord, open unto us; and He shall answer and say unto you, I know you not whence ye are: then shall ye begin to say, We have eaten and drunk in Thy presence, and Thou hast taught in our streets. But He shall say, I tell you, I know you not whence ye are; **depart from Me**, all ye workers of iniquity." Luke 13:24-27; Also Mt. 7:21-23

Instead of giving their "all" when Christ called, they shall have excused themselves, and continued onward in their own pursuits *(Lk. 14:16-24)*; refusing to give Him His rightful place as Ruler and Lord over every area of their lives. This includes their "free" time, their privacy and their pocket books *(Lk. 19:11-27)*. Putting off the commitment He requires of us today for some imagined future date *(Heb. 4:7)*, and deceived to believe that they were already "okay with the Lord" *(Rev. 3:17)*; they will have **neglected** their Salvation.

"Therefore we ought to give the more earnest heed to the things which we have heard, lest at any time we should let them slip. For if the word spoken by angels was stedfast, and <u>every</u> transgression and <u>disobedience</u> received a just recompence of reward; how shall we escape, if we **neglect** so great Salvation; which at the first began to be spoken by the Lord, and was confirmed unto us by them that heard Him." Hebrews 2:1-3

These are the multiplied millions of arm chair "Christians," perfunctory church goers and *"lukewarm"* religionists that the Lord calls *"evil"* because they squander their fleshly existence *(Rev. 3:16; Mt. 24:48)*; ostensibly living for Him, but in reality, living for themselves *(2 Tim. 3:2-5; Lk. 12:21)*. Behaving as though *"gain is godliness" (Rev. 3:16; 1 Tim. 6:5)*, and *"turning the grace of our God into lasciviousness" (Jude 4)*; they indulge—rather than deny—*"worldly lusts"* *(Tit. 2:11-14)*. Swept up in spiritual whoredom, covetousness, and the *"cares"* and *"pleasures"* of this life *(Lk. 12:15-21; 21:34; 2 Tim. 3:4)*, they *"put far away the evil day" (Am. 6:3; 2 Pet. 3:3-4)*.

"But and if that **evil servant** shall say in his heart, **My Lord delayeth His coming**; and shall begin to smite his <u>fellowservants</u>, and to eat and drink with the drunken; the Lord of that servant shall come in a Day when he looketh not for Him, and in an Hour that he is not aware of, and shall cut him asunder, and appoint him his portion with the <u>hypocrites</u>: there shall be weeping and gnashing of teeth." Matthew 24:48-51

Though they may speak joyfully of the First Resurrection, they live as though it were a great way off.

"The Holy Spirit is calling God's people to make their final move. We know that the end is near—and you and I have to make our move now as to what kind of person we are going to be in the last hours. You are going to become more worldly minded—or more Godly minded. You are going to buy and spend and waste more—or give and share and surrender more. . . . Let us stop all this glib talk about 'getting ready' until we are prepared to take drastic steps in getting free. Look over your world and all you own or hope to own. Then—emphatically, carefully, thoughtfully—cut loose from it all. . . . Disengage yourself from the bondage of things. You are entering a period of terrible warfare, and you must not be encumbered. Bring your body and all its appetites under subjection. Having food and shelter and raiment, be content! Be no longer a slave to the sin of covetousness. Trim your lamps and your budgets. Sacrifice with joy, and give to those in need."

David Wilkerson [1]

Such have reversed their priorities; putting more emphasis on the use of their God-given talents and resources to advance in the world, than to advance the Kingdom of God.

"Go to now, ye rich men, weep and howl for your miseries that shall come upon you. Your riches are corrupted, and your garments are motheaten. Your gold and silver is cankered; and the rust of them shall be a <u>witness against you</u>, and shall eat your flesh as it were fire. Ye have heaped treasure together for the Last Days. . . . Ye have lived in pleasure on the earth, and been wanton; ye have nourished your hearts, as in a Day of Slaughter."

James 5:1-3, 5

Jesus said: "Take heed, and <u>beware of covetousness</u>: for a man's life consisteth not in the abundance of the things which he possesseth. And He spake a parable unto them, saying, The ground of a certain rich man brought forth plentifully: and he thought within himself, saying, What shall I do, because I have no room where to bestow my fruits? And he said, This will I do: I will pull down my barns, and build greater; and there will I bestow all my fruits and my goods. And I will say to my soul, Soul, thou hast much goods laid up for many years; take thine ease, eat, drink, and be merry. But God said unto him, Thou fool, this night **thy soul shall be required of thee**: then whose shall those things be, which thou hast provided? So is he that layeth up treasure <u>for himself, and is not rich toward God</u>." Luke 18:15-21

Rather than being *"moved with fear"* to preach *"righteousness,"* like Noah before the flood *(Heb. 11:7; 2 Pet. 2:5)*, they shirk their responsibility to call others to repentance *(Eze. 3:17-21)*. Though they may support the evangelistic labors of others, in one way or another, they personally shrink back from defending Christ and His uncompromised Gospel.

Indeed, financial contributions to doctrinally sound missionary work and other worthy causes are commendable; but only as an <u>extension of</u> (not a <u>substitute for</u>) the risking of reputation and relationships that is inseparable from the one-on-one evangelism of neighbors, family and friends that

Jesus commands in His Gospel *(Mk. 16:15)*. This is cause for deep reflection in the lives of all God-fearing Christians. Our manner of life, as well as our words, are to be of such impeccable integrity that we *"shine as lights in the world"* *(Phil. 2:15, 16; 1 Cor. 10:32, 33; 2 Cor. 6:3, 4)*. Silence, under the auspices of "discretion"—if not truly led by the Holy Spirit—can be a subtle form of Christ denial.

"Whosoever therefore shall confess Me before men, him will I confess also before My Father which is in heaven. But whosoever shall deny Me before men, him will I also deny before My Father which is in heaven." Matthew 10:32, 33

". . . A Great White Throne"
The Final Judgment

These *"unprofitable"* servants *(Mt. 25:14-30)* shall be delivered up from the grave and the sea, as well as from death and hell, to stand trial <u>together</u> with the rest of the wicked, going all the way back to the beginning. There, a **Final Judgment** shall be held in the Presence of God Almighty *(2 Pet. 2:9b)*; a Potentate so awesome and so great that from before His face, both heaven and earth flee away.

"And I saw a **Great White Throne**, and Him that sat on it, from whose face the earth and the heaven fled away; and there was found no place for them. And I saw the dead, small and great, stand before God; and the books were opened: and another book was opened, which is the **Book of Life**: and the dead were judged out of those things which were written in the books, <u>according to their works</u>. And the sea gave up the dead which were in it; and death and hell delivered up the dead which were in them: and they were judged every man <u>according to their works</u>. And death and hell were cast into the Lake of Fire. This is the <u>second death</u>. And **whosoever was not found written in the Book of Life was cast into the Lake of Fire**." Revelation 20:11-15

This is *"the **Day of Judgment and Perdition of ungodly men**" (2 Pet. 3:7b)*: the *"appointed . . . Day, in the which He [God Almighty] will judge the world in righteousness **by that Man [Jesus Christ]** Whom He hath ordained" (Acts 17:31)*.

"I beheld till the thrones were cast down, and the Ancient of days did sit, Whose garment was white as snow, and the hair of His head like the pure wool: His throne was like the fiery flame, and His wheels as burning fire. A fiery stream issued and came forth from before Him: thousand thousands ministered unto Him, and ten thousand times ten thousand stood before Him: the **judgment was set, and the books were opened**." Daniel 7:9, 10

Thorough Examination

The defendants subpoenaed to stand trial before the Son at this Heavenly Tribunal shall be thoroughly examined based upon the records preserved in these books. They shall be judged *"according to the cleanness of . . . [their] hands in His eyesight" (Ps. 18:24b)*; not by the integrity of life they think they possess; nor by excuses, alibis, good intentions, or any other such thing.

"Every way of a man is right in his own eyes: but the Lord pondereth the hearts." Proverbs 21:2

"The heart is deceitful above all things, and desperately wicked: who can know it? I the Lord search the heart, I try the reins, even to give every man according to his ways, and according to the fruit of his doings." Jeremiah 17:9, 10

There, the entire portfolio of man's transitory life, from dust to dust, shall be laid bare before the all discerning *"eyes of Him with Whom we have to do" (Heb. 4:13b)*. But instead of having Jesus at their side as *"**Advocate**"* for the *"remission of sins" (1 Jn. 2:1)*—like the faithful saints *"accounted worthy"* of the First Resurrection *(Rom. 3:25; Lk. 21:36)*—the unjust shall stand *"naked and opened"* before Him as **Judge** *(Heb. 4:13)*. There, they shall be required to present their defense before a Righteous God, so profoundly pure that even *"the heavens"* are not *"clean in His sight" (Job 15:15)*.

". . . O Mighty God . . . Thou art of purer eyes than to behold evil, and canst not look on iniquity . . . " Habakkuk 1:12b, 13a

"Stand in awe of Him who encloses the heavens and the earth in the palm of His hand, who sends forth the fiery shafts of His lightening, the blast of the tempest, and makes the mountains to shake, who rules all things with the Word of His power, before whom every knee shall bow of things in heaven and things in earth and things under the earth, and to whom every tongue shall confess that He is Lord. When He calls, you must come to court . . . no matter who you are, how, or where. In that place there will be no escaping by flight, no counsel, no excuse. When He calls, you have to be there and give account, for you may be steward no longer. It will be but a little while and the wicked is no more . . ."

Menno Simons, ex-Catholic priest, A.D. 1496-1561 [2]

Judged by the Word

All unrepented *"actions"* shall then be *"weighed"* against the righteous commandments set forth in Christ's Holy Gospel *(1 Sam. 2:3)*—not by the allowances we make for ourselves and others; not by the "low bar" set by nominal social churches; not by religious activity void of a righteous life *(Gal. 6:15; Tit. 1:16)*; not by personal beliefs, church traditions or *"doctrines of devils"* that can't be substantiated by the Word of God *(1 Tim. 4:1)*; not by the "free passes" granted by wolves in sheep's clothing that teach a one sided "gospel" with no Cross and no Covenant conditions attached.

"He that rejecteth Me, and receiveth not My Words, hath one that judgeth him: **the Word that I have spoken**, the same shall judge him in the Last Day." John 12:48

Nothing shall remain hidden at this trial.

"For there is nothing covered, that shall not be revealed; neither hid, that shall not be known." Luke 12:2

All of the *"secrets"* from man's youth *(Rom. 2:16; Ps. 25:7)*, as well as the *"thoughts and intents"* of his heart *(Heb. 4:12)*; the *"fruit of his doings"* *(Jer. 17:10; 32:19; Col. 3:25)*; the use of his *"talents"* *(Mt. 25:14-30)*; the management of his resources *(Lk. 12:16-21; Jam. 5:1-3)*; the example he set; the words of his mouth *(Mt. 12: 36)*; the rearing of his children; and the way he treated others (i.e. his neighbors, the saints and the needy— *Oba. 15; Mt. 25:41-46)*; shall be revealed and cast into the balance for judgment.

Eternal Damnation: The Lake of Fire and Brimstone

Then, verdicts shall be reached and due recompense shall be rendered unto *"every man **according to his deeds**"* *(Rom. 2:6; Rev. 20:12, 13)*; **or, lack thereof** (sins of omission—*Jam. 4:17)*. In short, *"every transgression and disobedience"* shall receive its *"just recompense of reward" (Heb. 2:1-3)*. Religious opportunists (emulators, hireling shepherds) that preach corrupt "gospels" *(Gal. 1:6-9)*, engender false hope, and deceptively use the name of Jesus as a tool for exploitation, shall receive particularly harsh sentences. They shall be appointed unto *"greater condemnation"* and *"greater damnation"* than others, because of the **soul destroying** effects of their heretical doctrines and unfounded promises of false grace *(Mk 12:38-40; Jam. 3:1; Gal. 5:20)*. Notwithstanding, whatever the severity of sentencing that may be decreed, none of the *"unrighteous shall . . . inherit the Kingdom of God" (1 Cor. 6:9)*.

"And whosoever was not found written in the Book of Life was cast into the Lake of Fire." Revelation 20:15

Be not deceived. Salvation is promised only to overcomers that walk in obedience and daily repentance.

"For we are made partakers of Christ, **IF** we hold the beginning of our confidence stedfast unto the end." Hebrews 3:14

Those whose names are written in the Lamb's Book of Life, yet turn back to unrighteousness *(Eze. 3:20; 2 Pet. 2:20-22; Heb. 10:26, 27, 38, 39)*—and fail to repent—are in danger of having their names **blotted out** and *"written"* again *"in the earth" (Ps. 69:27, 28; Rev. 22:19)*.

"O Lord, the hope of Israel, all that forsake Thee shall be ashamed, and they that depart from me shall be **written in the earth**, because they have forsaken the Lord, the fountain of living waters." Jeremiah 17:13

"He that <u>overcometh</u>, the same shall be clothed in white raiment; and I will not **blot out his name out of the Book of Life**, but I will confess his name before My Father, and before His angels."
Revelation 3:5

"O my dear sheep, He can soon **blot us out** again, and write our apostate names in the earth (Jer. 17:13), <u>if</u> we do not faithfully, according to our weakness, walk in God's commandments unto the <u>end of our lives</u>; for we know that the Glorious promises given to the pious, and the crown of eternal life, lie neither in the beginning nor in the middle; but he that endures, and continues faithful **unto the end** shall receive the same from the hand of the Lord."
  Jelis Matthijss, imprisoned & slain by Catholic decree, A.D. 1564 [3]

Eternal banishment *"from the Presence of the Lord, and from the Glory of His power"* shall be the fate of all those that do not turn away from their sins <u>in this present life</u> and accept God's mercy and grace by faith through the blood of the Everlasting Covenant of His Son *(2 Th. 1:6-10)*. That means **irrevocable separation** from everything and everyone that is loving, peaceable, noble and good. Both unbelievers and *"unprofitable"* servants that profess the Christian faith, yet fail to remain *"stedfast"* in it, shall find themselves in the same dreadful place: *"outer darkness,"* where there *"shall be weeping and gnashing of teeth"* *(Mt. 25:30; Lk. 12:45-48)*. No more "last chances." Grace expires at death.

"And as it is appointed unto men once to die, but after this the Judgment." Hebrews 9:27

The Second Death

Physical death is by no means the end for the impenitent. That's why suicide is such a dangerous myth. Transgressors that die without making peace with their Maker through genuine repentance and faith in the shed blood of Jesus shall live on in a Lake of Fire—an abyss of unfathomable agony *"prepared for the Devil and his angels"* *(Mt. 25:41)*. There they shall suffer the *"blackness of darkness for ever"* with a host of demons and the most vile, violent and unscrupulous people that ever lived *(Jude 13)*. It is a place of **eter-**

nal **"hell fire,"** where the *"worm dieth not, and the fire is not quenched" (Mk. 9:47, 48)*. It is a <u>second</u> and <u>permanent death</u> from which there is **no future hope of deliverance or reprieve**; *"no rest day nor night"* from the *"smoke"* of its *"torment" (Rev. 14:10, 11)*.

"But the fearful, and unbelieving, and the abominable, and murderers, and whoremongers, and sorcerers, and idolaters, and all liars, shall have their part in the lake which burneth with fire and brimstone: which is the **Second Death**." Revelation 21:8

A terrifying glimpse of hell before it is cast into the Lake of Fire is featured in the New Testament to compel us to <u>daily repentance</u>; and motivate us to make wise choices everyday to live for the promise of the life to come (even when that means suffering for Christ's sake); <u>not</u> for the fleeting *"pleasures"* of the here and now *(Heb. 11:24-27)*.

"There was a certain rich man, which was clothed in purple and fine linen, and fared sumptuously every day: and there was a certain beggar named Lazarus, which was laid at his gate, full of sores, and desiring to be fed with the crumbs which fell from the rich man's table: moreover the dogs came and licked his sores. And it came to pass, that the beggar died, and was carried by the angels into Abraham's bosom: the rich man also died, and was buried; and in hell he lift up his eyes, being in torments, and seeth Abraham afar off, and Lazarus in his bosom. And he cried and said, Father Abraham, have mercy on me, and send Lazarus, that he may dip the tip of his finger in water, and cool my tongue; for **I am tormented in this flame**. But Abraham said, Son, remember that <u>thou in thy lifetime receivedst thy good things</u>, and likewise Lazarus evil things: but now he is comforted, and thou art tormented. And beside all this, between us and you there is a great gulf fixed: so that they which would pass from hence to you **cannot**; neither can they pass to us, that would come from thence. Then he said, I pray thee therefore, father, that thou wouldest send him to my father's house: for I have five brethren; that he may testify unto them, <u>lest they also come into this place of torment</u>. Abraham saith unto him, They have Moses and the prophets; let them hear them." Luke 16:19-29

This sobering account should motivate every true believer to rise up in the fear of God with renewed zeal in hopes of reaching as many people as possible (including kinsmen) with the saving Gospel **while we still can**.

"Knowing therefore the terror of the Lord, we persuade men . . ."
2 Corinthians 5:11a

No More Evil

Wickedness meets its final *"End"* when death and hell are cast into the Lake of Fire and Brimstone *(Rev. 20:14; 1 Cor. 15:24-28)*.

"The last enemy that shall be destroyed is **death**."
1 Corinthians 15:26

Once this final act of judgment has been executed, Christ shall have completed His mission on earth. For then He will have *"delivered up the kingdom to God,"* subdued *"all enemies under His feet"* *(1 Cor. 15:, 24, 25)*; and eradicated everyone that would not hearken to His Words, nor bow in sweet surrender to the Sovereign Lord that formed them. Thus shall be fulfilled the words which *"God hath spoken by the mouth of all His holy prophets since the world began"* *(Acts 3:21b)*.

"For Moses truly said unto the fathers, A Prophet shall the Lord your God raise up unto you of your brethren, like unto me; Him shall ye hear in all things whatsoever He shall say unto you. And it shall come to pass, that every soul, which will not hear that Prophet, shall be destroyed from among the people." Acts 3:22, 23

Hallelujah! In the end, *"death is swallowed up in victory"* *(1 Cor. 15:54b)*; the wicked are forever severed *"from among the just"* *(Mt. 13:49, 50)*; the redeemed of the Lord sin no more *(Zep. 3:13)*; and **everyone acknowledges that *"Jesus Christ is Lord, to the Glory of God the Father"*** *(Phil. 2:11b)*.

CHAPTER SEVENTEEN

Glory Hallelujah!

Eternal Life
With the Father and the Son

Words are insufficient for describing the beauty of life when we receive *"the end of ... [our] faith, even the Salvation of ... [our] souls" (1 Pet. 1:9)*, and <u>everything</u> is restored brand new. The Apostle Peter put it like this:

> "... Joy unspeakable and **full of Glory**."
> 1 Peter 1:8b

What a Glorious privilege it shall be to take part in the celebration when the heavenly laurels promised in the Gospel are bestowed upon the prophets, the apostles, the martyrs and all those (both small and great) who pressed their way through the *"straight gate"* into the wide heaven *(Mt. 7:13)*; consecrating their lives to the Lord Jesus, by **holding nothing back** from Him! To each shall be given the *"crown of life"* and full rights of citizenship in the everlasting Kingdom of God with the Father, Son and every faithful believer that ever lived *(Jam. 1:12)*. This beautiful family of worshippers shall dwell in a brand *"new heaven and a new earth"* *(Rev. 21:1)*, *"wherein dwelleth [only] righteousness"* *(2 Pet. 3:13)*. It shall be a perpetual Paradise *(Rev. 2:7b)*, governed by the **"Royal Law"** of God's Love *(Jam. 2:8)*, and perfectly suited for overcomers whose names are found written in the *"Lamb's Book of Life"* *(Rev. 21:27)*.

The Glory of Glories

In viewing the future world through the eyes of the Spirit, the Apostle John saw New Jerusalem descending out of heaven *"as a bride adorned for her husband"* *(Rev. 21:2)*.

Clothed in God's Glory, the radiance of it was *"like a jasper stone, clear as crystal"* (Rev. 21:11b).

He also heard a great voice saying that the actual *"Tabernacle of God"* shall be with men *(Rev. 21:3)*. Amazing as it is to comprehend, all the faithful who ever walked the earth shall one day behold the face of God and live *(Exo. 33:20; 1 Tim. 6:16; Rev. 22:4)*! Their *"eyes shall see the King in His beauty . . ."* and *"the Lord God will wipe away tears from off all faces"* *(Isa. 33:17a; 25:8)*.

". . . And He will dwell with them, and they shall be His people, and **God Himself shall be with them**, and be their God. And God shall wipe away all tears from their eyes; and there shall be no more death, neither sorrow, nor crying, neither shall there be any more pain: for the former things are passed away."
Revelation 21:3b, 4

There shall be no temple in this New Jerusalem, *"for the Lord God Almighty and the Lamb are the temple of it"* *(Rev. 21:22)*; neither shall there be any *"need of the sun, neither of the moon, to shine in it: for the glory of God . . . [shall] lighten it, and the Lamb is the light thereof"* *(Rev. 21:23)*. There *"shall be no night there,"* either *(Rev. 21:25)*; no anguish; no heartache; no sickness or death; no painful parting from those that we love; no grief; no evil doer; nor any curse whatsoever; for sin, sinner and Satan shall be no more *(Rev. 21:27; 22:15)*. Hallelujah!

"And there shall be **no more curse**: but the throne of God and of the Lamb shall be in it; and His servants shall serve Him."
Revelation 22:3

What shall we more say? The street of the City of God is *"pure gold"* *(Rev. 21:21)*. Its inhabitants are *"an innumerable company of angels . . . the general assembly and Church of the Firstborn, which are written in heaven, and . . . the spirits of just men made perfect"* *(Heb. 12:22b, 23)*. The twelve foundations of its stately wall are *"garnished with all manner of precious stones"* *(Rev. 21:19)*. In them are found the names of Christ's twelve apostles: the anointed men whose ground of holy doctrine now lights our way to the coming Fatherland

(Rev. 21:14). This wall, *"great and high,"* has twelve gates of pearl. They, too, are named. They are named after the *"twelve tribes of the children of Israel,"* the treasured nation through whom God chose to send His Beloved Son into the world *(Rev. 21:12, 21)*.

After having caught a glimpse in the Spirit of this eternal resting place, the great patriarch Abraham completely detached himself from the earth as his homeland. From then on, he confessed himself to be a stranger and pilgrim *(Heb. 11:13)*, on his way to a better, heavenly country; to a *"City which hath foundations, whose builder and maker is God"* *(Heb. 11:10b, 16)*. King David, likewise, passionately desired to come to this place, saying:

"One thing have I desired of the Lord, that will I seek after; that I may dwell in the House of the Lord all the days of my life, to behold the beauty of the Lord, and to enquire in His Temple."
Psalms 27:4

What Glorious promises await the faithful in Christ Jesus when God's Plan of Salvation and Eternal Life is fulfilled! At last the breach between man and His Maker caused by the <u>disobedience of Adam</u> shall be forever healed *(Rom. 5:19)*. Once again, God's chosen creatures, created for His pleasure *(Rev. 4:11)*, in His very own image, and that of His Beloved Son *(Gen. 1:26, 27)*, shall be welcomed back into Paradise, wherein lies the *"Throne of God and of the Lamb"* *(Rev. 22:1)*. There they shall have free access to the formerly guarded *"**Tree of [Eternal] Life**"* from which Adam and Eve were once banned *(Gen. 3:22-24)*. As it was in the beginning, so shall it be in the culmination. The redeemed of the Lord shall bask in the Father's loving favor and share in His dominion *(Gen. 1:26; Rev. 22:5)*, under the Sovereignty of the Lord Jesus, *"world without end"* *(Dan. 7:27; Isa. 45:17)*.

"And the Spirit and the Bride say, **Come**. And let him that heareth say, **Come**. And let him that is athirst **come**. And whosoever will, let him take the water of life freely." Revelation 22:17

CHAPTER EIGHTEEN

The Issues of Eternity

Issues of eternal destiny should be uppermost in the minds of us all. Yet so few—even in the Church—confront them with the gravity they deserve until forced by life threatening circumstances to do so. That's because the natural man (our lower nature) shies away from the reality of Christ as Judge; and more readily envisions Him according to the tender side of His nature. The bent of our soul is to see the Lord Jesus only as *"the Great Shepherd of the sheep"* (Heb. 13:20), gathering the little *"lambs with His arm,"* and gently leading *"those that are with young"* (Isa. 40:11). Yet, over and over, the Bible describes Christ as tender and tough. Revelation Chapter Five, for example, reveals Him first as ***"Lion"*** and then as ***"Lamb"*** (Rev. 5:1-8).

The concept of a Savior *"strong in love,"* while *"stern in anger against sin,"* and *"most strong in love when He forgives that which has moved Him to anger,"* is far removed from the mind-set of the unregenerate man.[1] He wants to live for the here and now, and inherently recoils from all thoughts of future punishment. His preference is to live unrestrained and without rebuke as his own judge; all the while believing that he has the blessing of God, and that heaven will be his ultimate end.

To support this errant belief he has redressed the Person of Christ, stripping Him of His *"garments of vengeance"* (Isa. 59:17), *"dipped in blood"* (Rev. 19:13); and leaving Him only with *"an helmet of Salvation upon His head"* (Isa. 59:17). In so doing, he has turned the Biblical portrait of Jesus into an idolatrous image of his own imagination. This false Christ most often resembles an accommodating, easygoing figure that overlooks (rather than executes judgment against) what Scripture defines as sin *(2 Cor. 11:4)*.

The Devil has been a great contributor to the formation of this delusion (if not the author of it), providing the wayward with an abundance of Scriptures that tell of the tender mercies of God, while at the same time <u>separating</u> these passages from the <u>conditions attached</u>. This has been one of Satan's primary devices for robbing the Church of its fire power and sending massive numbers of professing Christians straight down the road to apostasy. Preying upon the weakness of man, he has subtly **changed** the fundamental **doctrine of forgiveness**, from a thundering call to repentance, into a *"comfortable theory,"* that allows us to continue onward in our self-willed ways, without fear of reprisal in this life, or the life to come; as long as we maintain a nominal level of piety that suits our own choosing.

"Modern theology has taken away the reminder of the anger of God, and has pictured God as an amiable figure, who is not allowed to rebuke sin and cannot heal it. We have not dared to stand under the anger of God. We have selected for our comfort all the passages which speak of the love of God in the Bible, and we have ignored all the passages which speak of His anger, as though they found their way into the Bible through some human error. It is we who have erred. We have turned the doctrine of the forgiveness of God into a comfortable theory, which costs nothing and achieves nothing, that God in His mercy loves us as we are, and that we can therefore freely continue as we are. [Yet,] the doctrine of the forgiveness of God in Christ **starts with a Cross**, and there we must <u>first</u> learn how greatly we need to be forgiven." [2]

An earmark of those that have been snared by this heresy is the glaring absence of the **reverential fear of God**. Rather than centering their lives on daily repentance and amendment of life (the Cross), they feel at liberty to carry on in the whimsical pursuit of temporal gratification. Confident in an assumed assurance of Salvation, they are content with the careless adaptation of their lives to the progressively deteriorating secular and religious norms that dominate TV, movies, sports, modern forms of music and the Internet; rather, than to the **covenantal conditions** of Christ's saving Gospel.

Yet, consideration of our ultimate end **in Light of New Testament mandates** is an absolute must if we hope to be saved! The way we conduct ourselves today has everything to do with which resurrection we shall take part.

Right Standing with God

Implicit belief in the Lord Jesus Christ is a great big requirement for Salvation *(Jn. 3:16; Mk. 16:16)*.

> ". . . Believe on the Lord Jesus Christ,
> and thou shalt be saved . . ." Acts 16:31

The Apostle Paul did not haphazardly preach this condition. Rather, he spoke in <u>specifics</u>, teaching that it is those that *"**believeth <u>unto righteousness</u>**"* that shall be saved. In other words, in addition to one's profession of faith, there must also be **evidence of a changed life**; not mere participation in a *"form of godliness" (2 Tim 3:5)*, like church attendance or tithing, *"but . . . a renewal of soul in the image of God."* ³

"That if thou shalt confess with thy mouth the Lord Jesus, and shalt believe in thine heart that God hath raised Him from the dead, thou shalt be saved. For with the heart man **believeth unto righteousness**; and with the mouth confession is made unto Salvation." Romans 10:9, 10

John Wesley, a well known English Anglican priest turned reformer of the seventeen hundreds, came to this stunning realization on the eve of the profound spiritual awakening that mushroomed around his life. At that time, the Holy Ghost made known to him the utter impotence of his <u>self</u>-absolution and <u>self</u>-righteousness, based upon outward performance; in contrast to the actual forgiveness of sins and <u>God-given</u> righteousness, that is made manifest by the purging of the conscience and the miraculous transformation of our inward man by the blood of Jesus Christ *(Heb. 9:14; Eph. 4:24)*. Wesley's inadequate faith had not led him to this New Testament high-bar of Biblically defined faith; nor to Christ's "Touchstone Test" for determining whether or not we that profess to be His followers are actually walking in it. Notwithstanding, Wesley's fellow churchmen, subject to the same deficient religious ethic, thought this man to be quite pious.

". . . What I now hoped to be saved by, was, 1. Not being so bad as other people. 2. Having still a kindness for religion. And 3. Reading the Bible, going to church, and saying my prayers."
John Wesley [4]

The Great Discovery: The Cross of Christ

Smitten by the fear of God, and standing in doubt of his own Salvation, Wesley then discovered teachings on the **Cross**. As a result, he made a radical U-turn from rote-religion to regeneration. Then, he started preaching daily soul searching and repentance, in combination with the joyful giving (by faith) of *"the **whole heart** and the **whole life** to God."* [5] He also started small prayer bands all over the country where earnest believers gathered weekly to share their victories and their struggles; openly confessing their faults one to another, and praying for one another's freedom.

In Wesley's mind, **whole meant whole**; not the mere rendering of convenient bits and pieces of our lives that appease an inherent need for a sense of righteousness and eternal security; but pose no substantial threat to our earthly interests. Total surrender to the Lordship of Christ was what he called: *"My idea of Perfection."* [6]

Two centuries later, Frank Buchman—another disillusioned minister (this time a Lutheran from the United States)—had a comparable experience and came to the same conclusion.

"Any man who would follow Christ must surrender to Him all that he is and has—the whole man and his outfit. **Christ claims all**. He asks no more and He will take no less. Hudson Taylor [a missionary to China] used to say: 'If you don't crown Him Lord of all you don't crown Him Lord at all.'" [7]

Similarly revolutionized by a message he heard on the **Cross**, Buchman surrendered his life to Christ and went on to become a major life-changer—especially amongst those that he called *"the professionally religious."* But breaking through the white-washed walls of external piety was no small task. His own transparency in one-on-one encounters, as well as in small "house-parties," much like Wesley's prayer bands, set in motion another Glorious move of the Holy Spirit that spread into China, England, South Africa, the USA, etc.

"Frank . . . [took] nobody for granted. He may be a clergyman, an elder or a vestryman in a church, a Sunday-school superintendent, and yet need ruthless moral surgery. Frank declines to accept the division of the world into two classes—saved and unsaved. Christ was emphatic as to which of these two classes—the professionally religious, and the publicans and sinners—most needed changing, for with scathing irony He said, 'I came not to call the righteous, but sinners to repentance.' Frank believes the Pharisee is still as much in need of spiritual attention as the publican." [8]

Oswald Chambers, remembered for His classic devotional *My Utmost for His Highest,* was another "man of the cloth" that was brought to the **Cross** after coming to the end of conventional religion. And, just like Wesley and Buchman, he discovered that wholehearted surrender to the Lordship of Christ was a foundational mandate for Salvation; as well as the only answer to our deep hunger for righteousness and the divine communion it begets. This has been the experience of countless others over the centuries. Oswald's motto then became *"Be absolutely His."* [9]

"Go with Him all the way. The end and aim and meaning of all sanctification is **personal, passionate devotion to Jesus Christ**."
Oswald Chambers [10]

Robbed by a Lie!

Though a great many people have been tricked to believe that total surrender to Christ, and the wonder-working power of His Cross, are somehow an unbearable burden; those of us that have tasted of the Glory attached know for a certainty that just the opposite is true. So thoroughly convinced are we, that we spend our days and nights trying to introduce others to the same blessing. Yes, our flesh rebels when we make the choice to deny self by putting Christ and the advance of His Gospel first. And, yes, we experience hardship and persecution. But when we learn to embrace them, they are transformed by the sovereign hand of God into a mighty rushing wind of supernatural grace that fills our hearts with His love, lifts our spirits, and sends us deeper into the harvest *(Mt. 5:10-12; Acts 5:41; 8:1)*. In the midst of outward deprivation, we find ourselves spiritually *"out-living"* and *"out-loving"* others; including lukewarm "Christians" that are still deceived by the sensual entrapments of this transitory world.[11]

"To Frank and his friends this **unconditional surrender of everything between them and God** meant the grandest adventure of all time. . . . It meant the thrills of a Columbus voyage, pioneering trials in new countries, risks of going over the top, persistent poverty in the midst of luxury, living hour by hour on faith and prayer with exposure to ridicule inside and outside the churches, misunderstanding and ceaseless misrepresentation. It meant voluntarily facing up to every challenging obstacle that has lured the boldly aspiring and adventurous to triumph or disaster through all the ages. Moreover, it meant a relentless crusade to induce other men and women not only to believe in the possibility of living the victorious [and fulfilling] life [in Christ], but to [actually] live it . . . [in the midst of] the thousand enticements of sin in a luxury loving, security seeking, sensual civilization."[12]

First Love: The Plumb Line

This concept of *"First Love"*—demonstrated by the absolute surrender of our lives to God—is not one of man's invention *(Rev. 2:4)*. It has been in place since the beginning and lies at the hub of Christ's own doctrine on Salvation *(Mt. 13:44-46; Lk. 14:33)*. It is, and always will be, the *"first and great commandment"* *(Mt. 22:38)*. The Jewish people call it the Shema.

"Hear, O Israel: The Lord our God is one Lord: and thou shalt love the Lord thy God with **all thine heart**, and with all thy soul, and with all thy might." Deuteronomy 6:4, 5

Without fulfilling this fundamental of the faith, along with the second commandment that Jesus attached to it, not one of us can hope to be saved.

"And, behold, a certain lawyer stood up, and tempted Him, saying, Master, <u>what shall I do to inherit eternal life</u>? He said unto him, What is written in the Law? How readest thou? And he answering said, Thou shalt **love the Lord thy God** with **all thy heart**, and with all thy soul, and with all thy strength, and with all thy mind; and thy neighbour as thyself. And He said unto him, Thou hast answered right: **this do, and thou shalt live**."
Luke 10:25-28; See also Matthew 22:36-38

Love without limits for the God that made us is the attribute of devotion that set Abraham apart as a *"friend of God"* and the *"father of all them that **believe**"* (Jam. 4:8; Rom. 4:11; Gen. 22:1-18). It must be the same plumb line by which we measure our uprightness in God's sight, too.

"Ye are My friends, <u>if</u> ye do whatsoever I command you."
John 15:14

Behold the prayer of an exemplary martyr that gave up His life in this world so as to render unto our worthy Lord the wholehearted affection and homage He deserves.

". . . I acknowledge that I owe it to serve Thee, and to do only Thy will, with all my ability, yea with all my strength, so that I am to withhold nothing in this earth, whatever it be, not even my life, nor to refuse in my thoughts to pay Thee the willing debt of obedience, which I owe to Thee, and am to give Thee, not because I expect a reward from Thee, but only that I show thereby that I love Thee; so that we learn to hate all visible things for the Lover's sake, that we may love Him alone above all, and may also be loved by Him."
Matthias Servaes,
Tortured & beheaded in the Catholic Inquisition, A.D. 1565 [13]

Love & Obedience: *"Organically United"*

Knowing that abandoned love for our Lord Jesus Christ is the full expression of Christian belief (and therefore the

bedrock of righteousness and Salvation), we need to turn back to an old hymn and ask the questions in its refrain:

> "Tis a point I long to know,
> Oft it causes anxious thought,
> **Do I love the Lord, or no**?
> Am I His, or am I not?" [14]

"Too much hinges on the answer to pass the matter off lightly. . . . In seeking to learn whether we truly love our Lord we must be careful to **apply His own test**. False tests can only lead to false conclusions as false signs on the highway lead to wrong destinations. The Lord made it plain enough. . . . [He] told His disciples that **love and obedience were organically united**, that the keeping of His sayings would prove that we loved Him and the failure or refusal to keep them would prove that we did not." A.W. Tozer [15]

"He that hath My commandments, and **keepeth** them, he it is that **loveth Me** . . . He that loveth Me not keepeth not My sayings . . ."
John 14:21a, 24a

"For this is the love of God, that we **keep His commandments**: and His commandments are not grievous." 1 John 5:3

The Testing & Proving of our Faith & Love for God

Christ's own test brings us right back to the Garden of Eden. Everyday that we spend in this wicked world has a singular purpose, just as it did for Adam and Eve in the Garden, and the Israelites in the wilderness. That purpose is to **test our faith and love for the Lord**. It is to see if we, in all circumstances (no matter what the peril, price or temptation), will remain steadfast in our adherence to His true Gospel; and thus be granted entrance into His Kingdom *(Mt. 19:16, 17)*.

"And thou shalt remember all the way which the Lord thy God led thee these forty years in the wilderness, to humble thee, and to prove thee, to know what was in thine heart, whether thou wouldest **keep His commandments**, or no." Deuteronomy 8:2

To fail the test of obedience, is to suffer the Great Wrath of God *(Eph. 5:6; Col. 3:6)*, and be forever separated from the *"Presence of the Lord" (1 Pet. 4:17, 18)*.

"And to you who are troubled rest with us, when the Lord Jesus shall be revealed from heaven with His mighty angels, in flaming fire taking vengeance on them that know not God, and that <u>obey not</u> the Gospel of our Lord Jesus Christ: who shall be punished with **everlasting destruction from the presence of the Lord**, and from the Glory of His power; when He shall come to be Glorified in His saints, and to be admired in all them that believe (because our testimony among you was believed) in that day."
2 Thessalonians 1:7-10

Conditional Salvation

We cannot play "leapfrog" with the Gospel of Christ, hearing His commandments, yet bypassing the mandate to keep them. The faith we profess must be **accompanied by works**, otherwise it is *"dead" (Jam. 2:26)*.

"For faith follows upon hearing, obedience upon faith, and the **promise upon obedience**."
Menno Simons, ex-Catholic priest, A.D. 1496-1561 [16]

"Good works are **necessary**, but follow faith, as the fruit comes from the tree." Doctrine of William Tyndale [17]

Hearing the Word, believing the Word—and then walking obediently in the Light of that Word—has always been the highway to life. And when we slip, *"for in many things we offend all" (Jam. 3:2a)*, we speedily repent in Jesus' name *(1 Jn. 1:9, 2:1, 2)*, receive His forgiveness, and then we yield again to our obedience.

God established obedience as the bond of His Covenant in the very beginning with Adam and Eve. Moses carried it onward with the giving of the Law.

"Now therefore hearken, O Israel, unto the statutes and unto the judgments, which I teach you, for **to do them, that ye may live**, and go in and possess the land which the Lord God of your fathers giveth you." Deuteronomy 4:1

And Jesus brought it to remembrance when He introduced His Salvation to the world.

"And, behold, one came and said unto Him [Jesus], Good Master, what good thing shall I do, that I may have eternal life? And He said unto him, Why callest thou Me good? There is none good but One, that is, God: but **if thou wilt enter into life, keep the commandments**." Matthew 19:16, 17

These are not *"dead works"* of our own choosing *(Heb. 6:1, 9:14)*; nor of man's invention (as in the "sacraments" of Catholicism and other corrupt denominations). Rather, they are ***"works" of obedience*** outlined in the Scriptures, and personally mapped out for each of us on a daily basis by the Spirit of God.

"For we are His workmanship, created in Christ Jesus unto good works, which God hath before ordained that we should walk in them." Ephesians 2:10

"Let no one here understand Salvation by good works, but Salvation with good works; good works **without meriting Salvation** (mark well) for Salvation is of grace, thanks to our Lord Christ, as in Gal. 2:16, and still clearer in Eph. . . . ." Hendrick Alewijns, Tortured & burned to death by Catholic Decree, A.D. 1569 [18]

"For **by grace are ye saved through faith**; and that not of yourselves: it is the gift of God: not of works, lest any man should boast." Ephesians 2:8, 9

These divinely *"ordained"* works require sacrifice and surrender; like the **obedience** Abraham offered up, as an expression of his *"first love"* for God. The fulfilling of them ushers us into the righteousness that Christ purchased for faithful "Covenant-keepers" with His own blood.

"But wilt thou know, O vain man, that faith without works is dead? Was not Abraham our father **justified by works**, when he had offered Isaac his son upon the altar? Seest thou how faith wrought with his works, and by works was faith made perfect? And the scripture was fulfilled which saith, Abraham **believed God**, and it was **imputed unto him for righteousness**: and he was called the

Friend of God. Ye see then how that by works a man is justified, and **not by faith only**." James 2:20-24

Jesus Took the Lead...

Not only did Jesus teach us how to determine whether or not we possess the love He requires (as did Abraham), He also demonstrated it. He went to the uttermost extremity in His **obedience** to the Father; not counting His own life dear unto Himself; thus, paving the way into the Kingdom for all that would follow in His steps.

"Though He were a Son, yet learned He **obedience** by the things which He suffered; and being made perfect, He became the author of Eternal Salvation **unto all them that obey Him**."
Hebrews 5:8, 9

Death & Resurrection: There is No Other Way

Obedience, even unto death, was the substance that Jesus placed in God's hands to catapult Him from the *"lower parts of the earth,"* to the heights of heaven *(Eph. 4:9)*.

"And being found in fashion as a man, He humbled Himself, and became **obedient unto death**, even the **death of the Cross**. Wherefore God also hath highly exalted Him, and given Him a name which is above every name." Philippians 2:8, 9

"The servant is not greater than his Lord" *(Jn. 15:20)*. Obedience, even unto death (if need be), paves the way to Resurrection for us all. This does not necessarily mean death incurred through persecution (though some of us may be martyred). And it does not exclusively mean our future resurrection and change at the Lord's Appearance *(1 Cor. 15:51, 52)*. But also, presently speaking, **death** (as symbolized in water baptism) means the total relinquishment of all the demands of the flesh that put us at odds with God's purposes. Then, we are to *"walk in the newness of life."* We are to walk in the new man *"created in Christ Jesus unto good works"* *(Eph. 2:10)*.

"Therefore we are buried with Him by baptism into **death**: that like as Christ was raised up from the dead by the Glory of the Father, even so we also should **walk in newness of life**. For if we have been planted together in the likeness of His death, we shall be also in the likeness of His Resurrection: knowing this, that our old man is crucified with Him, that the body of sin might be destroyed, that henceforth we should not serve sin. For he that is dead is freed from sin." Romans 6:4-7

No wonder obedience to the Lord and His Word is such a threat to Satan! It leads to the **Cross** where our old man is put to death, the sinful nature is destroyed, and the Devil's yoke of tyranny is broken over our lives *(Col. 2:13-15)*.

The Patience of Job

In like manner as the Lord Jesus, and His faithful *"friend"* Abraham, Job also demonstrated his *"first love"* for God and his unwavering trust in the Lord's goodness—even when pushed to the outermost threshold of his faith. Undaunted by the discouragement of his own wife and close friends, he also made the fateful choice to take the path of surrender and obedience when he was put to the test.

"Though He slay me, yet will I trust in Him: but **I will maintain mine own ways before Him**." Job 13:15

Job feared God. He knew that it was His Father's prerogative both to give and to take away *(Job 1:21)*. So when Satan came to sift him with adversity in hopes of proving to God that Job's devotion was conditioned upon blessings—and not foremost upon love *(Job 1:8-12)*—this upright man did not allow the Devil to **move him away from obedience** and right standing *(Col. 1:23)*. He did not weaken in faith, and thereby impugn the character of His Maker *(Job 2:9, 10)*. Instead, he kept his eyes on the outcome of the trial *(2 Cor. 4:16-18)*; knowing that if he remained faithful to God in all his ways, the authenticity of his love would be revealed, and he would *"come forth as gold,"* after he was tried *(Heb. 10:36-39)*.

"... He knoweth the way that I take: when He hath tried me, I shall come forth as gold. My foot hath held His steps, His way have I kept, and not declined. Neither have I gone back from the commandment of His lips; I have esteemed the words of His mouth more than my necessary food." Job 23:10-12

In Job's *"patience" (Jam. 5:11)*, he *"possess[ed]" his soul (Lk. 21:19)*; proving by obedience and surrender that his love for God—as well as his fear of God—truly was **without bounds**.

"Cast not away therefore your confidence, which hath great recompence of reward. For ye have need of patience, that, **after** ye have done the will of God, ye <u>might</u> receive the promise." Hebrews 10:35, 36

The hope that was set before him kept his faith alive *(Heb. 12:1-3)*.

"For I know that my Redeemer liveth, and that He shall stand at the Latter Day upon the earth: and though after my skin worms destroy this body, yet in my flesh shall I see God: Whom I shall see for myself, and mine eyes shall behold . . ." Job 19:25-27a

Even so, there is no greater way for us to tell the Lord that we love Him, and that we emphatically believe in His faithfulness and care; that we cherish His lovingkindness <u>above all else</u>, including our closest relationships and life itself *(Ps. 63:3; Lk. 14:26, 33)*; than by similarly obeying His commandments, and following His Spirit, even when led into adversity and loss.

"If any man come to Me, and hate not his father, and mother, and wife, and children, and brethren, and sisters, yea, and his own life also, he cannot be My disciple. [Hate in this verse means that our affections for everything and everyone, without exception, are to be subordinate to our foremost love for God]." Luke 14:26

This testimony of faith, hope and love, expressed by **unwavering obedience** in all circumstances, and at all costs, must be operational in every true believer as we enter into the coming End-Time peril and persecution. Without it, we are sure to fail the Lord's own test. In so doing, there is great danger of being snared by the Devil; disqualified by default from the Christian Race *(2 Tim. 2:5)*; and swept up in the great falling away.

"That no man should be **moved by these afflictions**: for yourselves know that we are appointed thereunto. For verily, when we were with you, we told you before that we should suffer tribulation; even as it came to pass, and ye know. For this cause, when I could no longer forbear, I sent to know your faith, lest by some means the **Tempter** have tempted you, and our labour be in vain."
1 Thessalonians 3:3-5

Come what may, we must remain stedfast in our obedience and devotion to the Lord, knowing that our gracious Father is **testing our faith** today; and shall be using the acceleration of Tribulation (inclusive of brutal persecutions) to purge and prepare us for a Glorious end *(Rom. 8:28)*. New Jerusalem, here we come!

"Therefore will not we fear, though the earth be removed, and though the mountains be carried into the midst of the sea; though the waters thereof roar and be troubled, though the mountains shake with the swelling thereof. Selah. There is a river, the streams whereof shall make glad the City of God, the holy place of the tabernacles of the Most High." Psalm 46:2-4

Rights of Passage

Going all the way back to the Garden of Eden, the Devil has sought to divide asunder the Glorious **bond forged in obedience and love** between man and his Maker. Successful as his strategy was then, so it is now (if not more so); waxing so dominant in "Christian" thought that lawlessness is now glorified as "liberty," and obedience is all too commonly dismissed (even disdained!) as "legalism." Again, Satan turns everything upside down. He has turned the Lord Jesus into a *"stone of stumbling, and a rock of offense."*

"Unto you therefore which believe He is precious: but unto them which be **disobedient**, the Stone which the builders disallowed,

the same is made the Head of the corner, and a Stone of stumbling, and a Rock of offence, even to them which stumble at the Word, being **disobedient**: whereunto also they were appointed."
1 Peter 2:7, 8

In the Garden, the Serpent beguiled Eve into disobedience by suggesting that there were good things to be had outside the reach of God's commandments: a lie he still effectively uses today. Added to it is the popularly preached delusion that obedience to the commandments of God is a grievous and oppressive bondage (religious tyranny), rather than the **joyous liberty to wholeheartedly love and serve God**. It is quickly swallowed, because of the *"deceitfulness of sin" (Heb. 3:13)*.

"For when they speak great swelling words of vanity, they allure **through the lusts of the flesh**, through much wantonness, those that were clean escaped from them who live in error. While they promise them liberty, they themselves are the servants of corruption: for of whom a man is overcome, of the same is he brought in bondage." 2 Peter 2:18, 19

If, indeed, obedience is legalism, as some say, our Lord Jesus was (and still is) the "chief of legalists." He put uncompromised obedience at the center of His Salvation message; and personally refused to move to the right or left of a single word spoken by the Almighty when **tempted by the Devil** to do so.

"And when the **Tempter** came to Him, He said, If thou be the Son of God, command that these stones be made bread. But He answered and said, It is written, Man shall not live by bread alone, but by **every word** that proceedeth out of the mouth of God."
Matthew 4:3, 4

Jesus said: "Go ye therefore, and teach all nations, baptizing them in the name of the Father, and of the Son, and of the Holy Ghost: teaching them to **observe all things** whatsoever I have commanded you: and, lo, I am with you alway, even unto the end of the world. Amen." Matthew 28:19, 20

Stepping Stones to Glory

Jesus let absolutely nothing interfere with His obedience. He knew that it was (and still is) the necessary action that **insures** our fellowship in the Father's loving favor and abiding Presence. It is the conditional link to eternal security.

"And He that sent Me is with Me: the Father hath not left Me alone; for I do always those things that please Him." John 8:29

As it was for our Lord, so it is for us: **Faith** in the absolute goodness of God *(Mk. 10:18)*, working by **love** *(Gal. 5:6)*, and expressed through **obedience**, opens the door for both the Father and the Son to come in and sup with us and us with Them.

"Jesus answered and said unto him, If a man love Me, he will **keep My words**: and My Father will love him, and **We will come unto him, and make Our abode with him**." John 14:23

This "greatest of all blessings," hinged not only on Christ's atonement, but also on our belief in Him as Savior (as evidenced by obedience and repentance), applies not only to this life; but most importantly, the **life to come**. Rather forsake all, than suffer the severing of this vital bond, and thus be forever shut out from the Kingdom of God.

"Blessed are they that **do His commandments**, that they may have right to the **Tree of Life**, and may enter in through the gates into the City." Revelation 22:14

"In that day shall this song be sung in the land of Judah; We have a strong city; Salvation will God appoint for walls and bulwarks. Open ye the gates, that the righteous nation which **keepeth the Truth** may enter in." Isaiah 26:1, 2

CHAPTER 19

A Call to Examination

Speaking specifically about events pertaining to the last of the Last Days, the Apostle Peter left us with a sober call to thorough soul searching and repentance.

"Wherefore, beloved, seeing that ye look for such things, be **diligent** that ye may be found of Him in peace, without spot, and blameless. And account that the longsuffering of our Lord is Salvation . . ." 2 Peter 3:14, 15a

Spiritual "location" (evaluation) is a desperate need that we all share.

"**Examine yourselves**, whether ye be in the faith; prove your own selves . . ." 2 Corinthians 13:5a

We need to make sure that we're not self-deceived; thinking that we're "right with God," when in reality, our lives are not in alignment with the Gospel.

"But be ye **doers of the Word**, and not hearers only, deceiving your own selves." James 1:22

We need to be constantly checking our manner of life by the commandments of Christ; not by the declining standards of a world waxing stone cold in iniquity *(Mt. 24:12)*; or, by the liberal doctrines and backward virtues of modern churches that are progressively being moved by the **spirit of antichrist** into the mainstream of the presently forming structure of Babylon the Great.

"There is . . . a place for self-judgment and a real need that we exercise it (1 Cor. 11:32, 33). While our self-discovery is not likely to be complete and our self-judgment is almost certain to be biased and imperfect, there is yet every good reason for us to work along with the Holy Spirit in His . . . effort to **locate us spiritually** in order that we may make such amendments [while we still can!!!] as the circumstances demand." A.W. Tozer [1]

"Search me, O God, and know my heart: try me, and know my thoughts: and see if there be any wicked way in me, and lead me in the way everlasting." Psalm 139:23, 24

Take Heed

Think about the **warning** in Revelation chapters Two and Three that was sent to the seven churches of Asia. There, the Lord Jesus recounts in detail the attributes of Glory shining in the lives of His people: works, labor, patience, abhorrence for evil, rejection of false doctrine, charity, service, faith, even martyrdom. Though so many good fruits characterized the churches as a whole, the Lord had a controversy with five of the seven. These flawed fellowships varied in their virtues and vices. As a result, the Lord Jesus did not find their works (or their affections for Him) "*perfect before God*" *(Rev. 2:4; 3:2)*. So He sounded a **call to repentance** with full reconciliation and soul-security promised to His "*overcomers*" *(Rev. 3:5)*; and grievous judgments pronounced against those that continued onward without making the necessary changes *(Rev. 2:16, 22, 23)*. The consequences for impenitence included the potential removal of one's name from the Lamb's *"Book of Life."*

Knowing that *"all these things happened unto them for ensamples: and they are **written for our admonition**, upon whom the ends of the world are come" (1 Cor. 10:11)*, we must take heed, go to our knees and prayerfully examine our own lives and fellowships. We need to open to those chapters and invite the Holy Spirit to comb through our lives so as to determine whether or not any (or all) of the same sins that plagued the early Church have soiled our garments, too. …Heresy? Whoredom? Self-righteousness? Materialism? Assimilation into the local culture? The adoption of secular values? The pride of life? The operation of the spirit of Jezebel? If it offends our pride, and threatens the assessments we maintain of our own heart purity, to ponder the possibility of guilt in relationship to any of these things; that, in itself, is its own indictment. It indicates that we need to do some honest soul-searching. Without this kind of thorough and ongoing Holy Ghost examination **in Light of God's Word**, followed by repentance and reformation, we are in danger of eternal hell fire.

In an urgent call to repentance brought to the Church of Ephesus, one of the seven churches of Asia, Jesus said:

"I know thy works, and thy labour, and thy patience, and how thou canst not bear them which are evil: and thou hast tried them which say they are apostles, and are not, and hast found them liars: and hast borne, and hast patience, and for My name's sake hast laboured, and hast not fainted. Nevertheless I have somewhat against thee, because thou hast left thy **first love**. Remember therefore from whence thou art fallen, and **repent**, and do the first works; or else I will come unto thee quickly, and will remove thy candlestick out of his place, **except thou repent**." Revelation 2:2-5

The Beauty of Holy Separation

Heresy and whoredom (spiritual adultery) are two great sins revealed in the early Church that today's professing Christians too readily brush over, if not ignore altogether. This is primarily due to the prevailing spirit of ecumenism *("whoredoms"—Hos. 4:12, 5:4)* that has spilled over from the world, liberalizing most churches, and blinding members to Satan's intent for penetrating our lives through these doors. We are from what Jesus called an *"adulterous and sinful generation" (Mk. 8:38).* Hence, we don't adequately understand the jealousy of God; nor the reason for His mandate of holy separation; namely, spiritual protection. This critical commandment cuts us off from undue exposure to **seducing evil spirits**; whose sole design is first to deceive us; and then, to capture our devotion, distract us with idolatries, and **turn us away from God** to the inadvertent worship of Satan and/or the works of our own hands.

Both the Old and New Testaments teach that hairline movement to the right or left of the Word of God turns us **away from Christ** to other *"gods,"* either of our own imagination; or, to evil religious spirits masquerading as Christ *(2 Cor. 11:4, 14)*. For that reason, heresy provokes the Lord to jealousy and brings down upon our heads terrible curses.

Old Testament: "And thou shalt not go aside from **any** of the words which I command thee this day, to the right hand, or to the left, to go after **other gods** to serve them." Deuteronomy 28:14

New Testament: "I marvel that ye are so soon **removed from Him** that called you into the grace of Christ unto another gospel: which is not another; but there be some that trouble you, and would pervert the Gospel of Christ. But though we, or an angel from heaven, preach any other gospel unto you than that which we have preached unto you, **let him be accursed**." Galatians 1:6-8

The Lord wants us for Himself, wholly *"separated unto the Gospel of God" (Rom. 1:1)*; like a faithful wife given in **undivided love** to the desires and requests of her husband.

"For I am jealous over you with godly jealousy: for I have espoused you to one husband, that I may present you as a chaste virgin to Christ. But I fear, lest by any means, as the Serpent beguiled Eve through his subtilty, so your minds should be corrupted from the simplicity that is in Christ. For if he that cometh preacheth **another Jesus**, whom we have not preached, or if ye receive **another spirit**, which ye have not received, or **another gospel**, which ye have not accepted, ye might well bear with him [meaning, you wrongly tolerate his deception]." 2 Corinthians 11:2-4

The Holy Scriptures are not "soft" when it comes to matters of moral and doctrinal integrity. The Lord calls lying words spoken in His name *"**villany**" (Jer. 29:23)*. He calls false prophesy *"**horrible**" (Jer. 5:30, 31)*. He **loathes** them both!

"But I have a few things against thee, because thou hast there them that hold the doctrine of Balaam, who taught Balac to cast a stumblingblock before the children of Israel . . . . So hast thou also them that hold the doctrine of the Nicolaitanes, **which thing I hate**." Revelation 2:14, 15

Heresy is a *"**damnable**"* stumblingblock that can subvert one's inheritance in the Kingdom of God *(2 Pet. 2:1; Tit. 3:10, 11)*. It is condemned as a work of the flesh, equally as wicked as adultery, fornication and murder.

"Now the works of the flesh are manifest, which are these; adultery, fornication, uncleanness, lasciviousness, idolatry, witchcraft, hatred, variance, emulations, wrath, strife, seditions, **heresies**, envyings, murders, drunkenness, revellings, and such like: of the which I tell you before, as I have also told you in time past, that they which do such things **shall not inherit the kingdom of God.**"
Galatians 5:19-21

Yet, in today's ecumenical culture, heresy is often flippantly discounted as "no big deal." The tolerance of *"divers and strange doctrines"*—resisted unto blood since the outset of Christianity *(Heb. 13:9)*, and casual fellowship with those that walk therein—has now been widely accepted by the religious status quo as a fundamental expression of "Christian love and virtue." This outrageous amendment to the whole Spirit and constitution of the Bible is one of the most (if not the most!) *"pernicious"* influences in all of Christendom *(2 Pet. 2:2; 2 Jn. 9-11; 1 Cor. 10:20, 21)*. The same irreverent spirit of the Serpent that so lightly dismissed the importance and supremacy of the true Word of God in the Garden of Eden is just as active and subtle today.

We are commanded to *"earnestly **contend for the faith** which was once delivered unto the saints" (Jude 3)*—not to compromise it.

"And have **no fellowship** with the unfruitful works of darkness, but rather reprove them." Ephesians 5:11

Believers unable to get victory over particular maladies that seem to be indicative of some kind of a breach need to consider the possibility of compromise in this area. Closing the gap could be part of opening the door to deliverance and healing, as well as a key in the restoration of right standing with God and intimate fellowship with the Lord.

"And I heard another voice from heaven, saying, **Come out of her**, My people, that ye be not **partakers of her sins**, and that ye **receive not of her plagues**. For her sins have reached unto heaven, and God hath remembered her iniquities."
Revelation 18:4, 5; See also 2 Corinthians 6:14-18

"Now I beseech you, brethren, mark them which cause divisions and offences <u>contrary to the doctrine which ye have learned</u>; and **avoid them**." Romans 16:17

Learning from the Apostasy that Stole the Hearts of our Jewish Predecessors

Not only do today's Christians need to learn from the sins that surfaced in the churches of Asia; but also, from the apostasy of the Israelites. They were a highly favored people that withheld from the God that chose them the **obedience** and devotion He desires from those bound in Covenant love with Him. Once baptized into Christ, our lives, like theirs, are no longer our own *(Gal. 2:20; 1 Cor. 6:19, 20)*. From thenceforth, we are to be wholly given to His purposes; one of which, is to be a Light, <u>not a reproach</u>, unto the world around us *(Mt. 5:13-16)*. And if we transgress and abide not *"in the doctrine of Christ"* (2 Jn. 9), as they transgressed and departed from the Law, our end shall be no different than theirs; unless, of course, we truly repent.

"For if God spared not the natural branches [the Jews], take heed lest He also spare not thee. Behold therefore the **goodness** and **severity** of God: on them which fell, severity; but toward thee, goodness, <u>if</u> thou <u>continue</u> in His goodness: **otherwise thou also shalt be cut off**." Romans 11:21, 22

Their provision for mercy was the *"blood of goats and calves,"* but now ours (and theirs) is *"the precious blood of Christ, as of a Lamb without blemish and without spot"* (Heb. 9:12-14; 1 Pet. 1:19). We've been given a *"new"* and *"better Covenant"* (Heb. 8:8, 6); therefore, we are even <u>more</u> accountable than they were before Jesus came!

"He that despised Moses' Law died without mercy under two or three witnesses: of how much **sorer punishment**, suppose ye, shall he be thought worthy, who hath trodden under foot the Son of God, and hath counted the blood of the Covenant, wherewith he was sanctified, an unholy thing, and hath done despite unto the Spirit of grace? For we know Him that hath said, Vengeance belongeth unto Me, I will recompense, saith the Lord. And again, The Lord shall judge <u>His people</u>. **It is a fearful thing to fall into the hands of the living God**." Hebrews 10:28-31

It is no small matter to have the Gospel so readily available to us; and then, to ignore it, dismiss its conditions, knowingly disobey it for any reason (even the seemingly most justifiable); or, to put away the whisper of Holy Ghost conviction and restraint. To do so is to jeopardize one's Salvation and invite the Wrath of God.

"For if we sin <u>wilfully</u> **after that we have received the knowledge of the Truth**, there remaineth no more sacrifice for sins, but a certain fearful looking for of judgment and fiery indignation, which shall devour the adversaries." Hebrews 10:26, 27

"Lest there should be among you man, or woman, or family, or tribe, whose heart turneth away this day from the Lord our God .... and it come to pass, when he heareth the words of this curse [the warnings attached to disobedience], that he bless himself in his heart, saying, I shall have peace, though I walk in the imagination of mine heart, to add drunkenness to thirst: the Lord will not spare him, but then the anger of the Lord and His jealousy shall smoke against that man, and all the curses that are written in this book shall lie upon him, and the Lord shall blot out his name from under heaven." Deuteronomy 29:18a, 19, 20

Apostasy does not necessarily occur overnight; and the chances of recovery are slim *(Heb. 6:4-8; 12:14-17)*. Most often, it is the result of an accumulation of choices. It's the outcome of an ongoing pattern of resistance and disobedience that takes place gradually over time. Left unchecked, it eventually leads the snared believer so far from the Lord that he is given over to the very nature from whence he originally sought deliverance; and cannot discern his fallen condition. Like the Jews, he is blinded. Then, there is nothing left to restore such an one to right standing with God but chastisement; <u>if</u>, at that stage, there is anything of Christ's nature still within him that will suffer itself to be reproved.

The Cross of Christ: Our Remedy

Well aware of this propensity to backsliding inherent in us <u>all</u>, John Wesley counseled his disciples as follows:

"'Use every help, and remove every hindrance; always remembering, "He that despiseth little things shall fall by little and little."'" [2]

Oswald Chambers recognized the same precarious vulnerability. *"He realized . . . what the disposition of sin in him could do."* [3] For that reason, like Wesley, he preached the necessity of the **Cross**, and *"the pushing to the most painful point of resistance the experience of giving up the right to ones self."* [4] Chambers knew that nothing short of wholehearted obedience and abandon can satisfy our Bridegroom's passion for the undivided affections of His own.

We of the 21st century desperately need that same acknowledgment of fleshly weakness, as well as the same commitment to the Cross. Sin, in whatever form it takes, if not "nipped in the bud," is the potential ruin of us all; no matter how "holy," devout or renewed we believe ourselves to be *(Isa. 65:5; Lk. 18:9-14)*.

"Wherefore let him that thinketh he standeth **take heed lest he fall**. There hath no temptation taken you but such as is common to man: but God is faithful, who will not suffer you to be tempted above that ye are able; but will with the temptation also make a way to escape, that ye may be able to bear it."
1 Corinthians 10:12-13

Let's not forget...

". . . It was a group of religious people, priests and Pharisees, who sent Christ to the Cross. They did not want to be disturbed, but to be left alone in the snugness of their half-faith. They were respectable citizens, regular churchgoers. Read the story again. It is all so human, all so understandable. Now the Cross shows us to ourselves, exposes our excuses, unmasks our motives. . . . The Cross makes us to see the desperate nature of sin. Behind the tragedy of Calvary are the ordinary lives of men and women to whom little sins seemed harmless until at last they tried to murder God." [5]

The only thing, therefore, that can prevent us from falling into the *"perpetual backsliding"* that stole the affections of our Israelite predecessors *(Jer 8:5)*, is the grace of God at work in our hearts. This costly *"true grace" (1 Pet. 5:12)*—unlike the cheap false "grace" that allows us to continue as we are—teaches us to admit the weakness of our flesh amidst trials and temptations. It compels us to take the narrow *"way of escape"* (even in the seemingly "smallest" matters) that is abundantly provided **through the blood of Christ's Cross**.

"For the grace of God that bringeth Salvation hath appeared to all men, teaching us that, <u>denying</u> ungodliness and worldly lusts, we should live soberly, righteously, and godly, in this present world."
Titus 2:11, 12

The Children of Light

Scripture says that God dwells *"in the light which no man can approach unto" (1 Tim. 6:16)*. Knowing that we are soon to enter into the fullness of that Light, or to be cast into outer darkness; we need to force ourselves out of the shadows and squarely face our *"secret sins" (Ps. 90:8)*. We need to be openly confessing them first to the Lord *(Ps. 32:5)*; and then, when given the opportunity, confiding in trustworthy brethren and soliciting their prayers.

"Draw nigh to God, and He will draw nigh to you. Cleanse your hands, ye sinners; and purify your hearts, ye double minded. Be afflicted, and mourn, and weep: let your laughter be turned to mourning, and your joy to heaviness. Humble yourselves in the sight of the Lord, and He shall lift you up." James 4:8

"Confess your faults one to another, and pray one for another, that ye may be healed. The effectual fervent prayer of a righteous man availeth much." James 5:16

This is the **wonderful way of the Cross**, discovered by Wesley, Buchman and Chambers; taught by the apostles; and lived unto death by the Christian martyrs.

"Seeing then that we have a great High Priest, that is passed into the heavens, Jesus the Son of God, let us <u>hold fast</u> our profession. For we have not an high priest which cannot be touched with the feeling of our infirmities; but was in all points tempted like as we are, yet without sin. Let us therefore come boldly unto the Throne of Grace, that we may obtain mercy, and find grace to help in time of need." Hebrews 4:14-16

Faithful attendance upon the altar of repentance is a mandate for communion with the Father and the Son. It is also the necessary faith initiative that transforms routine church services into *"fellowship"* that is truly heavenly. It is a taste of exceeding Glory that surpasses even the deepest camaraderie shared by people of the world.

"But <u>if</u> we **walk in the light**, as He is in the light, we have fellowship one with another, and the blood of Jesus Christ His Son cleanseth us from all sin. If we say that we have no sin, we <u>deceive</u> ourselves, and the Truth is not in us. <u>If</u> we **confess our sins**, He is faithful and just to forgive us our sins, and to cleanse us from all unrighteousness." 1 John 1:7-9

Walking with a clear conscience in the Light of Christ under His atoning blood is the only sure way to <u>hold fast</u> to Salvation. It should be the number one priority of every earnest believer that is serious about Christ's charge to be *"ready"* for the First Resurrection *(Mt. 24:44)*.

"For yourselves know perfectly that the **Day of the Lord** so cometh as a thief in the night. For when they shall say, Peace and safety; then sudden destruction cometh upon them, as travail upon a woman with child; and they shall not escape. But ye, brethren, are not in darkness, that that Day should **overtake you as a thief**. Ye are all the **children of light**, and the children of the day: we are not of the night, nor of darkness. Therefore let us not sleep, as do others; but let us **watch** and be sober." 1 Thessalonians 5:2-6

"O House of Jacob, come ye, and
let us **walk in the light** of the Lord." Isaiah 2:5

Chastisement

There are no second causes in the lives of God's children. We have a Father in heaven that deals with us as sons.

". . . Behind all 'natural causes' [stands] the First Cause Himself."
John Wesley [6]

The Lord *"knoweth our frame" (Ps. 103:14)*; that apart from His marvelous inner working, we are earthly minded and *"bent to backsliding" (Hos. 11:7)*; prone to religious complacency and self-righteous pride. We tend to be like Esau, when he returned to his father with the requested venison, only to discover that the blessing he expected to receive had been stolen by his younger brother *(Gen. 27)*. In other words, we can be well pleased with ourselves, living in anticipation of great blessings and rewards, and yet be out-of-step with God and His Will. When His wrath falls upon the conscience to turn us from our sins, our first response is to rationalize and dismiss the case against ourselves (gainsay); or, to hide what remains of our adamic disposition under carefully sewn *"fig leaves"* of piety, so as to leave it in tact *(Gen. 3:7)*; or, even worse, to side with the Devil, and *"varnish over every form of wickedness and sin, as though they were nothing but virtue and righteousness."* [7] Thus, in our futile attempts to *"save"* our lives (our "dignity" ...our pride ...our inflated self-image), we can be tricked to lose them eternally *(Mt. 16:24-26)*.

"Sin has a power that blinds us to its nature and workings; this is what makes sin so deceptive. This answers why we so easily overlook our own sin and call it something else by giving it a more respectable label. . . . Only the judgment of God upon sin saves us from any self-justifying lightness about our own condition." [8]

This tendency to resist conviction magnifies enormously in "good times." That's when we're least apt to own up to our sins and receive the ongoing discipline and correction we so desperately need *(Rev. 3:17)*.

"I spake unto thee in thy prosperity; but thou saidst, I will not hear. This hath been thy manner from thy youth, that thou **obeyedst not My voice**." Jeremiah 22:21

Actually, relief from affliction; or, ease and comfort of any kind; usually prompts a slackening of our reigns, and a subsequent hardening of our hearts; just as it did in Pharaoh's life when the plague of frogs was stayed.

"But when Pharaoh saw that there was **respite**, he hardened his heart, and hearkened not unto them . . ." Exodus 8:15

Hence, in His great mercy and grace, our Heavenly Father brings upon us His **rod of correction** by virtue of circumstances; and allows us to be brought low through reproach and persecution, which also have a chastening effect; to open us up to the reality of our transgressions *(Job 36:10)*; and **turn us to the Cross**, as a means of bringing these stumbling blocks of Salvation to crucifixion.

"When we consider, worthy brethren, our very weak and sinful nature . . . how that we have a tendency at all times (although we do seek and fear God) to mind earthly and perishable things, then we see that the gracious God and Father, who through His eternal love always cares for His children, has left behind in His House an excellent remedy against all this, namely, the pressing **cross of Christ**. . . . Through the aforesaid Cross, that is, through much oppression, tribulation, anxiety, apprehension, bonds, seizure, and so forth, [we] let go of all the transitory things of the earth, and that which delights the eyes. And so we die unto the world and unto the flesh, **love God alone**, and seek the things that are above where Christ sitteth at the right hand of God." Menno Simons [9]

Thank the Lord for His chastisements and judgments *(1 Cor. 11:32; Heb. 12:5-13)*! They bring us to our knees (if we let them) and force us to consider things that we (of ourselves) would prefer to ignore. We would be wise to avail from these dealings. We need to receive them in good faith, as from the sovereign hand of our loving Father; knowing that the things that surround our lives (even those that seem harsh and happenstance) are to try our faith, and encourage us onward; or, to reveal our wanton hearts, and inspire us to *"consider"* our ways and repent *(Hag. 1:7)*; thus, saving us from trouble in this life, and damnation as our final end.

"For if we would **judge ourselves**, we should not be judged. But when we are judged, we are chastened of the Lord, that we should not be **condemned with the world**." 1 Corinthians 11:31, 32

Let's not be of a secular mind-set that separates "cause and effect;" or, of the errant religious mind-set that pins every adversity on the Devil. Yes, the Devil attacks, but God is sovereign over all, and it is His intent that every affliction we undergo drives us closer to Him. Instead, let us be of a Biblical mind-set, humbly discerning and accepting the fullness of His dealings. Only then shall they impact and change our lives; thereby producing in us the **redemptive fruits of repentance**, while at the same time preparing us for the upcoming harvest, and the Appearance of the Lord.

"Now no chastening for the present seemeth to be joyous, but grievous: nevertheless afterward it yieldeth the peaceable **fruit of righteousness** unto them which are exercised thereby."
Hebrews 12:11

Live Each Day as Though it were Your Last

Beloved Brethren: The issues of eternity are not something to be trifled with; dismissed; ignored; or put off for future deliberation.

"If we have not come into His righteousness in this life, then how shall we stand in His presence thereafter? God knows the unspeakable anguish of a man's eternal separation from Himself. There is, therefore, an **urgent finality** about eternity and judgment that needs to be registered upon our souls." [10]

God forbid that any of us, *"perish . . . in the gainsaying of Core" (Jude 11)*, because we fail to lay God's manifold warnings to heart, by using the "window of grace" we now have as an occasion to confront our duplicity, repent and render unto the Lord Jesus Christ the abandoned obedience and adoration He is due *(1 Cor. 16:22)*. Despite popular opinion, His unspeakable grace does have bounds; and they fall within the framework of what He calls *"To day."*

"Again, He limiteth a certain day, saying in David, **To day**, after so long a time; as it is said, To day if ye will hear His voice, harden not your hearts."
Hebrews 4:7

Prior to her torture and execution for the dissemination of anti-Nazi leaflets at the University of Munich in Germany, twenty-two year old Sophie Scholl left an entry in her diary that should impact us all. She lived during World War II when many watchful Christians thought the ends of the world had come. Regardless of the exact timing in the End-Time scenario she lived, however, Sophie knew that in her case, the *"Day of the Lord"* had come. Facing the sobering reality of martyrdom, she wrote:

"'Many people think that after our era the world will come to an end. The many terrible signs could make that belief plausible. But isn't this belief really only of incidental importance? For each of us, no matter in what age we live, have to be **prepared at a moment's notice to be called to account by God**. After all, do I know whether I'll be alive tomorrow?'" [11]

In other words: Live each day as if it were your last.

". . . Constantly and at every moment walk as you hope to appear before Him, and do not lie down to sleep with a troubled or gnawing conscience, but purify your heart before God and your neighbor, and always act and walk according to the right rule of the Scriptures. . . . Act not as though you might live many years yet, but walk before the Lord just as if you were to die immediately."
Jan Hendrickss, Burned at the stake by Catholic decree, 1572 [12]

Choices

"Our God is a consuming fire" (Heb. 12:29), but He is also a merciful Father that has made a way of escape from doom and damnation for us all. That Way is Christ crucified; and the stepping stones along the trail are daily repentance and amendment of life. If we fail to travel that road, and carve out one of "convenience," religious ritual, or even "good works" in its place, the fault lies with us, not with the Lord; for *"there is forgiveness with . . . [Him], that [He] mayest be feared"* (Ps. 130:4).

In this modern age of apostasy, dominated by religious inventions and the exaltation of human excellence, we've got to remember:

> "God is the only Being who is good,
> and the standards are set by Him." [13]

If we hope to receive the promise of Salvation we've got to make sure that we're serving Him *"**acceptably** with **reverence** and **godly fear**" (Heb. 12:28b)*, based on His Word; not on our own private set of morals and judgments; or, by an alternative plumb line set by anyone else, including wayward religious institutions, *"highly esteemed among men,"* but abominable in the sight of God *(Lk. 16:15)*.

When the Trumpet sounds at the First Resurrection, none of our flimsy excuses, justifications, or simulated righteousness will stand. No **half-measures** will insure our rising *(Rev. 3:16)*; no humanitarian works will provide acquittal *(Tit. 3:5)*; no denominational imprimatur will grant passage.

Only overcomers that are born again of the incorruptible Seed Christ *(Jn. 3:3-7)*; that **put Him first** and **love Him most**; that **obey His Word**; that repent when they commit iniquity; that bear His Cross *(Lk. 14:27)*; that fight the *"good fight of faith"* against the world, the Devil and their own wicked flesh *(1 Tim. 6:12)*; that confess His name before men regardless of the cost or consequence *(Mt. 10:32, 33)*; in short, that *"believeth unto righteousness,"* **as signified by the joyful surrender of all**; are sure to enter in through the gates into the Holy City, and there abide forever, *"world without end"* *(Rom. 10:10; Eph 3:21)*.

Others that draw back in fear *(Heb. 10:38, 39; Rev. 21:8)*; retain divided interests *(Mt. 6:24)*; abide in disobedience *(Col. 3:6)*; circumvent the Cross *(Phil. 3:18, 19)*; practice willful sin *(Heb. 10:26, 27)*; blaspheme the Holy Ghost *(Mt. 12:31, 32)*; or deny Christ by worshiping the Beast and his image and receiving his Mark in their forehead or hand, shall find themselves shut out from the Kingdom of God *(Rev. 14:9-11)*.

The choice is ours. The time to make correction is now.

"The Lord is not slack concerning His promise, as some men count slackness; but is longsuffering to us-ward, not willing that any should perish, but that all should come to repentance." 2 Peter 3:9

In the words of Jesus Christ Himself:

". . . Repent: for the Kingdom of heaven is at hand."
Matthew 4:17b

CHAPTER TWENTY

Seeking the Glory...

Dear Reader:

A wonderful awakening is taking place around the globe as the world heads towards its certain end in preparation for the Kingdom of God. One cannot help but sense the acceleration of travail; feeling sore vexed and out-of-step; as though being drawn towards an altogether different place; the Paradise of Scripture; where Truth and righteousness—justice and compassion—reign supreme.

No doubt about it: the earth has gone into labor; a labor marked by manifold climatic disasters; economic uncertainty; major gains in the Ecumenical Movement; and the ongoing development of a one world government, with a single currency, an international court, food bank, health care system, etc. Perhaps one of the greatest signs of the times is the rampant outgrowth of corruption in the political and the religious arenas, capped off by the abominable exaltation of sexual perversion and violence (including increasing acts of terrorism) that can only be described as demonic.

If you are one of Christ's lost sheep, shackled to this condemned world by the chains of sin, yet sensing an inner stirring, and desirous of being set free and included in the coming Kingdom; know for a certainty that the Lord is calling. We encourage you to seize this occasion to give your life to the One who made you for Himself. This is <u>not</u> a call to institutional religion, so repugnant to those of us that yearn to know our Creator as He truly is, and not as men have made Him to be. Rather, it is a call to the Lord Jesus Himself. It is an invitation to reconciliation with the Heavenly Father and eternal bonding with His Divine Family, wherever that precious and rare "Church of the Two or More" may be found *(Mt. 18:20)*.

This call is broad in its scope, not only entreating those that have never made a profession of Christ's ownership of their lives; but also, to those that are estranged from Him, knowing only "religion" and not "relationship." A great number of these, though affiliated with church activities from their youth, have not yet experienced the reality of the new birth; or, have lost contact with a vital union with Christ, not knowing how to maintain that nearness through the power of His Cross. And then, there are still others (and you know who you are), that are walking in downright disobedience: backslidden; serving self, and once again entangled in the spirit of the world.

To all these, we come as *"ambassadors for Christ, as though God did beseech you by us,"* saying:

> "We pray you in Christ's stead, be ye reconciled to God."
> 2 Corinthians 5:20

Here are the initial steps...

Absolute Surrender

Jesus tells all that would follow Him to first count the cost *(Lk. 14:28)*. That is because conversion (though Glorious!) is far reaching in its demands. It means much more than simply confessing Jesus as Lord, rendering token repentance and then settling into a comfortable religious niche to await His blessings. Conversion means commitment: a complete turn around. It means giving up "the gavel and the bench" as the moral arbiters of right and wrong; and standing instead before the Judgment Seat of Christ, with His Word as the final moral authority over all matters of conscience and conduct that affect our lives. It means unseating self and putting Christ first by the ongoing surrender of our lives to Him: *"the whole man and his outfit."* [1] This includes the good and bad; our time, our assumed "rights," careers, interests, finances, talents and relationships. Anything that is held back (be it ever so "small") becomes an impediment to spiritual growth that hinders our capacity to receive and give the love of Jesus. Left in tact, it falls into the category of *"idola-*

try" (1 Cor. 6:9, 10), thus robbing one's inheritance in the Kingdom of God.

Repentance & Confession

Jesus Christ is there to meet "whosoever" is willing to honestly approach Him at His unseen (but very real) altar of repentance *(Heb. 4:15, 16; 10:22)*. This is a place of open and spontaneous confession where we continually lay bare our selfish hearts to God. Then, if possible, we share our inner struggles with meek Christians, who also freely confess their sins one to another without fear of belittlement *(Jam. 5:16)*.

This does not mean carefully manufactured self-deprecation or a broad based confession of sin in general. It means a humble acknowledgment of the manifold sins that so easily beset us, and an earnest cry for God's grace to overcome them one day at a time. Sin comes in many forms: in word and deed; as well as in overall attitudes of the heart; and self-centered imaginations of the mind, rooted in covetousness, lust and vanity.

The saints with whom we confide do not stand aloof in patronizing condescension; nor do they render excessive sympathy so as to take the necessary sting out of conviction. They simply draw near and pray with us (and for us) in mutual expectation of the forgiveness, healing and deliverance promised to the penitent in God's Word. Often times the Holy Spirit uses these cherished brethren to shine further light on our sins; or, to render helpful counsel and practical support for helping us to do spiritual warfare to overcome them.

There is no skirting around open confession, followed by the receipt of the loving prayers of fellow Cross-bearers. It makes forgiveness come alive by striking a major blow at self-deception and pride: Satan's "aces" for keeping captives enslaved to demon powers, hidden lusts, sexual fantasies, lingering grudges, haunting memories, vain imaginations, and evil thoughts. Once we breakthrough the *"inhibitions of moral cowardice"*[2] and allow ourselves to be seen by others in weakness, there comes an inrush of divine life and light (the outcome of forgiveness received); as well as an awareness of the Presence of a power that does not come of ourselves, but of God. As a result, our roots go deeper into the love of Jesus; our faith grows; and we are knit more closely together in Spirit with our Christian brothers and sisters *(Col. 2:2)*. To cap it off, we begin to notice within ourselves real change; a welcome blessing to those that know all about us—the good and the bad.

Forgiveness

To receive this unspeakable Atonement for our own sins, and the freedom it begets, we must <u>first</u> forgive (with God's help) the trespasses of others (no exceptions!). This is a condition built into the Gospel. Scripture teaches that the heart that nurses bitterness, resentment, grudges, or malice of any kind shall never know the Salvation of God. Love and hate share no common ground—not now, or in eternity.

> "And when ye stand praying, forgive, if ye have ought against any: that your Father also which is in heaven may forgive you your trespasses. But <u>if</u> ye do not forgive, <u>neither</u> will your Father which is in heaven forgive your trespasses." Mark 11:25, 26

Whatever wrongs we have suffered at the hands of others, we must be willing to admit that we have not always (if ever) been of a "right spirit" in our own journey through life. From this posture of genuine humility and penitence in regards to our own sins (in combination with a profound appreciation for the price Jesus paid to free us from their penalty), springs the love of God. This is a supernatural impartation of God's power that enables us to pray for those that despitefully use and abuse us, or others. It enables us to see <u>beyond the personal injury</u> to the need that we all share (as sinners) for Christ's forgiveness and the transformation of disposition that follows *(Mt. 5:43-45)*. The love that truly forgives is not an emotion, although it can be felt, at times; nor is it something we can drum up on our own. Rather, it is a mercy that the Lord expresses through us, if we willingly surrender ourselves to Him in our time of need.

Corrie ten Boom, a Dutch Christian imprisoned with her sister Betsie in a concentration camp for hiding Jews during the Holocaust, was given the opportunity to learn from her own experience how to manifest the forgiveness that she had so often spoken about to others.

"It was at a church service in Munich that I saw him, the former SS man who had stood guard at the shower room door in the processing center at Ravensbruck. He was the first of our actual jailers that I had seen since that time. And suddenly it was all there—the roomful of mocking men, the heaps of clothing, Betsie's pain-blanched face. He came up to me as the church was emptying, beaming and bowing. 'How grateful I am for your message, Fraulein,' he said. 'To think that, as you say, He has washed my sins away!' His hand was thrust out to shake mine. And I, who had preached so often . . . the need to forgive, kept my hand at my side. Even as the angry, vengeful thoughts boiled through me, I saw the sin of them. Jesus Christ had died for this man; was I going to ask for more? *Lord Jesus*, I prayed, *forgive me and help me to forgive him.* I tried to smile, I struggled to raise my hand. I could not. I felt nothing, not the slightest spark of warmth or charity. And so again I breathed a silent prayer. *Jesus, I cannot forgive him. Give Your forgiveness.* As I took his hand the most incredible thing happened. From my shoulder along my arm and through my hand, a current seemed to pass from me to him, while into my heart sprang a love for this stranger that almost overwhelmed me. And so I discovered that it is not on our forgiveness any more than on our goodness that the world's healing hinges, but on His. When He tells us to love our enemies, <u>He gives, along with the command, the love itself</u>." [3]

Restitution & Amendment of Life

Restitution is another necessary component of repentance that attests to the sincerity of our confession. To the best of our ability, we are taught to make every effort to compensate for the damage we have done to others when appropriate (and if circumstances allow), by "righting our wrongs," and admitting our transgressions to those that we have hurt by asking for their forgiveness. This is not something to be done haphazardly; but rather, prayerfully, with great sensitivity, wisdom and discretion, as impressed in conscience by the Holy Spirit. Such actions are not always received in goodwill and may even be met with resistance, doubt, contempt or vitriol. Nevertheless, we must remain constant in our love; going the "extra mile" to restore trust and praying for the wounded party/parties. Only then will our prayers for personal forgiveness be answered and our worship and service be received of the Lord.

"Therefore if thou bring thy gift to the altar, and there rememberest that thy brother hath ought against thee; leave there thy gift before the altar, and go thy way; <u>first</u> be reconciled to thy brother, and <u>then</u> come and offer thy gift."   Matthew 5:23, 24

Many times the opportunity to make recompense is no longer available. Hence, we cannot pay the debt that we owe; return the kindness that was due; give the love and attention we failed to render; or set aside "quality time" to spend with others who needed our attention when we were too caught up in ourselves to show adequate interest, etc. Then, the restitution that God accepts is the heartfelt giving of ourselves (seasoned by past failure) to the precious souls that are in our lives <u>today</u>!

The Cross of Christ

Jesus said: ". . . If any man will come after Me, let him deny himself, and take up His Cross <u>daily</u>, and follow Me."   Luke 9:23

The Cross of Christ, so often misunderstood, other than in the historic sense as it relates to the crucifixion of Jesus, is an essential component of the true Christian life. In a nutshell, it is the *"power of God"* unto Salvation; the force that separates us from the world and the world from us *(1 Cor. 1:18; Gal. 6:14)*. This divine power is unleashed in our lives through the complete surrender of ourselves to God's will, Word and ways amidst the reproach and persecution of men; as well as the chastisements and disciplines brought to bear upon us by virtue of the providences that surround our lives. Operating amidst heated trials, the Cross has a wondrous way of putting us in confrontation with our sinful nature; giving us the opportunity to confess our iniquities, repent, amend and make restitution.

Herein lies real change—not "a one time deal"—but rather, a lifetime of transformation from *"Glory to Glory"* by the Spirit of the Lord *(2 Cor. 3:18)*. Like no other instrument, the Cross opens us up to the searchlight of the Holy Spirit and reveals our attachment to the world. It has a remarkable way of casting light into the dark corners of our hearts, exposing secret faults; and the things we try to hide from ourselves, from others, and even from the Lord.

"It strips us of the silken robes of self-excusing and tears off the masks wherewith we disguise our condition." [4]

"Who can understand his errors? Cleanse Thou me from secret faults. Keep back thy servant also from presumptuous sins; let them not have dominion over me: then shall I be upright, and I shall be innocent from the great transgression. Let the words of my mouth, and the meditation of my heart, be acceptable in thy sight, O Lord, my strength, and my Redeemer." Psalm 19:12-14

Miraculous in its working, the Cross releases heavenly virtue that hurts but heals, bringing deliverance and Salvation. Without it, the seed of Christ initially sown into the heart quickly dies out and all that is left is *"a form of godliness"* with no *"power thereof"* *(2 Tim. 3:5)*. The stagnated Christian becomes unfruitful and dissatisfied; in constant need of artificial religious stimuli to keep "pumped up." Eventually, *"in time of temptation,"* those thus snared *"fall away"* *(Lk. 8:13)*. Religious activity may continue, but the true essence and Spirit of Christianity departs.

"And these are they likewise which are sown on stony ground; who, when they have heard the Word, immediately receive it with gladness; and have no root in themselves, and so endure but for a time: afterward, when affliction or persecution ariseth for the Word's sake, immediately they are offended. And these are they which are sown among thorns; such as hear the Word, and the cares of this world, and the deceitfulness of riches, and the lusts of other things entering in, choke the Word, and it becometh unfruitful." Mark 4:16-19

The Cross is the key to intimacy and fulfillment in Christ. It answers our hunger and thirst for righteousness *(Mt. 5:6)*. If you lose contact with Jesus, return to the Cross and you're sure to find Him there.

"The nearer I come to the Cross, the nearer I come to God; and the farther I am from the Cross, the farther I remain from God."
The Apostle Andrew,
Crucified at Patras in Achaia, around the year A.D. 70 [5]

A Wretch Like Me...

As a help to those that feel somewhat at a loss as to just how to approach the Lord, we set forth a prayer. May it be a lamp to your feet and a light to your path as you take your first steps on the uphill Road to Glory.

Heavenly Father,

Thou art the Potter and I am the clay.

"But now, O Lord, Thou art our Father; we are the clay, and Thou our Potter; and we all are the work of Thy hand."   Isaiah 64:8

Please put me on the wheel and fashion me anew, in the image of Your Son, just like Adam in the beginning before the fall. I ask you to forgive me for the sins of my fathers and my own, as well *(Neh. 9:2)*—those that I recognize and those that I don't yet see. In Jesus' name, forgive me for all these trespasses . . . . and empower me to overcome them and make appropriate restitution. Your Word teaches me to forgive everyone that I have had *"ought against" (Mk. 11:25)*, so that you (in turn) will forgive the enormous debt I owe You, yet am unable to pay. Thank you Jesus for the price you paid at the Cross in my behalf. I know that it is not in me to do this on my own, so I ask for Your strength to forgive from the heart, and not the mouth only; and to keep doing it, until all ill-will is driven from my soul, and nothing remains but love. Help me let go; to trust You with everything; and to move on. Help me to even forgive myself.

Make me to understand the consequences and effects of my sins so that I come to hate them; and as a result, willingly yield up my adamic nature; so that you can *"create in me a clean heart" (Ps. 51:10; 139:23, 24)*, just like you intended in the beginning: unselfish in its bent, and filled with divine love through and through.

I yearn to be set free from the burden of sin. I give You the reigns of my life ...the Lordship ...the control. I want to be born again. I am willing (by faith) to relinquish all that separates me from Your Presence; all that binds me to this wicked world and opens me up to its demonic influences. This includes not only my dreams, desires and aspirations, but also my pride, my very "self"—which I acknowledge to be *"the corrupt and self-defeating center of my life."* [6]

I desperately need the Spirit of Your Son and the baptism of the Holy Ghost to give me the moment-by-moment power to *"walk in newness of life" (Rom. 6:4).* My old nature won't readily give up its accustomed ways. Yet, I trust that as I surrender my will to You, and call upon You for strength, You will be there to succor me and see me through.

> "Holy Spirit from above, tender, undefiled Dove,
> In my spirit have Thy way, o'er my actions hold full sway.
> Blest Companion from on high, in Thy comfort ever nigh;
> Bind my heart to Christ in love, O Thou Precious Heavenly Dove.
> . . . Weak I in myself may be, but my strength shall be in Thee.
> Sweet provision of God's grace, in Thy gift His love I trace.
> I could not Thy coming earn, could no more Thy wooing spurn,
> Take control and bless and use, as the Infinite may choose.
> . . . Thou jealous love, Thou burning Flame,
> Oh, burn out all unlike Thy Name.
> Make soft my heart in Thy strong flame,
> To take the imprint of . . . [Christ's] Name." [7]

Fill me with Your Presence, O God. Help me to taste of Your favor. I desire the peace and joy you promise in this life; and I yearn to be a full participant in the Glory of the life to come.

> Jesus, please come into my heart
> and be my Messiah and Lord.

Baptize me with Your Holy Spirit *(Mt. 3:11; Lk. 11:9-13; Acts 1:8; 2:4; 10:44-47, etc.).* Wash me thoroughly, change me. Make me a blessing and a lifeline to others. Guide my steps into Your foreordained plan and purpose for my life; something eternally consequential that I acknowledge to be far more fulfilling than anything I could come up with on my own. Help me to joyfully take up the Cross of reproach and persecution for Christ's name sake; and to submit to the daily disciplines of self denial necessary to crucify the sinful nature I inherited from Adam. Teach me Your ways. Open my understanding to Your Word.

In Jesus' name, I renounce Satan's claim on my life. I commit myself to seek out water baptism by immersion as an open declaration of my faith in Jesus Christ; and of my determined purpose to leave the world behind and reach for the Kingdom of God. I confess Jesus Christ as King of kings and Lord of lords; and myself, a pilgrim on my way, like the great patriarch Abraham, to a Heavenly City whose builder and maker is God. I have found Eternal Glory!

Glory Hallelujah! I am born again!
My name is written in the Lamb's Book of Life.

" . . . It is certain that the crown is not to be found in the beginning or in the middle, but at the end. (O that this would be considered, as it should!) But as necessary as it is to finish well, so necessary it is also to begin well, and, having begun, to go on well; for without a good beginning and a good progress it is impossible to attain to a good end. . . . Let us be patient together, then, most beloved in the Lord, till the Day come, which, _if_ we remain faithful unto the end, will assuredly bring us that which we here wait for in hope."

T.J.V. Braght [8]

Our Arms are Open...

Welcome to the Divine Family, where there is neither Jew nor Gentile, bond or free, black or white, American, African or European: *". . . But Christ is all, and in all (Col. 3:11).*

"Unto Him be Glory in the Church by Christ Jesus throughout all ages, world without end. Amen." Ephesians 3:21

As a beginning we encourage you set aside quality time for prayer and Bible Study. Get a 1611 King James Bible (not a modern translation) and ask the Lord to lead you to a sound Christian fellowship (or at least one other truly Christ-centered relationship) where the unadulterated Word of God is spoken and lived out in fullness. In this day of ecumenical compromise such fellowship can be difficult to find.

Look for what the martyrs called "The Little Flock"— meaning one of the rare and special assemblies of penitent believers scattered here-and-there where the Cross is not a mere emblem on a steeple; but rather, a divine work of the Holy Spirit changing the lives of the people.

Discernment is paramount. There is great danger in these Last Days of falling into religious apostasy. Without even realizing it, vulnerable believers can settle into a nominal form of godliness; making peace with their sins, rather than exposing and forsaking them. Better to stand alone in Christ, until led by the Holy Spirit into a God-fearing body of fellow Cross-bearers, than to get caught up in the religious idolatry now sweeping the world.

"<u>Be warned</u>: It doesn't matter what anyone tells you about a great 'revival' or moving of the Spirit taking place; it doesn't matter how many multitudes are involved, or how loud their praises are; it doesn't matter how 'successful' a particular ministry may appear to be. If the <u>Cross of Jesus Christ</u> is not the door through which people come, you can rest assured—<u>it is not a work of God</u>." [9]

And of course, share Christ with others!
He is the *"Hope of Glory" (Col. 1:27)*.
There is no more noble reason for being alive!

"Ye are the light of the world. A city that is set on an hill cannot be hid. Neither do men light a candle, and put it under a bushel, but on a candlestick; and it giveth light unto all that are in the house. Let your light so shine before men, that they may see your good works, and <u>Glorify your Father</u> which is in heaven."
Matthew 5:14-16

"The whole human race was created
to <u>Glorify God</u> and enjoy Him forever."
Oswald Chambers [10]

Endnotes

Unlocking the Mystery

1. Parker and Charles, "There's a Land of Begin Again." WWII song of hope, 1945.

Chapter One: Born to Love

1. Thieleman J. van (TJV) Braght, *The Bloody Theater or Martyrs Mirror of the Defenseless Christians*, (Scottdale, PA: USA: Herald Press, 1749), pp. 695, 696.
2. H.A. Walter, Soul Surgery, (stepstudy press, www.stepstudy.com), p. 112. Walter quotes Fosdick, *The Meaning of the Faith*, p. 253.

Chapter Two: God's Plan of Salvation: A Messiah Shall Arise

1. Editor David Daniell, *William Tyndale The Obedience of a Christian Man*, (London, England: Penguin Books, 2000), p.7.
2. Scholl, Inge, *The White Rose, Munich 1942-43*, (Middletown, CT, USA: Wesleyan University Press, 1970, 1983), p. 48. Originally published in German in 1952.
3. Jesse Penn Lewis with Evan Roberts, *War on the Saints*—Unabridged Edition, (NY, USA: Thomas E. Lowe, Ltd., First Printing 1973), p. 8. This unabridged Ninth Edition is the outcome of a diligent search made in the nineteen sixties by Hannah Lowe, widow of Thomas Ernest Lowe, to find the whole volume of the authors' text. The republication of it—having been out of print for years—was *"strenuously opposed, but in 1973, with the help of likeminded believers, Mrs. Lowe had the joy of seeing the book once again made available exactly as its authors intended."*

Chapter Three: Born Again

1. C. Irving Benson, *The Eight Points of the Oxford Group, An Exposition for Christians and Pagans*, (Melbourne, London, Edinburgh, Toronto, Bombay and Madras: Humphrey Milford, Oxford University Press, 1938), p. 3.
2. Hannah Hurnard, *Hearing Heart*, (Wheaton, IL, USA: Tyndale House Publishers, Inc., 1978), pp. 26, 27. American edition copyright 1978 by The Church's Ministry Among the Jews.
3. Ibid, p. 25.
4. Ibid, p. 25.
5. Attributed to S. Sundar Singh, "I Have Decided to Follow Jesus," (Timeless Truths.org.).

Chapter Four: The Cross of Christ and Regeneration

1. C. Irving Benson, *The Eight Points of the Oxford Group, An Exposition for Christians and Pagans*, (Melbourne, London, Edinburgh, Toronto,

Bombay and Madras: Humphrey Milford, Oxford University Press, 1938), p.7.
2. Jesse Penn Lewis with Evan Roberts, *War on the Saints*—Unabridged Edition, (NY, USA: Thomas E. Lowe, Ltd., First Printing 1973), Editor's Forward.
3. Editor J.C. Wenger, Translated from Dutch by Leonard Verduin, *The Complete Writings of Menno Simons*, (Scottdale, PA, USA: Herald Press, 1956), pp. 994, 995.
4. H.A. Walter, Soul Surgery, (stepstudy press, www.stepstudy.com), p. 101. Walter quotes Frederick Lawrence Knowles from *Love Triumphant*, (Boston, MA, USA: Dana, Estes & Co.), pp. 92, 93.

Chapter Seven: Christ's End-Time Message

1. Frances J. Roberts, "My Kingdom is at Hand," *Come Away My Beloved*, (Ojai, CA, USA: The King's Press, 1970), pp. 158, 159.
2. Ibid, "As the Sounding of a Trumpet" & "My Kingdom is at Hand," pp. 189, 158.
3. Thieleman J. van (TJV) Braght, *The Bloody Theater or Martyrs Mirror of the Defenseless Christians*, (Scottdale, PA, USA: Herald Press, 1749), p. 570.

Chapter Eight: Interpreting End-Time Events

1. Art Katz, *True Fellowship: Church as Community*, (Bemidji, MN, USA: Burning Bush Press, 2009), p. 45.
2. Oswald Chambers, *My Utmost for His Highest*, (Ulrich, OH, USA: Barbour Publishing, 1935), Entry 7/29.
3. Mary Stewart Relfe, Ph.D., *When Your Money Fails: The "666 System" is Here*, (Montgomery, AL, USA: Ministries, Inc., 1981), p. 191.
4. Thieleman J. van (TJV) Braght, *The Bloody Theater or Martyrs Mirror of the Defenseless Christians*, (Scottdale, PA, USA: Herald Press, 1749), p. 592.

Chapter Nine: The Seventieth Week of Daniel

1. Thieleman J. van (TJV) Braght, *The Bloody Theater or Martyrs Mirror of the Defenseless Christians*, (Scottdale, PA, USA: Herald Press, 1749), p. 743.

Chapter Ten: The Great Tribulation

1. David Wilkerson, "The Vision," Cassette recording, (Lindale, TX, USA: World Challenge), Vision received in 1973.
2. Thieleman J. van (TJV) Braght, *The Bloody Theater or Martyrs Mirror of the Defenseless Christians*, (Scottdale, PA, USA: Herald Press, 1749), p. 730.
3. Editor David Daniell, *William Tyndale The Obedience of a Christian Man*, (London, England: Penguin Books, 2000), pp. 17, 102.

4. Jesse Penn Lewis with Evan Roberts, *War on the Saints*—Unabridged Edition, (NY, USA: Thomas E. Lowe, Ltd., First Printing 1973), pp. 13, 26.
5. Ibid, pp. 9, 10.
6. Thieleman J. van (TJV) Braght, *The Bloody Theater or Martyrs Mirror of the Defenseless Christians*, p. 363.
7. Ibid, p. 516.
8. Ibid, pp. 355, 356.
9. Ibid, p. 360.
10. Ibid, p. 929. Quote taken from a letter written by the husband of Adriaenken Jans, a martyress burned at the stake in 1572 by Catholic decree.
11. Ibid, p.839.
12. Ibid, p. 11.

Chapter Thirteen: The Time of Jacob's Trouble

1. References: Martin Luther, *On Jews and their Lies*, Wittenberg, 1943. Also, Editor Kevin A. Miller, "Christian History," Issue 39, Volume XII, No. 3, pp. 38, 39. Information quoted in "Christian History" was taken from Yale Collection of German Literature, Beinecke Rare Book and Manuscript Library.
2. Art Katz, *The Holocaust Where Was God?*, (Bemidji, MN, USA: Burning Bush Press, 1998, 2008), pp. 64, 62.
3. Ibid, p. 64.
4. Ibid, p. 69-71.
5. Ibid, p.72.

Chapter Fourteen: Jesus Christ Returns to Earth with All His Saints

1. Julia Ward Howe, "Battle Hymn of the Republic," 1861, (Seattle, WA, USA: Webster Publishing, Multimedia 2000, Inc., 2005). Webster's 2005 Encyclopedia CD-Rom.

Chapter Sixteen: The Resurrection of Damnation

1. David Wilkerson, *Racing Towards Judgment*, (Lindale, TX USA: World Challenge), pp. 116, 112, 113.
2. Editor J.C. Wenger, Translated from Dutch by Leonard Verduin, *The Complete Writings of Menno Simons*, (Scottdale, PA, USA: Herald Press, 1956), pp. 612, 613.
3. Thieleman J. van (TJV) Braght, *The Bloody Theater or Martyrs Mirror of the Defenseless Christians*, (Scottdale, PA, USA: Herald Press, 1749), p. 673.

Chapter Eighteen: The Issues of Eternity

1. Geoffrey Allen, *He That Cometh*, (New York, USA: The MacMillan Company, 1933), p. 167.
2. Ibid, p. 167, 168.

3. Edited by Elizabeth Jay, *The Journal of John Wesley. A Selection*, (Oxford, NY, USA: Oxford University Press, 1987), p. 39.
4. Ibid, p. 30.
5. Ibid, p. 158.
6. Ibid, pp. 158, 159.
7. C. Irving Benson, *The Eight Points of the Oxford Group, An Exposition for Christians and Pagans*, (Melbourne, London, Edinburgh, Toronto, Bombay and Madras: Humphrey Milford, Oxford University Press, 1938), p. 6.
8. A.J. Russell, *For Sinners Only*, (Tucson, AZ, USA: Hats Off Books, 2003), p. 122. First published in 1932.
9. David McCasland, *Oswald Chambers: Abandoned to God*, (Grand Rapids, MI, USA: Oswald Chambers Publications Association, Ltd., Discovery House Publishers, 1993), p. 261.
10. Ibid, p. 107.
11. A.J. Russell, *For Sinners Only*, p. 122.
12. Ibid, pp. 46, 47.
13. Thieleman J. van (TJV) Braght, *The Bloody Theater or Martyrs Mirror of the Defenseless Christians*, (Scottdale, PA, USA: Herald Press, 1749), p. 694.
14. A.W. Tozer, *That Incredible Christian*, (Harrisburg, PA, USA: Christian Publications, 1964), p. 132.
15. Ibid, p. 132-134.
16. Editor J.C. Wenger, Translated from Dutch by Leonard Verduin, *The Complete Writings of Menno Simons*, (Scottdale, PA, USA: Herald Press, 1956), p. 376.
17. Editor David Daniell, *William Tyndale The Obedience of a Christian Man*, (London, England: Penguin Books, 2000), p. ix.
18. Thieleman J. van (TJV) Braght, *The Bloody Theater or Martyrs Mirror of the Defenseless Christians*, p. 747.

Chapter Nineteen: A Call to Examination

1. A.W. Tozer, *That Incredible Christian*, (Harrisburg, PA, USA: Christian Publications, 1964), 102.
2. Edited by Elizabeth Jay, *The Journal of John Wesley. A Selection*, (Oxford, NY, USA: Oxford University Press, 1987), pp. 12, 16, 17.
3. David McCasland, *Oswald Chambers: Abandoned to God*, (Grand Rapids, MI, USA: Oswald Chambers Publications Association, Ltd., Discovery House Publishers, 1993), p. 83.
4. Ibid, pp. 169, 170.
5. C. Irving Benson, *The Eight Points of the Oxford Group, An Exposition for Christians and Pagans*, (Melbourne, London, Edinburgh, Toronto, Bombay and Madras: Humphrey Milford, Oxford University Press, 1938), p. 17.
6. Edited by Elizabeth Jay, *The Journal of John Wesley. A Selection*, (Oxford, NY, USA: Oxford University Press, 1987), p. xii.
7. Thieleman J. van (TJV) Braght, *The Bloody Theater or Martyrs Mirror of the Defenseless Christians*, (Scottdale, PA, USA: Herald Press, 1749), p. 728. TJV Braght quotes Valerius the Schoolmaster, executed by Papal decree in 1568.

8. Art Katz, *And They Crucified Him*, ((Bemidji, MN, USA: Burning Bush Press, 2011), pp. 16, 17.
9. Editor J.C. Wenger, Translated from Dutch by Leonard Verduin, *The Complete Writings of Menno Simons*, (Scottdale, PA, USA: Herald Press, 1956), p. 614.
10. Art Katz, *The Holocaust Where Was God?*, (Bemidji, MN, USA: Burning Bush Press, 1998, 2008), p. 73.
11. Scholl, Inge, *The White Rose, Munich 1942-43*, (Middletown, CT, USA: Wesleyan University Press, 1970, 1983), p. 48.
12. Thieleman J. van (TJV) Braght, *The Bloody Theater or Martyrs Mirror of the Defenseless Christians*, p. 934.
13. Frances Chan with Danae Yankowski, *Crazy Love*, (Colorado Springs, CO, USA: David C. Cook, 2008), p. 34.

Chapter Twenty: Seeking the Glory

1. C. Irving Benson, *The Eight Points of the Oxford Group, An Exposition for Christians and Pagans*, (Melbourne, London, Edinburgh, Toronto, Bombay and Madras: Humphrey Milford, Oxford University Press, 1938, p. 6.
2. Ibid, p. 23.
3. Corrie Ten Boom with John and Elizabeth Sherril, *The Hiding Place*, (Peabody, MA, USA: Hendrickson Publishers, 2009), pp. 261, 262.
4. C. Irving Benson, *The Eight Points of the Oxford Group, An Exposition for Christians and Pagans,* p. ix.
5. Thieleman J. van (TJV) Braght, *The Bloody Theater or Martyrs Mirror of the Defenseless Christians*, (Scottdale, PA, USA: Herald Press, 1749), p. 88.
6. Arthur Katz, *Ben Israel, Odyssey of a Modern Jew*, (Bemidji, MN, USA: Burning Bush Press, 2000), p. 118.
7. Frances J. Roberts, "Tender Dove," *Come Away My Beloved*, (Ojai, CA, USA: The King's Press, 1970), p.103. Also, Hannah Hurnard, *Hinds' Feet in High Places*, (Wheaton IL, USA: Living Books, Tyndale House, 1977), p. 243.
8. Thieleman J. van (TJV) Braght, *The Bloody Theater or Martyrs Mirror of the Defenseless Christians*, p. 11.
9. David Wilkerson, "They Have Done Away with the Cross," *Times Square Church Pulpit Series*, (Lindale, TX USA: World Challenge), Dec. 23, 1996.
10. Oswald Chambers, *My Utmost for His Highest*, (Ulrich, OH, USA: Barbour Publishing, 1935), Entry 9/21.

www.ingramcontent.com/pod-product-compliance
Lightning Source LLC
Chambersburg PA
CBHW061641040426
42446CB00010B/1526